Computational Finance and its Applications III

WIT PRESS

WIT Press publishes leading books in Science and Technology.
Visit our website for the current list of titles.
www.witpress.com

WIT eLibrary

Home of the Transactions of the Wessex Institute.
Papers presented at COMPUTATIONAL FINANCE III are archived in the WIT elibrary in volume 41 of WIT Transactions on Information and Communication Technologies (ISSN 1743-3517).The WIT electronic-library provides the international scientific community with immediate and permanent access to individual papers presented at WIT conferences.
http://library.witpress.com.

THIRD INTERNATIONAL CONFERENCE ON COMPUTATIONAL FINANCE

COMPUTATIONAL FINANCE III

CONFERENCE CHAIRMEN

M. Costantino
Royal Bank of Scotland, UK

M. Larran
University of Cádiz, Spain

C.A. Brebbia
Wessex Institute of Technology, UK

INTERNATIONAL SCIENTIFIC ADVISORY COMMITTEE

Organised by
Wessex Institute of Technology, UK
University of Cádiz, Spain

Sponsored by
WIT Transactions on Information and Communication Technologies

WIT Transactions

Transactions Editor

Carlos Brebbia
Wessex Institute of Technology
Ashurst Lodge, Ashurst
Southampton SO40 7AA, UK
Email: carlos@wessex.ac.uk

Editorial Board

Computational Finance and its Applications III

EDITORS

M. Costantino
Royal Bank of Scotland Financial Markets, UK

M. Larran
University of Cádiz, Spain

C.A. Brebbia
Wessex Institute of Technology, UK

WIT*PRESS* Southampton, Boston

M. Costantino
Royal Bank of Scotland Financial Markets, UK

M. Larran
University of Cádiz, Spain

C.A. Brebbia
Wessex Institute of Technology, UK

Published by

WIT Press
Ashurst Lodge, Ashurst, Southampton, SO40 7AA, UK
Tel: 44 (0) 238 029 3223; Fax: 44 (0) 238 029 2853
E-Mail: witpress@witpress.com
http://www.witpress.com

For USA, Canada and Mexico

Computational Mechanics Inc
25 Bridge Street, Billerica, MA 01821, USA
Tel: 978 667 5841; Fax: 978 667 7582
E-Mail: infousa@witpress.com
http://www.witpress.com

British Library Cataloguing-in-Publication Data

A Catalogue record for this book is available
from the British Library

ISBN: 978-1-84564-111-5
ISSN: 1746-4463 (print)
ISSN: 1743-3517 (online)

The texts of the papers in this volume were set individually by the authors or under their supervision. Only minor corrections to the text may have been carried out by the publisher.

Printed in Great Britain by Athenaeum Press Ltd

Preface

This book contains the edited version of the papers presented at the conference Computational Finance 2008, held in Cádiz in Spain 2008. This conference follows the success of the first International Conference on Computational Finance and its Applications which was held in Bologna, Italy, in 2004 and the second International Conference of Computational Finance and its Applications held in London in 2006.

The main topic discussed in the preface of the 2006 conference was the explosion of the price of commodities, in particular oil which, back then, reached the price of 74 dollars. Analysts at that time were worried of the implications of this on the wider economy, in particular regarding the threat of inflation.

Since then, two years later, the price of oil reached 110 dollars. This, in addition to the dramatic increase of the price of many other commodities, from metals to gold and lately, to wheat and other main agricultural products, has indeed now fed through to the wider economy in terms of inflation and the implications are starting to be felt by the consumers and, in turn, in terms of economic growth.

The other major event of the last two years has been the recent "credit crunch", which occurred primarily from the second half of 2007. This started in the United States in the form of raising defaults on the sub-prime mortgages – mortgages offered to people with a poor credit record. While this looked initially like a very self-contained event, as time went on, it began spreading to the wider financial system, reaching Asia as well as Europe. In essence, debt had been packaged in the form of mortgage-backed securities which was then sold on to other financial institutions, but also pension funds and, in some cases, private investors. When US home owners began to default on their mortgages in bigger numbers, banks started to suffer major losses and, in some cases, some almost went out of business. This also very quickly fed to the end consumer. Banks unable to secure enough funding had to quickly withdraw their best mortgage deals and to restrain lending to people with the best credit records. This in turn caused house prices to collapse even further in the States (the impact is starting to be felt in the UK) which triggered more repossessions and new waves of mortgage defaults.

This in itself was still reasonably self-contained. However, as time went on, panic started spreading through the financial markets and banks became reluctant to lend to each other on the open market. Some of the weaker players, which relied mostly on the wholesale market for funding, found themselves without enough cash to be able to fund normal operations and they had to turn to the Central banks for help. This famously occurred to the UK bank Northern Rock but, more shockingly for people working in finance, was the almost collapse of Bear Sterns, one of the oldest and most respected US investment banks.

Central banks now faced a big dilemma: on one hand they had rising commodities prices which were causing inflation requiring higher interest rates, on the other they had financial institutions which were unable to borrow money on the open market and they were desperate for help to be able to continue working. The priority was clear; the central banks (the Fed in particular) had to safeguard the most important thing – the correct functioning of the financial markets. Therefore, a huge amount of funds were directly injected into the economy by both the Fed and the Bank of England and the American interest rates were cut dramatically. This, in turn, caused both the US dollar and the British pound to fall sharply, with currencies seen as safer, for example the Euro and the Yen to raise sharply, undermining both countries' efforts to restrain inflation. Finally, the stock market has also dropped significantly, in particular bank shares, on worries that this could start to affect the wider economy and several western countries could fall into a deep recession.

Analysts are now divided as to what will happen next. Most of them, though, seem to agree with the fact that the economy is entering a period of uncertainty which may lead to a recession. How deep and prolonged this will be is however highly controversial.

Events of this type are the most difficult to forecast and handle by automatic systems and intelligence techniques. They are unexpected and techniques purely based on short-term time series of prices can perform very badly. On the other hand, situations like this also offer the best opportunities. Smart and experienced traders who may have lived through similar events, such as the .dot com bubble, can profit from taking the right positions and outperform the markets significantly. Techniques such as algorithmic trading and intra-day automatic market making can also be extremely profitable, because they do not rely on a particular market direction but profit from the increased volatility on the market.

Even in such difficult times, therefore, financial institutions are always keen to explore new strategies and tools which could outperform their rivals and to continue the dialogue with the research communities to explore the best solutions.

It is in this context that Computational Finance 2008 brought together leading experts from both the industry and academia to present and share the results of their research, with the aim to become one of the main forums where such collaboration takes place.

This book contains many high quality contributions reporting advances in the field and focussed on the following areas: Forecasting, Advanced Dynamics and Simulation; Derivatives Pricing; Portfolio Management and Asset Allocation; Market Analysis, Dynamics and Simulation; Risk Management.

This volume would have not been possible without the help of the members of the International Scientific Advisory Committee, whose help is gratefully acknowledged. Their help in reviewing the papers has been essential in ensuring the high quality of this volume.

The Editors
Cádiz, Spain, 2008

Contents

Section 1
Forecasting, advanced dynamics and simulation

Control systems identification in finance and economics

O. Criner
Texas Southern University, Houston, Texas U.S.A.

Abstract

The research program that views economies as complex dynamic systems has received significant development over the past several decades and has become known as "Complexity Economics". The amount of information that economies create has grown exponentially. Most markets on formal exchanges have become electronic and they are consolidating into new organizational structures. The data from worldwide economic activity are widely available. However, the methods of analysis and interpretation of these data have not kept pace.

Everyday hundreds of parameters are reported by corporations, governmental and nongovernmental agencies. Corporations make their earnings reports, financial events, and other information available. This flood of information is continuously analyzed in the various media. However, the effect of this influence is subject to varied interpretation.

The research reported here seeks to define a method by which to quantify this influence using several globally-traded financial instruments. The methodology applies data analysis techniques analogous to those used for control of dynamical systems and links the response of trading activity to reports of economic activity. The important issues are (1) identification of the reports that have significant effect on trading activities in specific markets, and (2) determination of the extent, magnitude, and duration of the influence.

We design a computational dynamical systems model from the derivatives of the market prices and use the external economic data as driving functions on the dynamical system. We explore a financial market system model consisting of the derivatives markets in crude oil, stock indices, and currencies.

Keywords: dynamical systems, financial events, economic indicators, event trading.

WIT Transactions on Information and Communication Technologies, Vol 41, © 2008 WIT Press
www.witpress.com, ISSN 1743-3517 (on-line)
doi:10.2495/CF080011

1 Introduction

Dynamical systems applications in financial markets are receiving considerable attention as the information from financial markets and the ability to process that information becomes widely available. Scientific and engineering techniques are being widely used in the analysis of financial markets. Model building is the essence of scientific inquiry. So, it is natural to consider model building for financial systems. Constructing dynamical systems models of financial markets is an "inverse" problem, since there are no fundamental first principles of market finance as there are for physics or engineering. There are no long standing empirically verified equations describing fundamental first principles from which models can be formulated.

Indeed, the traditional theories of finance have come under question as unsatisfactory descriptions of the market processes [1,2]. The rigorousness of the mathematics does not compensate for a theory the assumptions of which are not supported by empirical scientific evidence. Further, grand theories "in the large" should not be attempted, since the processes we are attempting to model are nonlinear, time varying, and, possibly, chaotic. This research is concerned with the transient responses of financial markets to changes in parameters or financial events. Hence, we attempt to model limited but significant processes that may provide insight on the influence of certain events on the behaviour of market systems.

Information from financial and economic activities has become ubiquitous as the global economy expands. Concerns about economic activity, the prices of essential commodities and services, and the wellbeing of national economies are expressed throughout the media and especially on the all-news media outlets. The development of financial and economic web sites has made a great deal of economic and financial data available to individuals worldwide. Websites offering trading and investment services now number in the tens of thousands. Cursory searches on World Wide Web for various permutations on the strings "investment advisors" and commodity trading advisors" produces millions of hits. This suggests that there is an exceptionally large group of people attempting to "make sense" of economic systems, i.e., people are attempting to make models to analyze and explain the phenomena they observe in the marketplace. This has let to a large number of books, tools and procedures for the study of financial time series.

The range of people engaged in this process is very broad and extends from the professionals responsible for very large investment pools to the individual investor and trader with a small IRA or personal account. There is so much activity that the reporting of financial and economic news now is a major industry in itself, which is in stark contrast to the situation forty years ago when the industry was essentially opaque. The opacity may have been due largely to the lack of an efficient and inexpensive financial and economic information infrastructure. A new trading technique, "event trading", has been developed where traders look for specific events to trigger profitable price movement. This fact suggests that these specific events have specific responses in the market and these responses have been characterized by the event traders. One result of this research is to formalize the event surveillance process and to integrate it into a model of the market system. Since financial and economic surveillance has become so all encompassing of the major economic systems and large datasets are more available, it is now possible to construct models to forecast economic and financial events more accurately. Not withstanding the view of markets as complex dynamical systems that behave counterintuitively to many stimuli, we assume that complex systems can behave "linearly" in certain instances, also. Such instances have been observed and are presented herein.

This paper examines the transient response and time-wise local effects of announcements of economic information upon the prices of several derivative instruments. Several sources of economic data are available along with the well known price time histories of the Dow Jones Industrials, the S&P500, the Russell 2000, and the NASDAQ stock indices and their associated futures markets. We choose to examine the effects of economic data that have been rated as very important to the markets by several authorities. Baumohl [3] and Yarmone [4] provide in-depth discussions and importance rankings for many indicators. Briefing .com [5] provides synoptic information and aggregated daily data reporting for many indicators. Several other websites publish current economic data as do the originating institutions of government, private economic research groups, and industry organizations. Trading sites also provide this information in conjunction with the subscriptions for the use of the trading facilities of the site. The website fxcm.com DailyFX Plus combines Thomson IFR's streaming news and market commentary, real-time charting from DailyFX, and live foreign exchange rates from FXCM's Trading workstation platform [7]. This mass of economic information requires extraordinary effort to combine it with the price time histories of trading instruments of interest and to analyze, interpret, and infer some action on the part of an investor or trader. Clearly some computational techniques need to be developed to assist in these analyses. We analyze the design requirements for such systems, also.

We assume that the stock indices and their associated futures are descriptive of the overall marketplace for exchange traded instruments. The currency markets and their associated derivatives markets are another set of indices of the relative position of economies with respect to each other and they respond rapidly to the announcement of economic data and other events. The commodity markets for raw materials that drive these economies are another major indicator of economic activity and crude oil heads the list of important commodities for a number of indices. The extremely high importance of oil in the economies of the world is indicated in the data by the weights given for inclusion in the various commodity indices. In the Rogers International Commodity Index [8], crude oil is 21% and Brent oil 14% of the weights of the index of 36 commodities. The next highest weights are for wheat at 7%, corn at 4.75%, Cotton at 4.05%, copper and aluminium at 4%, Gold at 3% and all of the others are at 3% or less. Gold is singled out because of its popularity and purported inflation hedge characteristics.

2 Dynamical systems model design

Dynamical systems model construction depends on the existence of a set of candidate models and systems identification is the name of the process of selecting the parameters for the chosen model of the process from the set. We formulate the problem of market tracking on electronic exchanges as a very elaborate example of the fundamental tracking problem in the control theory of dynamical systems. Figure 1 is a simplified diagram of the tracking problem using the Maxwell viscoelastic model. A spring with spring "constant" k is hung from a rigid support beam above and an inertial mass m is attached to the spring and constrained by the walls to move only in one direction. The walls have been coated with a sticky substance with viscosity *v* that resists motion in proportion to the speed of the motion of the mass. The Little Man, our financial operator, is instructed to keep to keep the pointer $p_o(t)$ on the mass of the system as close as possible to the pointer $p_i(t)$ being observed from outside the system by applying a force F(t) to the mass m. Grodins [9] uses the Little Man controller in the study of biological control models, which are, in many ways, very similar to economic and financial control models.

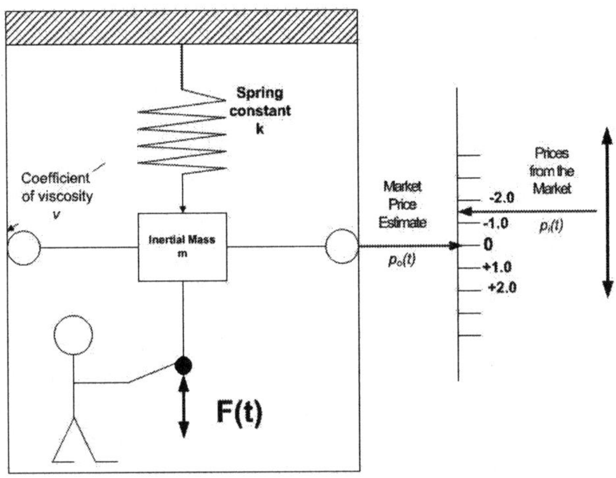

Figure 1: Little Man market tracker.

How is this system to be modeled given, what we know about the incoming data of observed prices? Can the transients, oscillations, and the steady state be identified? In this model the mass, spring "constant", and the viscosity may not be constant at all and may vary in unusual ways. The volume of trading or the open interest in a market may be associated with the mass in the model, in which case it is not a constant. A very thin market will have a small mass and the model will have difficulty tracking the market as the forcing function *F(t)* attempts to model the volatility. Extremely large volume markets were usually thought of as being less volatile and smoother, but with the advent of programmed trading, volatility appears to have increased.

An essential difference between biological dynamical models and economic and financial dynamical models is that, in most cases, the biological system can be studied and modeled in a laboratory. Computational science provides the ability to study phenomena that cannot be studied in a controlled laboratory environment. Models of economic and financial systems are very much like models of the environment and ecological systems, neither of which can be enclosed in a laboratory. However, dynamical models of this kind are well studied and have applications throughout science and engineering. This paper considers a design of how this class of dynamic models may be applied in finance and economics. This simple model can be used as a prototype component for a much more elaborate lumped mass dynamical model of a market.

Many people have observed that some price data have familiar patterns of behavior. Indeed, “technical analysis” is predicated upon pattern recognition; however, the patterns in dynamical systems are different. As an example, one such pattern, a shock took place on October 31, 2007 at around 9:30 a.m. central time, when the U.S. Energy Information Administration (EIA) released its report of crude oil inventories held outside of the strategic oil reserves. Figure 2 shows the real time dynamic price reaction of electronic trading in crude oil futures for delivery in December. The shape of the upper curve is very similar to the response of a linear dynamical system experiencing a step function force. The price movement amplitude before and after the announcement event is small compared to the magnitude of the jump. The announcement occurred at 10:30 a.m. Eastern Time or 9:30 Central Time, where the writer observed the phenomena and took this screen shot. This is a classic trajectory formation in applied mathematics that is widely modeled and used in dynamical systems. The

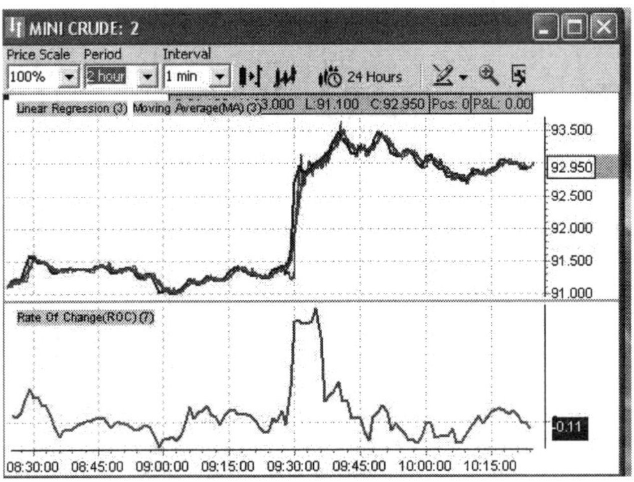

Figure 2: Real-time crude oil futures trading prices.

lower curve is the dynamic real time rate of change or first mathematical derivative of the upper curve. The rate of change is exactly what is expected of the derivative of a step function, an approximation to the impulse function.

This phenomenon suggests that this event process can be modeled with a linear system over small time intervals. This event may be characterized historically by analyzing the average evoked response of the crude oil market to the change in inventories announcement event.

Piecewise linearization of a nonlinear function is common in applied mathematics as a method for handling nonlinear processes. In cases for which there is almost no fundamental theory one can argue, by analogy with systems having similar responses, what the underlying dynamic process might be, and, therefore, the model for which parameters should be sought. A step function or a sinusoid with a step could be used as a model of the crude oil futures market in the neighborhood of an inventory announcement. These are simple well known functions that could be used to characterize the response of the market, provided that a table of responses as a function of inventory is compiled from history. Such data would constitute the transfer response function of the crude oil market system to the step function announcement event.

Figure 3 shows a closer examination of the event after the fact using two minute historical sampled data. Clearly, some information was lost from the real time data of Figure 2. However, the step function and its derivatives are clear. The mathematical model of this data is shown in Figure 4 as a sine function superimposed on a linear function with a step. The first panel is the actual data and a smoothed estimate of the data. The second panel graph is of the first derivative of the smoothed estimate of the price and the third panel graph is the second derivative. Figure 4 shows the same calculations for the model.

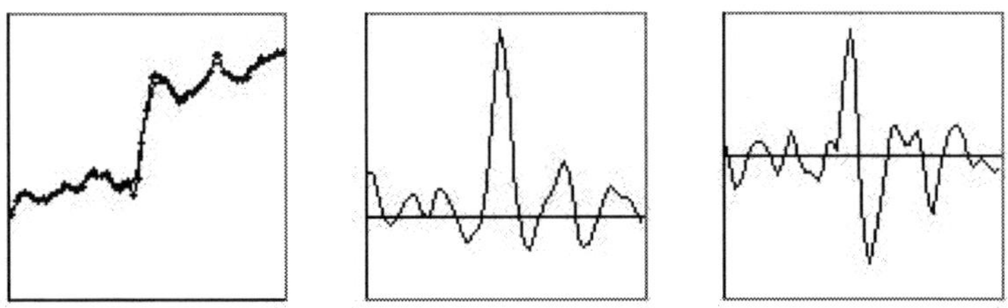

Figure 3: Two minute historical data around the event.

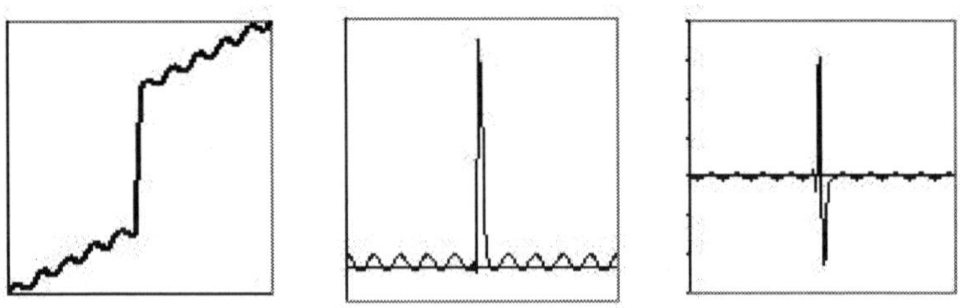

Figure 4: Sinusoid with a step and derivatives.

Step functions are widely used in applied mathematics and dynamical systems engineering and have well known properties.

3 Models of the event data

Since the price of crude oil is the heaviest component of most of the commodity indices, it is important to have an estimator of the futures prices that is based upon the actual market reaction to the economic data from which the change in inventories is derived. The source data are made available in a weekly updated time series of crude oil stocks from the US. Energy Information Administration (EIA). The announcement that is widely reported is of the change in the inventories. The change in inventories, when taken alone, is too volatile to make any reasonable estimates, as most differences of raw data are erratic. However, the actual inventory of oil stocks is a much smoother function. Figure 5 shows a graph of the EIA oil stocks data, a smoothed estimate of the data, 1st and 2nd derivatives of the smoothed estimate, a polynomial model of the smoothed data, and a histogram of the announcement event data. The announcement event data is the difference of the value on one oil stocks inventory report and on the previous report. Since the economic data are sampled at longer intervals and are generally low frequency data, models for these data are easier to construct. They can be constructed automatically using the Microsoft Office Suite. Hence, this capability is widely available.

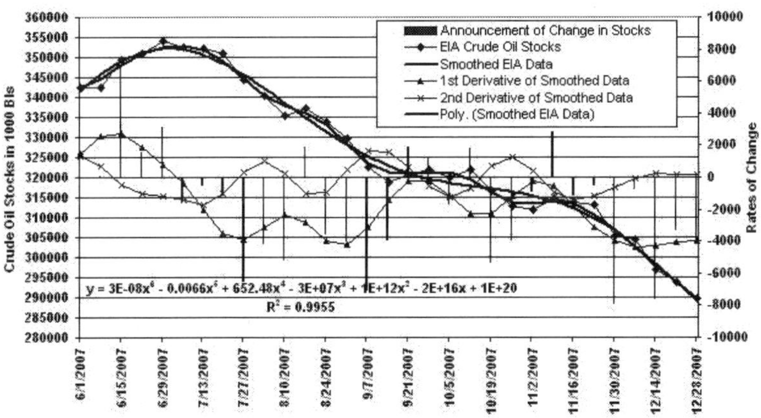

Figure 5: Crude oil stocks and change data.

The smoothed EIA data are used to compute the derivatives. The least squared polynomial is computed on the smoothed data set and its R-squared value is .9955, which indicates that the smoothed data are very close to the values of the least squared polynomial over that interval. The smoothed data can be reproduced within the interval from the derivatives using a modified predictor-corrector integration scheme and a forecast can also be made.

4 Lumped parameter models

In financial markets we consider the time series of the price-time history of a traded instrument to be its trajectory. So, each instrument has a trajectory or time series that its dynamical system model must track. In addition these tracking dynamical system models are not independent of each other. A more realistic and complex model would be a lattice of mass-spring-dashpot models connected together in order to model the mutual influence of the values of multiple instruments.

Dynamical systems modeling using lumped parameters have been used to study extremely complex applications in mechanics, nanotechnology, and medicine in recent years. There does not appear to be many such operating models in economics and finance, even though there are many papers addressing dynamic systems in economics and finance. We want to study the transient response of several instruments to economic events using a model like that described above.

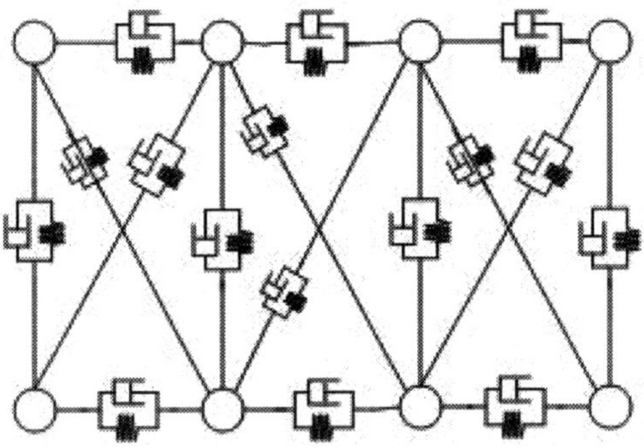

Figure 6: Two dimensional mass-spring-dashpot lattice model.

Figures 7 and 8 shows the trajectories of six related instruments traded on electronic futures markets on 31 October 2007. We consider the time series of prices of the 100 oz Gold, U.S. Dollar Index, Euro Currency, British Pound, Emini Dow Jones Industrial index, and Emini S&P500 index contracts, respectively. An examination of Figures 7 and 8 show the effect of the crude oil announcement at around 09:30, since the announcements are Eastern Time and the time series are Central Time. However, the FED event produces the strongest reaction in these markets.

The electronic crude oil and the Japanese Yen futures are also considered. Each node will represent one of these instruments. The research will seek to determine the real time transient response that propagates through the markets as a result of events and announcements. The effect of economic events, the reports of economic parameters on interrelated markets, or the relationship between the dominant commodity, crude oil, and the other trading instruments can be modeled in this manner. The scheduled economic events are shown in Figure 9.

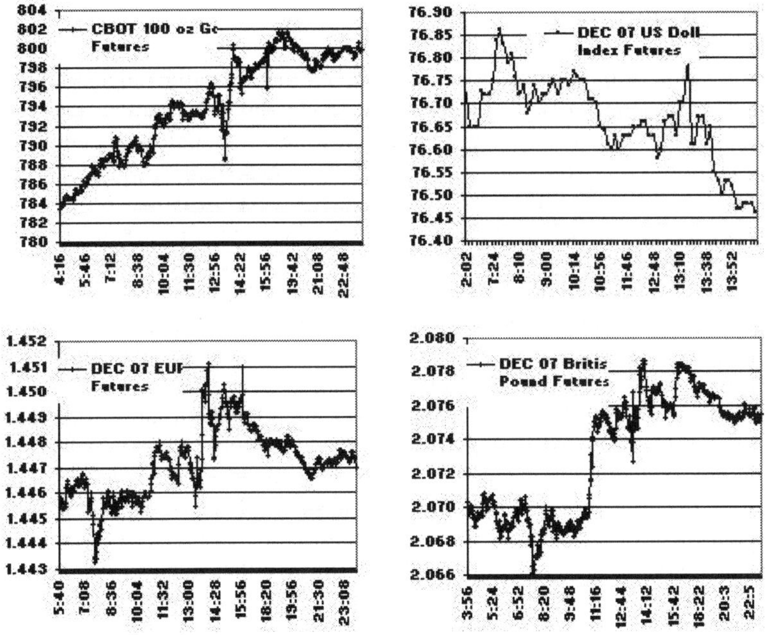

Figure 7: Real time trajectories of 4 related instruments on 31 Oct 2007.

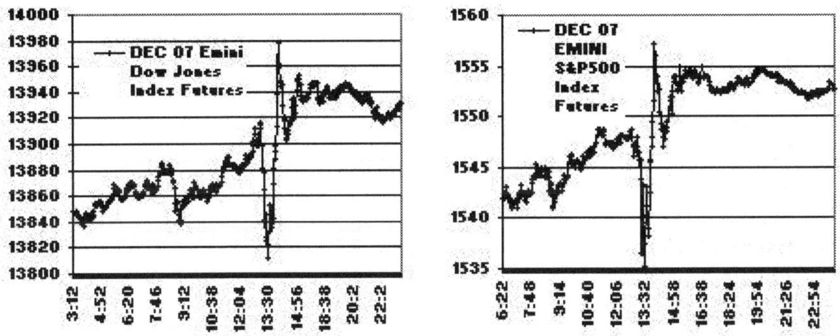

Figure 8: Real time trajectories of 2 related instruments on 31 Oct 2007.

10/31/07	8:30	Gross Domestic Product -- Advanced.
10/31/07	8:30	Chain Deflator-Advanced
10/31/07	8:30	Employment Cost Index
10/31/07	9:45	Chicago Purchasing Managers Index
10/31/07	10:00	Construction Spending
10/31/07	10:30	Crude Inventories Change
10/31/07	14:15	FED Open Market Committee policy statement

Figure 9: Economic events and announcements on 31 Oct 2007.

5 Conclusion

An observation of the behaviour of the crude oil market in the neighbourhood of a scheduled announcement of a monitoring event showed a pattern that is well known in the study of linear time invariant dynamical systems. The contemporary assumption of markets as nonlinear time varying complex dynamical systems precludes such behaviour, in general. However, one of the characteristics of complex systems listed by Forrester [10] is that complex systems behave counterintuitively. What could be more illustrative of counterintuitive behaviour of a complex system than for it to behave as if it were linear? One of the complex behaviours of such systems is that it may be linear at certain times or under certain conditions. This means that the dynamical system models must also be capable of similar behaviour.

This study of the behaviour of markets in the neighbourhood of significant scheduled events showed that they entered into a quiescent period before the announcement. During that period the behaviour could be modelled as a linear system in the way that mechanics is linear for small deformations. After the event, they behave as struck by impulse functions or step functions. The impulse and step responses decay with time. These observations suggest that nonlinear dynamical system modelling using arrays of masses, springs, and dashpots in lumped models would be a fruitful research program for modelling markets in real time.

References

[1] James R. Thompson and Edward E. Williams, "Future Enrons await, unless business schools must stop teaching faulty formulas," *The Houston Chronicle*, Outlook Section, May 27, 2006.

[2] Eric D. Beinhocker, *The Origin of Wealth – Evolution, Complexity, and the Radical Remaking of Economics,* Cambridge, MA: Harvard Business School Press. 2006.

[3] Baumohl, Bernard, *The Secrets of Economic Indicators – Hidden Clues to Future Economic Trends and Investment Opportunities,* Upper Saddle River, NJ: Wharton School Publishing, 2007.

[4] Richard Yarmone, *The Traders Guide to Key Economic Indicators*, Princeton, NJ: Bloomberg Press, 2004.

[5] Briefing.Com, Economic Calendars, <http://www.briefing.com/Investor

[6] /Public/Calendars/ EconomicCalendar.htm>, Accessed November 30, 2007.

[7] FXCM Web Site for FOREX Capital Markets, www.fxcm.com/dailyfx-plus.jsp

[8] Rogers, Jim, *Hot Commodities – How Anyone can Invest Profitable in the World's Best Market,* New York: Random House Trade Paperbacks, 2007.

[9] Fred S. Grodins, *Control Theory and Biological Systems*, New York, NY: Columbia University Press, 1963.

[10] Jay Forrester, Urban Dynamics, Cambridge, MA: The M.I.T. Press, Massachusetts Institute of Technology, 1969, p. 109.

Multifractal analysis and multiagent simulation for market crash prediction

V. Romanov, V. Slepov, M. Badrina & A. Federyakov
Plekhanov Russian Academy of Economics, Russia

Abstract

In this paper the results of multifractal analysis by means of partitions and scaling function calculation are described, as well as wavelet analysis, which were applied to USA 1987 October Black Monday DJ data. For the partition calculation and Legendre transform a special program was elaborated. As our aim is predicting crash situations, we are trying to find out the best indicator that uses multifractal analysis and wavelet analysis methodology. With this aim in mind we have tested different methods of preprocessing the original time series to discover the best indicator. The wavelet analysis data were calculated on a 256 day moving window. The changes in the multifractal analysis features were studied while approaching crisis point and after the crisis. From the multiagent market model we can observe the crisis evolution and the dynamic of changing parameters such as share prices, trading volumes, price increments and statistical distribution dependent on traders' strategies.
Keywords: stock market, market dynamics, multiagent simulation, wavelet analysis.

1 Introduction

The prediction of tough crucial changes in the finance market is very difficult because of the non-linear structure of the processes. It doesn't allow us to effectively use common statistical methods. Hurst exponent values estimation can be used for time series properties determination and for choosing the proper method of data processing. Unfortunately in the case of the multifractal time series, the Hurst exponent value is not constant and at different time scales takes different values, generating a spectrum of values.

Multifractal analyses potentially give us the possibility of predicting sharp changing market states. In this paper we are making an attempt to apply

WIT Transactions on Information and Communication Technologies, Vol 41, © 2008 WIT Press
www.witpress.com, ISSN 1743-3517 (on-line)
doi:10.2495/CF080021

mathematical theories and methods that are known from the literature [1–7] for detection of approaching crises situations at the stock market. Results of the experiment on processing real and artificial data by this special program, realizing Gibb's partition method and fractal dimension spectrum estimation, are presented in this article. It was also shown that wavelet analysis with Daubichies-12 expansion gives another possibility for approaching crises detecting.

2 Methodology

2.1 Scaling function estimation

It is known that fixed time scale is inappropriate for analysis of complex dynamic systems such as the stock market. For estimating the fractal dimension spectrum the partitions method may be used. Let us have time series $\{x_t\}$; $t \in [0,T]$. On the interval $[0,T]$, we compute the logarithmic price increment:

$$Z = \{z_t\},\ z_t = \ln x_{t+1} - \ln x_t\ ,\ t=0,\dots,T \qquad (1)$$

We divide interval $[0, T]$ on N subintervals, where N integer, $1 \le N \le N_{max}$, so that each segment will contain $int(\frac{T}{N}) = A$ values of time series Z_t. With such a partition the total amount of processed readings will be AN. Let us denote the segment index K, where $1 \le K \le N$. For each segment let us denote the current number of readings l_K, running in the range $1 \le l_K \le A$. The correspondence between indexes l_K and t is:

$$t = (K-1)\,A + l_K \qquad (2)$$

In the literature [1–7] an opinion is expressed that the spectrum of the local Hölder exponent is widening at the moments, preceding the crash and it's plot widths jump sharply after the crash. So the aim of our research is to discover observable distinctions between time series fractal parameters before and after the crash point. These differences may be used later as early detectors and warnings of stock market crashes. As we are looking for the best possible indicators, we will test several methods of preprocessing the original time series. We consider the following variants:

-the original time series itself $Z_0 = \{z_t\}$;

-the preprocessed time series (accumulated sum at each interval) $Z_1 = \left\{ \hat{Z}_K \right\}, K = 1,2\dots N,$ where

$$\hat{Z}_K = \frac{1}{A}\sum_{l_K=1}^{A} Z_{K,l_K} \qquad (3)$$

-the preprocessed time series (subtract the mean and divide by the mean square deviation)

$$Z_2 = \left\{ \frac{Z_{(K-1)A+l_K} - \hat{Z}_K}{S_K} \right\} \qquad (4)$$

$$S_K = \sqrt{\frac{1}{A}\sum_{l_K=1}^{A}\left(Z_{K,l_K} - \hat{Z}_K\right)^2} \tag{5}$$

-the preprocessed time series (subtract mean)

$$Z_3 = \left\{Z_{(K-1)A+l_K} - \hat{Z}_K\right\} \tag{6}$$

The partition gives us the possibility of representing the time series in different time scales, so we take one reading from each interval and in such a way we compress the scale.

Then we compute one dimensional array for every fixed N and for different values q, $Q_{min} \leq q \leq Q_{max}$ – the scaling function for all four variants:

$$\hat{\tau}_N^0(q) = \frac{\log \pi^{(0)}{}_N(Z,q) + \log A - \log N}{-\log A} \tag{7}$$

$$\hat{\tau}_N^1(q) = \frac{\log \pi^{(1)}{}_N(Z,q) + \log A - \log N}{-\log A} \tag{8}$$

$$\hat{\tau}_N^2(q) = \frac{\log \pi^{(2)}{}_N(Z,q) + \log A - \log N}{-\log A} \tag{9}$$

$$\hat{\tau}_N^3(q) = \frac{\log \pi^{(3)}{}_N(Z,q) + \log A - \log N}{-\log A} \tag{10}$$

For all four variants we estimate the local Lipschitz-Hölder exponents describing the singularity strength as a two dimensional array for different values of q:

$$\alpha_i = \frac{d\hat{\tau}^i}{dq} = (\hat{\tau}^i(q) - \hat{\tau}^i(q-1)) / \Delta q = \Delta\hat{\tau}^i(q)/\Delta q \text{ , } i = 1, 2, 3, 4. \tag{11}$$

Carrying out the Legendre transform of scaling function $\tau(q)$ we find multifractal singularity spectrum $f(\alpha)$ as the Hausdorff dimensions of the fractal subset with Lipshitz-Hölder local exponent α:

$$f_i(\alpha) = \arg\min_q \; [q\alpha - \hat{\tau}_i(q)] \approx ([q\Delta\hat{\tau}^i(q)/\Delta q - \hat{\tau}^i(q) \text{ , } i=1,2,3,4 \tag{12}$$

For determining the position of τ *(q)* plot we use properties τ (0) = -1 and $\tau(\frac{1}{H}) = 0$. From another side, τ *(q)* is a monotonically increasing function. We can regard the scaling function as the slope of the partition function in bi-logarithmic coordinates. In expression (12) the Legendre transform expresses reciprocal correspondence between statistic moments and the singularity exponent. The width of α spectrum may be estimated as different between the maximum and minimum values of α:

$$\Delta\alpha = \alpha_{max} - \alpha_{min} \tag{13}$$

Spectrum analysis of the time series interval near the crash events may detect the presence of market forecasting signals. Despite the partition method making it possible to explicate global stable relations, as we stated, it not sensitive enough to fast local changes. This method also demands significant value of calculations and elaboration of corresponding software. Wavelet analysis is to some extent free from these drawbacks.

2.1.1 Wavelet analysis of multifractal time series

Wavelet analysis doesn't use the assumption of stationary and ergodic properties of the time series, and like the partition method wavelet analysis allows us to analyze the time series behaviour at different time scales. Due to the compactness of the carrier, wavelet analysis can detect short living events at short time segments as a trend at long intervals.

Wavelet is a function with zero mean and finite energy. Unlike the Fourier analysis the wavelet analysis method operates locally in time and doesn't need cycle stationary components. The wavelet transform may be presented as an integral expression:

$$W(\tau,\alpha) = \int_{-\infty}^{+\infty} x(t)\psi_{\tau,\alpha}(t)dt \tag{14}$$

where $\psi_{\tau,\alpha}(t)$ is the function with zero mean centred around zero with time scale α and time horizon τ. A family of wavelet vectors is created from the mother function by displacement and scaling:

$$\psi_{\tau,\alpha}(t) = \frac{1}{\sqrt{\alpha}}\psi\left(\frac{t-\tau}{\alpha}\right) \tag{15}$$

The scaling functions re the set of function φ_k composing the span of subspace V_0 of space $L^2(R)$. So any function $f(t) \in V_0$. V_0 may be represented as a linear combination of scaling functions. Any discrete signal $f(t) \in L^2(R)$ may be represented in wavelet function terms:

$$f(t) = \sum_{k=-\infty}^{\infty} \alpha_{j_0}\phi_{j_0,k}(t) + \sum_{j \geq j_0} \sum_{k=-\infty}^{\infty} \beta_{j,k}\psi_{j,k}(t) \tag{16}$$

$$\alpha_{j_0,k} = \int f(t)\phi_{j_0,k}(t)dt \tag{17}$$

$$\beta_{j,k} = \int f(t)\psi_{j,k}(t)dt \tag{18}$$

where j_o is a constant, representing the highest level of resolution for which the most acute details are extracted.

The decomposition process of discrete values segments into averaged or approximating values and detail values for different scales are named as multiscale or multiresolution analysis. Multiresolution analysis is invariant to integer value translations and distortions, which are proportional to the power of two.

We have performed some experiments on processing real time series using multifractal analyses as wavelet analyses. The method of multifractal analyses, described above, has also been applied for the October 1987 USA financial crises, using Dow Jones index (Fig. 1).

Fig. 2 shows fractal dimension spectrum F2(α), which have been calculated according to (12).

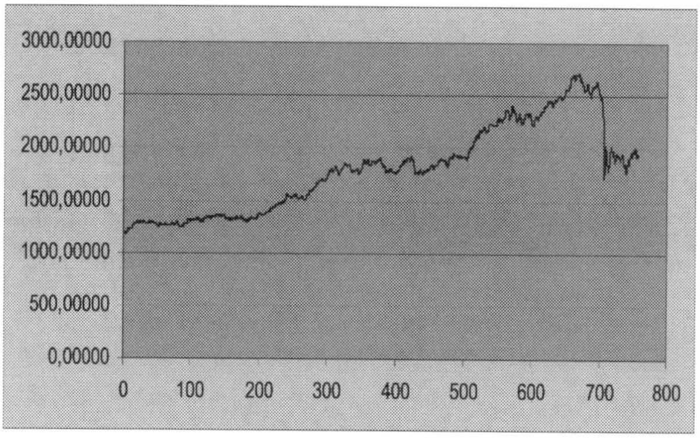

Figure 1: Dow Jones industrial average data for period 01.02.1985–31.12.87. Axis X contains serial numbers of readings.

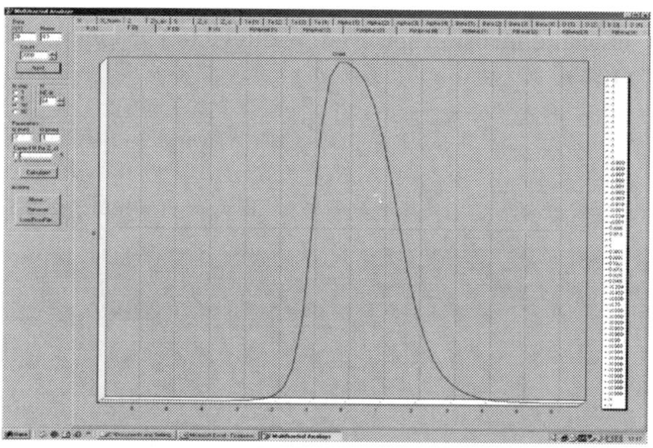

Figure 2: Fractal dimension spectrum F2 (α) for DJ industrial average series for period 10.10.85–19.10.87.

Fig. 3 and Fig. 4 show the plots of the multifractal spectrum width changing before and after crisis. The plots of different colours correspond to different levels of intersection of the fractal dimension spectrum graph and the lines of constant values 0, 0.6, 0.8.

From these plots we can see that there are peaks, both for the F1(α) and F2(α) versions of the multifractal spectrum preceding to the crises point and corresponding to dates 08.10.87 for F1(α) and 07.10.87 for F2, which permit us to assert that there are some kinds of predictive signals at least 8 days before crises. However, we continued the search of crisis indicators the using wavelet analysis method. In our research we choose Daubichies wavelets. Daubichies wavelets fit very well for coding of sequences, having intervals of slow changing or relatively constant values. From another side, Daubichies wavelets have some number of zero moments, which allow one to discriminate thin details.

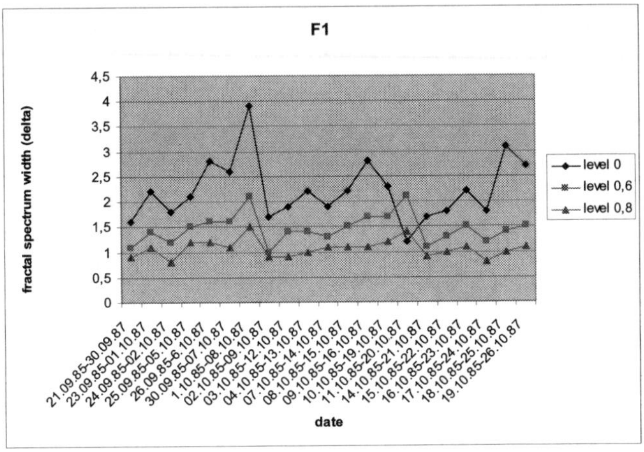

Figure 3: Fractal dimension spectrum width F1 (α) changing before and after crises.

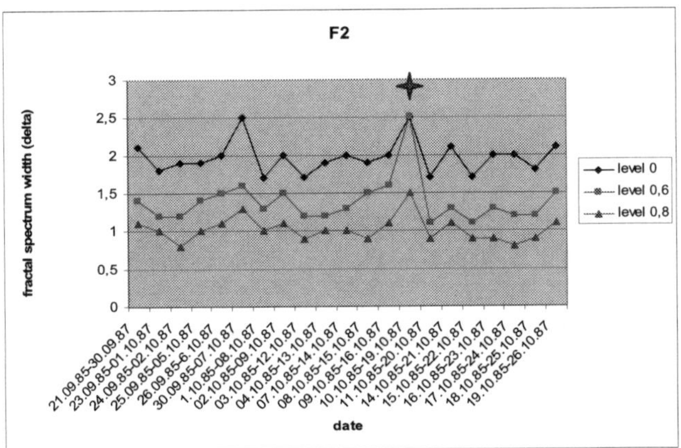

Figure 4: Fractal dimension spectrum width F2 (α) changing before and after crises.

The aim of the experiments was to extract a signal by means of time series processing, which could predict the following sharp changes in time series. We use Daubichies-12 expansion approximation and detail coefficients for 5 levels. We have processed 21 intervals each containing 256 readings from 02.09.86–29.10.87. For each interval we find the expansion coefficient at all 5 levels. Then we take the differences of maximum values from adjusting the intervals. The plots of maximum values and their differences are presented in Fig. 5 and Fig. 6.

The curve in Fig. 5 has a maximum at point 12.10.87. At the same point in Fig. 6 the curve is intersecting axis X. So we can make a conclusion that in both cases we obtain some indicators (maxima points) of forthcoming crisis, but these indicators are relatively weak. Obviously, this information can be used to detect a coming crash.

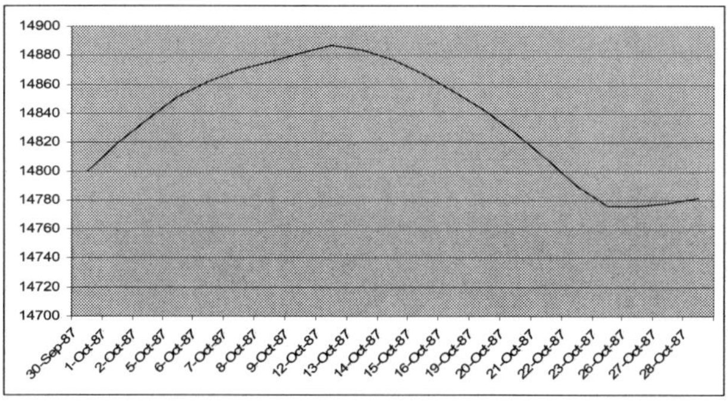

Figure 5: The plot of changing maximum values detail coefficients Daubichies -12 expansion.

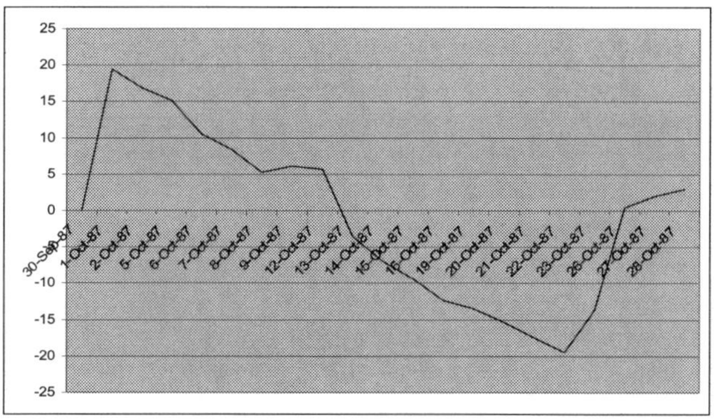

Figure 6: The plot of maximum differences.

In order to study how the crisis evolves in time we have made a financial market multiagent model, which was partly published in [8]. The choice of initial parameters of a virtual market makes sure that the virtual market is a reduced copy of an average real market. This in some way guarantees that the virtual market will behave in a similar way to the real market during the experiments. In this case, shown in Fig. 7, we used the following parameter values:

MARKET_MAKER_TRADER_COUNT = 2;
RANDOM_TRADER_COUNT = 0;
FUNDAMENTAL_TRADER_COUNT = 500; BROKER_COUNT = 5;
MARKET_COUNT = 1;
COMPANY_COUNT = 10;
COMPANY_MAX_ASSETS = 50000000; // 50kk
COMPANY_MIN_ASSETS = 1000000; // 1kk
MIN_BROKER_MARKET_ACCOUNT_MONEY = 100000; // 100k.
MAX_BROKER_MARKET_ACCOUNT_MONEY = 150000; // 300k.
BROKER_MONEY = 10000; // 10k.

The experiment is based on the “FundamentalTraders.fms” scenario. Its goal is to determine how fundamental traders’ actions can influence share price changes.

The main goal of fundamental traders in the system is to make the share price follow some predefined “want-to-be” price. There are several events in this scenario: at first the company increases its assets, then it decreases them very quickly, and at the end of this 3-month experiment it again increases them. Traders’ fundamental price is directly linked with companies’ assets, so we can expect that the market price will be influenced by traders’ expectations and somehow be linked to the fundamental l price too. In Fig. 7 we can observe how an artificial “crisis” is evolving in time: a period of significant price jumping is changed by comparatively modest deviations.

In Fig. 8 price distributions are presented. As we can see, share prices distribution is very close to distributions on the real markets. Only the average price distribution has a rather low peak value. Also the last transaction price has a very high peak. It may have been caused by high spread value or a very high

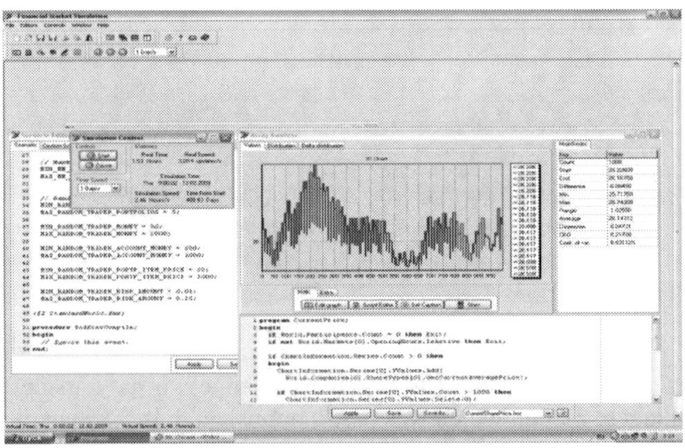

Figure 7: Stock market dynamic model.

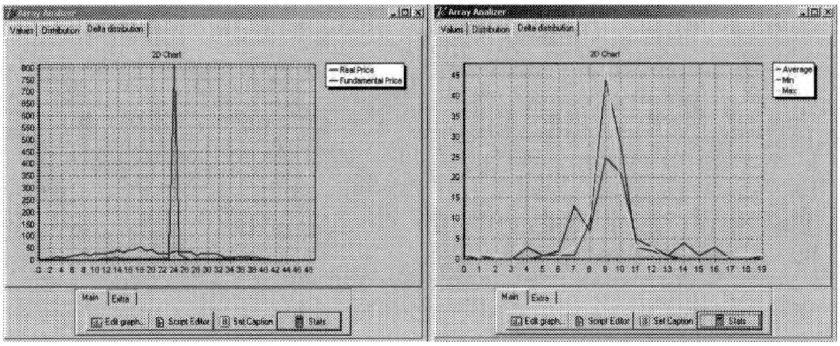

Figure 8: Distribution of share prices in the "FundamentalTraders.fms" scenario.

number of transactions (around 1000). It's a well known fact – the longer the initial array, the higher peak on its distribution. Almost flat distribution of fundamental price is an expected result, because it is generated from the company's assets, which change based on a simple algorithm that uses the standard Delphi random number generator.

3 Conclusion

In spite of positive research results in the detection of forthcoming crash situations by means of multifractal as wavelet analysis, there are some difficulties in getting appropriate patterns for adjusting the model's parameters. So it seems reasonable to use an agent based market simulation for generating artificial data, containing some patterns, which may be further applied for improving multifractal and wavelet models.

This approach can promote investigation in the domain of forecasting market time series by means of supplying necessary data for exploring forecasting methods market time series behaviour.

References

[1] Cornelis A. Los (EMEPS Associates, Inc.), Rossitsa M. Yalamova (University of Lethbridge), Multifractal spectral analysis of the 1987 stock market Crash. http://papers.ssrn.com/sol3/papers.cfm?abstract_id=588823

[2] Stefan Reimann, "An elementary model of price dynamics in a financial market Distribution, Multiscaling & Entropy". http://ideas.repec.org/p/zur/iewwpx/271.html

[3] Thomas Lux: "Detecting multi-fractal properties in asset returns: The failure of the 'scaling estimator'". http://ideas.repec.org/p/zbw/cauewp/ 1124.html

[4] Seong-Min Yoon, Kyungsik Kim and J. S. Choi: "Multifractal Features in Ko-rean Financial Markets". http://cat.inist.fr/?aModele=afficheN&cpsidt =16772737.

[5] Francois Schmitt, Shaun Lovejoy: "Multifractal fluctuations in finance". http://arxiv.org/abs/cond-mat/0102369
[6] Marco Corazza, Anastasios G. Malliaris: "MultiFractality in Foreign Currency Markets". http://sba.luc.edu/research/wpapers/990303.pdf
[7] I. A. Agaev, Yu. A. Kuperin: "Multifractal Analysis and Local Hoelder Expo-nents Approach to Detecting Stock Markets Crashes". http://arxiv.org/abs/cond-mat/0407603
[8] http://sourceforge.net/projects/fimas

Fast and flexible libor model pricing: two-stage Monte Carlo and on-the-fly payoff processing

M. Auer & S. Biffl
Institute of Software Technology and Interactive Systems,
Vienna University of Technology, Austria

Abstract

The Libor market model is the standard interest rate model. Yet its application relies on Monte Carlo simulation, which is slow, especially in a flexible, product-independent model setup.

This paper proposes an alternative software design of the Monte Carlo simulation to achieve fast and flexible pricing. The design is fast because it separates the computation of forward rate paths from that of payoffs to avoid redundant calculations; it is flexible because it adapts to new types of payoff functions at run-time via on-the-fly compilation.

The approach is arbitrarily accurate—it supports a high discretization resolution and even full factors without affecting the response time. It also features a small-footprint software design that is cheap to maintain and product-independent.
Keywords: Libor market model, Monte Carlo simulation, derivative pricing, user interface responsiveness.

1 Introduction

The Libor market model [1, 7] is the standard interest rate model. Its application requires Monte Carlo simulation, and thus some sort of software implementation. Ideally, this software should provide fast, accurate results, at low setup and maintenance costs, and independent of product types. Yet these are conflicting goals.

Consider a conventional software implementation of the Libor model, like a Euler scheme applied to the logarithm of the forward rates. It provides arbitrarily accurate results, and it is straightforward and cheap to set up and to maintain, but it will have too slow a response time for traders who need quotes fast.

WIT Transactions on Information and Communication Technologies, Vol 41, © 2008 WIT Press
www.witpress.com, ISSN 1743-3517 (on-line)
doi:10.2495/CF080031

One way to speed it up is to sacrifice some accuracy. If, for example, a higher standard error is acceptable, the number of Monte Carlo runs can be reduced; if a low-factor approximation to a correlation structure is acceptable, the number of operations per Monte Carlo run can be reduced.

Other approaches do not compromise the accuracy, but they increase the size and complexity of the software implementation, and thus its setup and maintenance costs. One example is to parallelize the implementation, which is very suitable for Monte Carlo type models [8], as Monte Carlo simulation is an "embarrassingly parallel" computational task. Alternatively, a variety of variance reduction techniques can reduce the number of Monte Carlo runs required to obtain a desired accuracy [6]. Drift correction, in turn, allows reduction of the discretization resolution and thus the number of operations per Monte Carlo run. Yet these approaches increase the setup costs: they require additional hardware and/or the implementation of additional source code. But more importantly, they also increase the dominant maintenance costs: larger and more complex source code is more expensive to document, learn, modify, test, port and maintain. (An overview of such optimization methods is given in [5].)

Finally, there are some product-specific optimizations. For example, some financial products only rely on certain rates and fixing dates, which makes jump procedures feasible [9]. Such product-specific code—in addition to increasing code size and maintenance costs—makes the model implementation unsuitable to flexibly adapt to new product types.

In short, the goal of a fast and accurate model that is cheap to set up and to maintain, and product-independent, is difficult to achieve in a conventional Monte Carlo implementation.

This paper proposes an alternative software design that overcomes some of these limitations. The design specifically tackles two issues: (a) provide a very fast response time for model users, and (b) allow for product-independent pricing, i.e., process arbitrary, unforeseen payoff function types at run-time.

The former is achieved by separating the computational effort of the Monte Carlo simulation in two parts: the costly forward rate evolution and the elementary payoff aggregation. This avoids redundant computations in the typical case where many products have to be priced.

The latter issue—adapting to arbitrary new types of payoff functions at run-time without changes to the software implementation—is addressed with an on-the-fly compilation of the payoff functions.

The approach does not compromise accuracy: in fact, the approach easily allows for arbitrarily accurate results (i.e., using millions of Monte Carlo paths, a fine-grained discretization, and potentially full factors (Schoenmakers [10], e.g., illustrates the disadvantages of low factor models)), without affecting the response time.

Also, the source code can be implemented in an unoptimized, straightforward way, minimizing its size and complexity, and thus reducing its maintenance costs.

To sum up, the approach achieves arbitrarily accurate pricing with a response time of seconds (even when using full factors), with a small-footprint software design that is cheap to maintain and flexible, i.e., not tailored to any specific product.

However, there are a few drawbacks. The approach does not help with the inverse problem of parameter calibration. If products' tenor dates don't correspond to the model ones, interpolation is required during simulation. The approach also increases the setup costs due to the recommended 64-bit computer architectures. Finally, intraday calibration might require some degree of parallelization, partially offsetting the achieved software size/maintenance cost reductions.

1.1 Implications for practitioners

The proposed software design for implementing the Libor model has implications regarding two main concerns of decision makers: the usability of a model, and the costs of creating and maintaining it. First, our approach provides fast response times for end users like traders—it is user-friendly. (Note: several major financial data providers still refrain from providing the Libor model due to the problem of slow response times with traditional Monte Carlo.) Second, our approach is cheap: it runs on lean hardware, and requires no expensive optimization of the source code. Especially the maintenance costs can be cut, as graduate-level software engineers are perfectly able to implement and maintain the system; whereas hand-optimized Libor models might well require PhD-level mathematicians.

Section 2 illustrates the background and the benefits of the proposed approach in greater detail. Section 3 describes the implementation details and recommends some programming idioms to keep the software design transparent. Section 4 outlines some drawbacks of the approach. Section 5 concludes and outlines possible improvements.

2 Approach and benefits

The Libor model describes the arbitrage-free evolution of forward rates. Sticking to the notation of Glasserman [6], a (forward measure type) Libor model evolves according to

$$\frac{dL_n(t)}{L_n(t)} = - \sum_{j=n+1}^{M} \frac{\delta_j}{1+\delta_j L_j(t)} \vec{\sigma}_n(t)^\top \vec{\sigma}_j(t) L_j(t) dt + \vec{\sigma}_n(t)^\top dW(t)$$

The numeraire under the forward measure, required for the appropriate discounting, is given by

$$B_{M+1}(t) = B_{\eta(t)}(t) \prod_{j=\eta(t)}^{M} \frac{1}{1+\delta_j L_j(t)}$$

To actually price a product in this model setup using Monte Carlo, numeraire-adjusted payoff functions must be averaged:

$$p(0) = B_{M+1}(0)E^{Q_{M+1}}\left[\frac{p(T)}{B_{M+1}(T)}\right]$$

So there are two parts in Monte Carlo pricing: evolving the forward rates (and the numeraire), and aggregating the payoffs. In the typical case where many products have to be priced, the first part is redundant and should be computed only once. This leads to the following separation:

1. Evolve and store all forward rate paths. All forward rate paths, as well as the corresponding numeraire paths, are pre-computed and stored. This is computationally expensive, but it is done only once for every new Libor model calibration, or when a new forward rate snapshot has to be used as initial condition.

2. Aggregate payoffs for each product. Given the pre-computed forward rate paths, the pricing of products boils down to averaging numeraire-adjusted payoff functions of the stored forward rates. This is computationally cheap.

Separating the two parts of the computation makes the pricing of individual products fast—prices are obtained within seconds. But it has an additional advantage: if there is enough time to perform the evolution of the forward rates, it is possible to have a high-accuracy model while keeping the corresponding software design very simple. It is, e.g., possible to use a high discretization resolution, and a large number of Monte Carlo runs. This increases the accuracy but will not impact the speed of the pricing step, which accesses the same, just more accurately pre-computed, forward rate paths. Also, it is possible to simply use a full-factor model as opposed to a reduced-factor one [3] without affecting the pricing speed.

For all this, a simple software design can be used (object-oriented data structures, no obscure and error-prone optimizations, etc.), which greatly reduces maintenance costs. Also note, that no product-specific optimizations (like those required for jump procedures) take place: all forward rate paths are pre-computed and stored, making the implementation flexible, i.e., suitable for a vast array of product types.

Some Libor model implementations we are aware of benefit from this possible separation to some extent: they compute several payoffs in a given portfolio simultaneously, i.e., using the same paths. This paper extends the approach to handle new, unforeseen types of payoff functions or products that might emerge during a trading day and need to be priced with a fast response time. This is achieved by compiling new payoff functions on-the-fly into an executable, and accessing the pre-computed forward rate paths via a shared memory architecture.

The approach thus consists of the following steps:

0. Calibrate Libor model (minutes)
1. Evolve all forward rate paths and store them in shared memory (hours/single processor; minutes/multiple processors)

2. For each new product: aggregate payoffs (seconds)
   (a) compile the product's payoff function on-the-fly;
   (b) average numeraire-adjusted payoffs.

The following section describes the implementation of this distribution of computational workload. Several programming idioms are proposed to provide flexibility for new types of payoff functions and products, and to handle the large amount of memory required to store and access the pre-computed forward rate paths.

2.1 Evolve and store rates

The main idea of the proposed approach is to pre-compute and store all forward rate paths required for the Monte Carlo simulation. If this has to happen only once per day, a single-processor setup is sufficient. Yet in our approach, the forward rates must be re-computed not only when a new calibration takes place, but also when a new snapshot of initial forward rates—i.e., $L_i(t = 0)$—has to be used. This is likely to be necessary several times during a trading day, but a modest parallelization would achieve an acceptable performance for this step: a (parallelized) server application can (1) pre-compute the forward rate paths starting with the current forward rate snapshot; after completion, it will (2) designate this set of newly computed forward rates to be the one used for payoff aggregation; finally, it will (3) pre-compute the next set of forward rate paths based on the updated, most current forward rate snapshot.

Calculating the forward rates thus seems feasible. But storing them is less trivial. Our approach proposes to store them in main memory, to obtain optimal pricing speed. Thus, main memory size becomes the limiting factor. For n Monte Carlo runs, and M forward rates, $n*(M^2+M)/2$ values are required to store all forward rate paths (note: as rates expire, not every rate has to be tracked over the whole simulation period). An additional n*M values are required to hold all numeraire paths.

In a typical setup (n=107 Monte Carlo runs, and 20 years to simulate, with M =40 semi-annual forward rates), $8.6*10^9$ values need to be stored. Each value, if stored at double precision, requires 8 bytes, yielding a total of 68.8 gigabytes. In the scenario of intra-day updates, twice this memory is required to store both the forward rate paths being used for pricing at a given time, and those being precomputed from an updated forward rate snapshot (and bound to be used for pricing at completion). Unfeasible a few years ago, such an amount of memory can nowadays be handled well by 64-bit computer architectures.

2.2 Aggregate payoffs

When all forward rate paths are known, pricing a product becomes averaging its (numeraire-adjusted) payoffs. One preliminary aspect is how to handle payoff functions.

There are various ways to handle different product types or payoff function types in a Monte Carlo implementation. A common one is a "semi-hardcode" approach: each product type corresponds to some data structure, and users can parameterize those structures, e.g., by setting a strike parameter.

Another approach is to let users enter a payoff function as a text string, which in turn is evaluated by a software interpreter (much like a Basic-type mini-language). This is more flexible (new product types do not require changes to the software implementation of the model), but inefficient.

A similarly flexible, but faster alternative is, again, to allow the user to enter the payoff function as a text string, but then to compile this string on-the-fly into an executable (Examples for software tools that use a similar on-the-fly compilation technique are cash flow engines that need to adapt flexibly to a variety of cash flow structures.). C++ is the language of choice for this, especially because its operator overloading capability makes the payoff function look very intuitive.

For example, a user could enter the following line to define a specific caplet payoff:

```
B(0)/B(8)*max(0,delta(7)*(L(7,7)-0.03))
```

A parser then checks the input for syntax errors, adds code for the Monte Carlo loop, and slightly transforms the user input by adding Monte Carlo path indices:

```
double price = 0.0;
for (int n=0; n<10000000; n++) {
price +=
B(n,0)/B(n,8)*max(0,delta(7)*(L(n,7,7)-0.03));
}
price /= 10000000.0;
```

The various elements in the transformed code above are:

- delta(t): distances between the tenor dates.
- L(n,j,t): C++ object with overloaded parenthesis operator that accesses the precomputed forward rate paths and returns the j-th forward rate at time index t in the n-th Monte Carlo run.
- B(n,t): Another memory access object that accesses the numeraire paths for time index t in the n-th Monte Carlo run.

The payoff executable—which averages numeraire adjusted payoffs—is then executed to obtain the price. Note: the code transformation, the compilation, and the execution take place in the background and are invisible to the user, hence it is a "runtime" solution.

The executable's speed will mainly depend on the memory access patterns within the "L"-object, and on the processor's cache hierarchy. But even with sub-optimal memory access patterns, and with millions of Monte Carlo paths, the payoff executable will yield a price within seconds.

2.2.1 Operator overloading

To access data structures like arrays in C, the []-operator is used, e.g., DATA [2][7]. In C++, objects can be wrapped around the basic data structure to provide safe and maintainable code, e.g., DATA.getElement (2,7). More elegantly, C++

allows redefinition of the ()-operator, yielding highly readable code like DATA (2,7).

There are several reasons to use parenthesis operator overloading:

- It makes function calls and memory access operations look consistent.
- The data structure that is accessed is not a conventional n*M*M array, as rates only have to be stored up to their fixing date. Access with the standard []-operator would therefore look inelegant, and is best hidden behind the parenthesis notation.
- If the layout of the data structure is modified (e.g., to optimize the number of cache misses), it only requires changes within the parenthesis operator, but no changes to the operator's interface.
- Exception handling inside the operator can be used to signal invalid memory access during development.
- There is no performance penalty, as the parenthesis operator can be implemented as an inline function.

2.2.2 Memory access

Finally, some remarks about memory access. It is preferable to keep the pre-computed forward rate paths in main memory all the time to avoid delays when loading the data from a hard drive. It is also not advisable to let each payoff executable have their own copy of the forward rates, which would waste memory and cause disk activity due to virtual memory architectures if several payoff executables run at the same time. It is better to store and access only one copy of all forward rate paths in main memory, and let the payoff executables access them via shared memory constructs.

The pricing speed will now mainly depend on the memory access and the number of cache misses it causes. It is advisable to store the forward rate paths in such a way that the arguments to most products' payoff functions are stored close to each other in memory. If, for example, most payoffs are expected to require the 5- and 10-year forward rates, the Monte Carlo instances of these rates should be stored in one continuous area of the main memory.

3 Drawbacks

The benefits of the proposed approach may not always outweigh the drawbacks:

- Only the pricing step is fast (this ensures fast response times for users); precomputing the forward rate evolutions is—if the model implementation is deliberately kept simple to reduce costs—unoptimized and slow. Thus, the approach is not helpful for the inverse problem of finding suitable model parameters.
- Some products' fixing times will not coincide with the model's tenor structure. In that case, interpolation techniques like the geometric Brownian bridge (outlined by Brigo and Mercurio [2]) can be used. Other interpolation methods are described by Fries [4]. The approach's acceptance will depend on a comparison between interpolating spot rates in the simulation versus the conventional approach of interpolating the input data to achieve product-specific model tenors.

- If the model has to be calibrated several times during the trading day, more computational resources are needed to pre-compute the forward rate evolutions, potentially requiring some parallelization. This can offset some of the maintenance cost reductions achieved with the smaller and simpler code base. In addition, the proposed 64-bit computer architecture will adversely affect the setup costs (we consider those costs to be dominated by maintenance costs, though).
- Access to shared memory is implemented differently on different operating systems, which can affect the code's portability. As the size of these code segments is very small, this negative impact is small.

4 Conclusion

This paper proposes to separate the computational workload in a typical Libor model setting in two parts: an initial stage that pre-computes and stores forward rate paths, and a pricing stage, that merely aggregates payoffs to obtain a product's price. It also suggests compilation of payoff functions on-the-fly in order to adapt flexibly to unforeseen payoff function types at run-time.

This approach is fast for an end-user: product prices are obtained in seconds. It is arbitrarily accurate: it is possible to use a large number of Monte Carlo runs, a high discretization resolution, and even full factor models without affecting the pricing speed. The implementation is cheap to maintain: the software design is simple and the code base is small. The implementation is also flexible: a vast variety of products can be priced without tailoring the implementation to certain product types.

The approach, however, does not help with the inverse problem of parameter calibration; it is best implemented using 64-bit computer architectures with large memory capacity; and the individual products' tenor structure can require some interpolation during the simulation.

There is ample space for improvements: choosing a cache efficient storage order for the forward rate paths can minimize cache misses and further speed up the pricing; accounting for "single instruction, multiple data" (SIMD) commands common in modern processors could improve performance; various interpolation techniques need to be analyzed to assess the pricing accuracy on dates that do not correspond to model tenor dates.

References

[1] Brace, A., Gatarek, D., and Musiela, M. The market model of interest rate dynamics. Mathematical Finance 7, 2 (1997), 127–147.

[2] Brigo, D., and Mercurio, F. Interest Rate Models—Theory and Practice: With Smile, Inflation and Credit. Springer, 2006.

[3] Fan, R., Gupta, A., and Ritchken, P. On pricing and hedging in the swaptions market: how many factors really? Journal of Derivatives 15, 1 (2007), 9–33.

[4] Fries, C. Mathematical Finance: Theory, Modeling, Implementation. Wiley, 2007.

[5] Gatarek, D., Bachert, P., and Maksymiuk, R. The Libor Market Model in Practice. Wiley, 2006.

[6] Glasserman, P. Monte Carlo Methods in Financial Engineering. Springer, 2003.

[7] Jamshidian, F. Libor and swap market models and measures. Finance and Stochastics 1 (1997), 293–329.

[8] Moritsch, H., and Pflug, G. High-performance numerical pricing methods. Concurrency and Computation: Practice and Experience (2002), 665–678.

[9] Rebonato, R. Modern Pricing of Interest-Rate Derivatives. Princeton University Press, 2002.

[10] Schoenmakers, J. Robust Libor Modelling and Pricing of Derivative Products. Chapman and Hall, 2005.

Novel pruning based hierarchical agglomerative clustering for mining outliers in financial time series

D. Wang[1], P. J. Fortier[2] & H. E. Michel[2]
[1]*Western Asset Management, USA*
[2]*Department of Electrical and Computer Engineering, University of Massachusetts, Dartmouth, USA*

Abstract

Investors must make informed decisions using partial and imperfect information. As accuracy and completeness of information held by the investor rise, the probability for better decision making also rises. Similarity search based outlier detection in financial time series is key to making better decisions for many investment strategies and portfolio management techniques. This motivates people to utilize numerous data mining techniques to discover similarities from massive financial time series data pools. The research introduces a novel pruning based Hierarchical Agglomerative Clustering (HAC) algorithm to search for similarity among financial time series in high dimensional space using securities in the S&P500 index as experimental data. The algorithm is based on vertical and horizontal dimension reduction algorithms [11] and a unique similarity measurement definition [12] with the time value concept. This paper discloses a series of experiment results that illustrate the effectiveness of the algorithm.
Keywords: outlier, data mining, computational finance, financial time series, similarity search, high dimension, clustering.

1 Introduction

We propose a novel similarity search in high dimensional financial time series by using a pruning based HAC algorithm. The similarity search is performed after dimensionality reduction, which composes of an Attributes Selection (AS) algorithm [11] and a Piecewise Linear Representation (PLR) based Segmentation

www.witpress.com, ISSN 1743-3517 (on-line)
doi:10.2495/CF080041

and Pruning (SP) algorithm as presented in Wang [11], and a unique similarity measurement definition [12] based on PLR represented financial time series objects.

The paper is organized as follows: Section 2 presents the problem statement to be addressed and summarizes the major contribution of this work toward academia. The background and related work of this topic is reviewed in Section 3. Section 4 states the business similarity. Similarity definition and measurement in Wang [12] is re-presented in Section 5. Section 6 describes the pruning based HAC algorithm to search similarity. The experiments and result analysis are presented in Section 7. The conclusion and future work are discussed in Section 8.

2 Problem statement and contribution

Investors usually have different investment and portfolio management strategies [10]. Some strategies include, cash surrogate passive strategy, passive strategy, outlier active strategy, and portfolio diversification [7] across segments etc. The key is to measure the similarity of the financial time series based on historical data before further mining. Existing similarity search algorithms [4, 6, 13] look for similar sequence based on given whole time series sequence or subsequence in non-high dimensional space and assume all historical data has equivalent weight for similarity. In real financial markets, the financial time series are driven by a high number of dimensions and historical data has time value. More recent data is more relevant to decision making based our research. Sophisticated unsupervised similarity search algorithms are needed to help investors compute similarity from hundreds or even thousands of securities. The goal is to develop a method that not only improves the efficiency in identifying similarity, but also provides a very high level of accuracy. If that is achieved, investors can expect to reduce the risk component in their investment decision making process. The developed similarity search algorithm contributes to the academic research fields in many ways.

- ◆ The first to study applying data objects time value function to high dimensional financial time series.
- ◆ Developed a novel pruning based HAC algorithm based on dimensional reduction algorithms.
- ◆ Developed a unique similarity measurement definition and calculation.
- ◆ Provided a similarity measurement foundation for developing potential models in financial markets.

3 Background and related work

3.1 Time series and sequence data mining research

A time series is a sequence of real numbers, representing the measurements of a real variable at equal time intervals. A time series database is a large collection of time series data such as that found in the NYSE, and NASDAQ stock databases. Classical time series analysis can be categorized into identifying patterns [5] and forecasting. Similarity search is one of the major research topics within time series data and is used in subsequence similarity, clustering, indexing, and rule discovery. Existing similar sequence matching algorithms, map a data sequence of length n to a point in an n-dimensional space. Most of the algorithms define similarity between two data sequences using the Euclidean distance (ED) between two corresponding points. ED is easy to compute and scales to other problems such as clustering, and indexing. However, it doesn't allow for different baselines (i.e. stock A fluctuates at $80 and stock B at $10) and different scales (i.e. Stock A fluctuates between $80 and $120, stock B between $5 and $15). The challenge is to design solutions that attempt to strike a balance between accuracy and efficiency. Since search performance degrades exponentially as the dimensionality of the index structures increases, most of the existing algorithms reduce the dimensionality by mapping the n-dimensional points into the f-dimensional ones (f<n).

Wu, Salzberg and Zhang [13] proposed a subsequence based similarity search method particularly for stock market prediction analysis. However, the paper employs a b% indicator, a popular indicator derived from Bollinger Bands, and utterly relies on zigzag price movement to do prediction and therefore is not a high dimensionality approach. In reality, most sophisticated investors will consider not only the price, but also other dimensions (EPS, daily trading volume, 52 weeks low and highs, etc.) in making investment decisions.

3.2 Hierarchical agglomerative clustering

Hierarchical clustering is a deterministic algorithm. The hierarchical based algorithms use a distance matrix as clustering criteria and do not require the number of clusters k as an input, but require a termination condition. Two well-known heuristic methods are k-means and k-medoids algorithms [6].

In our study we use HAC to build a hierarchical classification of objects through a series of binary merges. The algorithm starts by merging the individual objects followed by merging these initial clusters. A slice across the hierarchy can then be taken at any level to provide the desired number of clusters. We experienced different rules for agglomeration, i.e. merge two clusters with the smallest distance between two inter-cluster elements.

4 Business similarity

The business definition of similarity is the foundation of our algorithm and implementation. Financial Analysts believe that individual stocks with a similar price change, a similar slope change, a similar length of change period and with other attributes such as similar trading volume, solid earning per share and price per earning are considered to be similar objects. Financial Analysts believe the reflect characteristics at the current time.

Price is the most important attribute in financial markets and is the foundation of the similarity definition in this study. The properties of subsequence of the price attributes movement over time are typically of more concern by financial analysts.

For example, in the Figure 1, S1 and S3, S2 and S4 have same amplitudes with different time differences. S1 and S2, S3 and S4 have the same time difference with different amplitude differences. Financial analysts consider S1 and S3, S2 and S4 more similar while S1 and S2, S3 and S4 are less similar. So we apply different weights for normalized amplitude change and time difference. Based on similarity principles above from the business world, we proposed our similarity definition and measurements [12] in section 5.

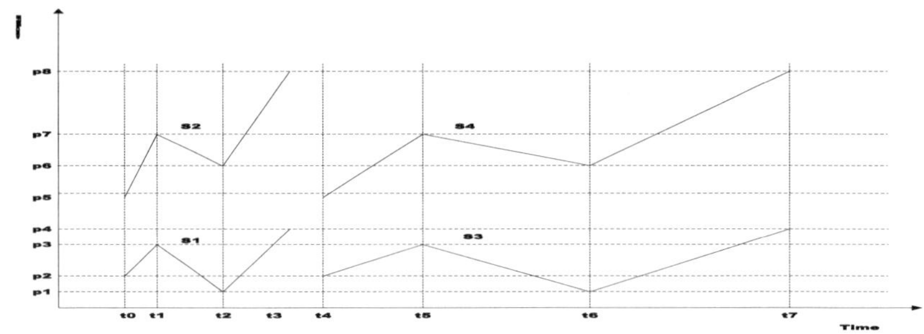

Figure 1: Price dimension similarity amplitude vs. time difference.

5 Similarity definition and measurement

Various indexing based similarity searching techniques have been explored for large databases. The biggest challenge in our research was how to implement similarity search in high dimensional data space across all time series data objects. The general idea is outlined below. Based on characteristics analysis of time series and data transformation, the following measurements are proposed: First, the zigzag shape of the Price dimension must be similar. We use a method similar to that proposed in Wu et al [13] based on permutation of the changing points and Euclidean distance between the objects based on the PLR. Second, the trend is always very important in a time series and should be part of the similarity search. We consider the Price attribute trend only for approving the concept. Third, for the remaining selected attributes, we calculate weighted distance based on the normalized values at changing points' time stamps. This is based on the correlation coefficient value of the attributes calculated during the Attribute Selection algorithm [11] against the Price dimension. Fourth, a time value function is applied to all data points. Based on the above analysis and observation, we proposed a similarity definition between two time series objects in Wang [12]:

Definition 1: Similarity measurement
Given two time series object S and S',

$S = ((t_1, \overrightarrow{D_1}, \overrightarrow{T_1}), (t_2, \overrightarrow{D_2}, \overrightarrow{T_2}) \ldots (t_n, \overrightarrow{D_n}, \overrightarrow{T_n}), t_0, t_c),$

S'= ((t'$_1$, $\overrightarrow{D'_1}$, $\overrightarrow{T'_1}$), (t'$_2$, $\overrightarrow{D'_2}$, $\overrightarrow{T'_2}$)…(t'$_n$, $\overrightarrow{D'_n}$, $\overrightarrow{T'_n}$), t'$_0$, t'$_c$), where $\overrightarrow{D_n}$ = (D_{1n}, D_{2n}, D_{3n}, …, D_{kn}), $\overrightarrow{T_n}$ = (T_{1n}, T_{2n}, T_{3n}, …, T_{kn}) and k the number of final dimensions. S and S' are similar if S and S's satisfy the following properties:

- S and S' have the same number of segments and permutation of the Price dimension. This is the pre-condition for any of the following properties.
- Distance(S, S') < ε_1, where ε_1 is the given error threshold and Distance(S, S') $= \sum_{i=1}^{k}\sum_{t=0}^{n} \gamma_i * f(t) * d(S.A_{it}, S'.A_{it})$, γ_i is the aggregated correlation coefficient value of ith dimension A_i. *f(t)* is the Time Value Function. The distance refers to the amplitude change difference of Price and the other selected dimensions.
- Distance(T,T') < ε_2, where ε_2 is given an error threshold and Distance(T,T') = $\sum_{t=1}^{n} f(t) * d(S.T, S'.T')$. T in this study is only for the Price dimension. *f(t)* is the Time Value Function and $f(t) = 1 - \lambda^{t_c - t}$ in this study where λ is an experiment value i.e. λ=0.95.

The similarity calculation uses backward order to calculate the value of each segment based on a time value function. According to the time value function, older data points within a selected time window contribute less to the final similarity value. The segment is the base unit for whole calculation. The similarity value is the average of the sum of the similarity of each segment. Each pair of segment similarities is calculated based on the price dimension, trend of the price dimension and other values from the final selected attributes with the time value function.

Equation 1: Segment similarity between two objects: [12]

$$
\begin{aligned}
& Sim(seg_1, seg_1') \\
&= (1 - \lambda^{(h - \frac{t_1 + t_2}{2})}) * \left\| \left\{ \begin{array}{l} \left[\alpha * |P_1 - P_2| + \beta * |T_{1\sim2}| + \alpha * \sum_{j=1}^{m} \left(\gamma_j * |A_{j1} - A_{j2}|\right) \right] \\ - \left[\alpha * |P_1' - P_2'| + \beta * |T_{1\sim2}'| + \alpha * \sum_{j=1}^{m} \left(\gamma_j * |A_{j1}' - A_{j2}'|\right) \right] \end{array} \right\} \right\| \\
&= (1 - \lambda^{(h - \frac{t_1 + t_2}{2})}) * \left[\alpha * \left(\left\| P_1 - P_2| - |P_1' - P_2' \right\| + \sum_{j=1}^{m} \left(\gamma_j * \left(\left\| A_{j1} - A_{j2}| - |A_{j1}' - A_{j2}' \right\| \right) \right) \right) + \beta * \left\| T_{1\sim2}| - |T_{1\sim2}' \right\| \right]
\end{aligned}
$$

where $(1 - \lambda^{(h - \frac{t_1 + t_2}{2})})$ is the time value function and h is the number of business days within the user specified time period. t_1 is the date for ending changing point and t_2 is the date for starting changing point of seg_1, where seg_1 stands for segment 1. P_1 and P_2 stand for the ending and starting plast value. α and β

stand for the relative contribution scale of the attributes amplitude and trend to the similarity respectively. $T_{1\sim2}$ stands for the trend degree value for seg_1 with end point as 1 and start point as 2.

6 Hierarchical agglomerative clustering

6.1 Pruning based HAC algorithm

We customized the traditional HAC algorithm through application of a pruning condition. After our PLR based Segmentation and Pruning algorithm [11], the initial data set is divided into groups based on the number of segments. Moreover, the groups are divided into subgroups based on a permutation. The data objects with the same permutation are grouped into sub groups. We consider these objects as having more similar characteristics. First, the similarity values only need to be computed within subgroups. Second, the clusters formation can not be across sub groups. With these two conditions, we prune the cluster formation based on the traditional HAC algorithm. The following is our customized HAC algorithm pseudo code.

```
/*************customized HAC algorithm pseudo-code****************/
 Begin;
Read in all PLRed stock file names;
Initialize HAC instance hac;
//step 1: grouping by number of segments
  hac.groupBySegNumber();
// step 2: Inside each group, filter stock by permutation algorithm
  hac.groupByPermutation(){
        Perform permutation inside each segment group;
        For every two stocks inside each segment group
                sort two stocks' low points by plast attribute;
                if all low point index are same;
                        continue to high points permutation;
                Else
                        Skip these two stocks because they can not be permuted;
                sort two stocks' high points by plast attribute;
                If all high point index are same;
                        Put in one sub group under the segment group;
                Else
                        Skip these two stocks because they can not be permuted;
}
//step 3: HAC clustering based on segment grouping and permutation sub grouping
Load each sub group within segment group as individual group;
Create HACMatrix for each individual group;
Perform HAC clustering based on HACMatrix(){
        //Compute Similarity
         For every two stocks inside HACMatrix group{
                Compute similarity value;
                Store the similarity value along with two stocks index in an Array;
                Compute similarity calculation;
        }
        //customized clustering based on minimum distance between clusters
         Find minimum stocks' similarity value;
        Produce a cluster by joining the stocks with this minimum similarity value;
        Update HACMatrix;
        Recompute similarity value between new grouped stocks and other stocks;
}
/*************customized HAC algorithm pseudo-code****************/
```

As depicted in the pseudo code above, first objects are grouped by the number of segments. Second further group objects to produce subgroups inside each group through the permutation process. The permutation process divides all changing points of any two objects into upper changing points and lower changing points. If the index is the same for each point, the two objects belong to the same subgroup. The third step performs HAC based on the produced subgroups. The algorithm creates a HAC matrix to store the similarity values for each individual subgroup. After the cluster is generated at each step, the algorithm updates the matrix and re-computes the similarity values between the new cluster and other clusters or objects.

7 Experiment and result analysis

7.1 Raw data and attribute set

The Standard & Poor 500 Composite (S&P 500) stocks from BLOOMBERG© were selected as our raw data. We obtained 15 years of historical data with 95 attributes ranging from the pricing attributes to fundamental financial attributes. In order to adapt the environmental effect, also collected were 11 key economic indicators for the United States over those 15 years from DATASTREAM.

7.2 Attribute selection and construction

The selection of the initial attribute set was conducted using inputs from financial market domain experts. Three categories of attributes: market attributes, financial attributes, and environmental attributes were selected. Besides these directly accessible attributes, others were created to better measure stock performance. For instance, $\ln\frac{Price_t}{Price_{t-1}} = \gamma_{t-1}$: which reflects the ratio of return between the current day and last day.

7.3 Sample clusters analysis

Figure 2 below represents groups of detected similar objects based on pxlast pruning thresholds equal to 12.5% with the data ranging from January 2, 2002 to December 30, 2003. We explain each figure in detail according to our framework but will only focus on Price amplitude change and trend degree.

All three objects CVX, CSX, and UCL have 6 segments. All three objects have the same upper and lower points which ensure that the basic shapes of all three objects are the same. CVX and UCL joined as one cluster first. CSX is joined to the cluster in second step. As you can notice from figure above, the reason why CVX and UCL are joined as one cluster first is due to the time value function. The first segment (backward) of CVX and UCL is more similar since both segments are very short with similar amplitude change. The difference between these three objects is mostly seen in segment #3 and #4. Segment #3's objects have very close amplitude change which is 2 times the weighted trend change in our experiment. The amplitude change plays a more important role. Also, note that the trend change is not too far away.

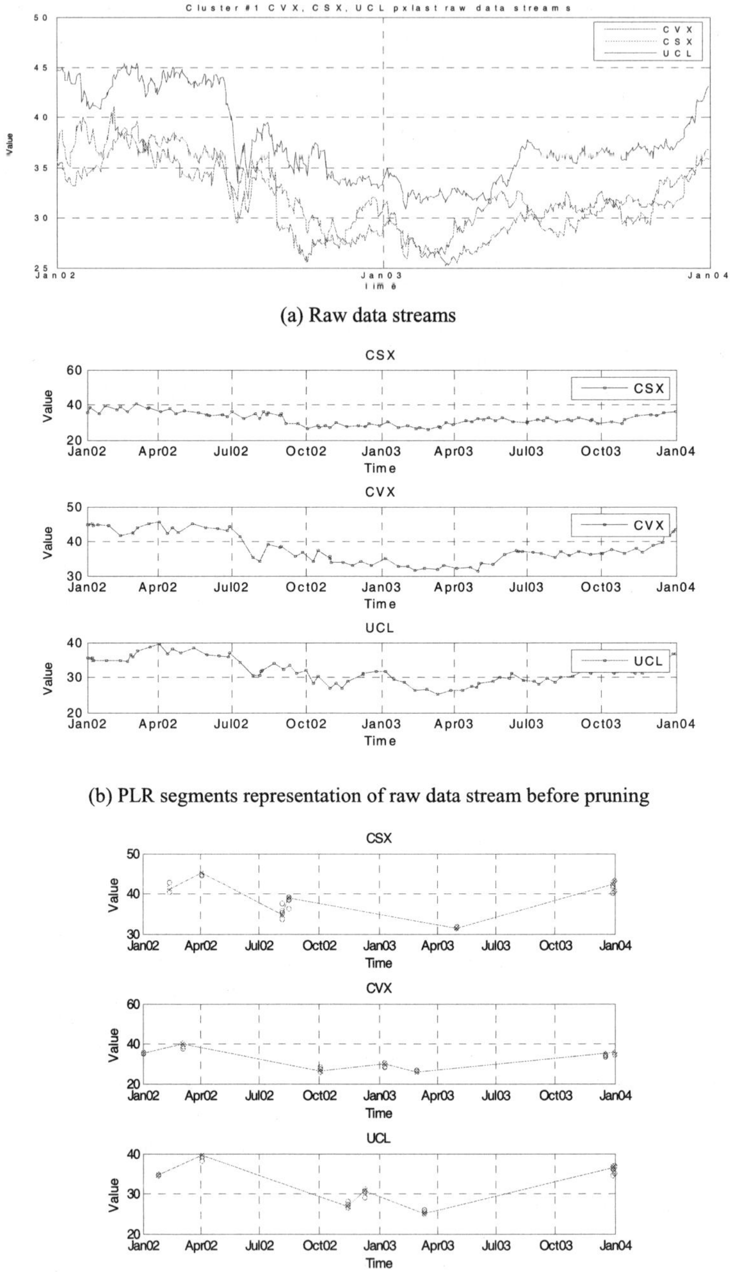

(a) Raw data streams

(b) PLR segments representation of raw data stream before pruning

(c) Pruning result used to compute the similarity

Figure 2: Cluster #1 CVX, CSX, and UCL with 12.5% puning threshold.

Therefore they are considered to be very close by the algorithm. There are also other selected attributes denoted as “o” in the figure and their amplitude changes contribute to the final similarity value as well. You can see they are similar over the Price dimension in fact, especially the CVX and UCL stock objects.

8 Conclusion

In this study, we introduced a pruning based Hierarchical Agglomerative Clustering algorithm over high dimensional financial time series. The pruning based Hierarchical Agglomerative Clustering algorithm is based on a piecewise linear represented multi-dimensional data object, produced by our Segmentation and Pruning algorithm over high dimensional financial data along with our Attribute Selection algorithm. Our experiments show that our vertical (Attribute Selection algorithm) and horizontal (PLR based Segmentation and Pruning algorithm) dimension reduction algorithms [11] are able to present the objects in concise and accurate form to be further processed by our HAC algorithm.

We also proposed a unique similarity measurement [12] which is composed of three parts, the Price dimension amplitude similarity, Price dimension trend similarity, and other selected attributes amplitude similarity. Our similarity measurement properties were derived from finance industry analysts, giving this research a realistic method for identifying similarity. Moreover, we introduced a new time value concept to the similarity measurement. We find that more recent data contributes more significantly to the similarity measurement. Consideration of an entire time series history is not meaningful to current decision making according to financial analysts in the industry.

The experiments illustrate that our algorithms are able to find similarity efficiently within a large set of high dimensional data.

In this study, we focused on static time series data. We can improve the algorithms presented in this research to dynamic (incrementally updated) time series data by dealing with the moving perspective of the data. In addition, our high dimensional dimension reduction algorithms can be utilized to predict the dependent variable data characteristics in next time interval based on classification.

References

[1] Adam Blazejewski, Richard Coggins. Application of Self-organizing Maps to Clustering of High-frequency Financial Data. The second workshop on Australasian information security, Data Mining and Web Intelligence, and Software Internationalisation - Volume 32, Pages: 85–90, 2004.

[2] Steve Craighead and Bruce Klemesrud. Stock Selection Based on Cluster and Outlier Analysis. Fifteenth International Symposium on Mathematical Theory of Networks and Systems University of Notre Dame, August 12-16, 2002.

[3] Martin Gavrilov, Dragomir Anguelov, Piotr Indyk, Rajeev Motwani. Mining the Stock Market: Which Measure Is Best? The sixth ACM SIGKDD International Conference on Knowledge Discovery and Data Mining, Pages: 487–496, 2000.
[4] Dimitrios Gunopulos(UC, Riverside), Gautan Das(Microsoft Research). Tutorial PM-2 Time Series Similarity Measures. The sixth ACM SIGKDD International Conference on Knowledge Discovery and Data Mining, Pages: 243–307, 2000.
[5] Jiawei Han, Guozhu Dong, Yiwen Yin. Efficient Mining of Partial Periodic Patterns in Time Series Database. The fifteenth International Conference on Data Engineering, pages 106–115, 1999.
[6] Jiawei Han and Micheline Kamber. Data mining: Concepts and Techniques. 2001 by Academic Press.
[7] Mehmed Kantardzic, Pedram Sadeghian, Chun Shen. The Time Diversification Monitoring of a Stock Portfolio: an Approach Based on the Fractal Dimension. The 2004 ACM symposium on Applied computing, Pages: 637–641, 2004.
[8] Boris Kovalerchuk and Evgenii Vityaev. Data Mining in Finance: Advances in Relational and Hybrid Methods. 2000 by Kluwer Academic Publisher.
[9] Jessica Lin, Eamonn Keogh, Wagner Truppel. Clustering of Streaming Time Series Is Meaningless. The 8th ACM SIGMOD workshop on Research Issues in Data Mining and Knowledge Discovery, Pages: 56–65, 2003.
[10] Robert R. Trippi, Jae K. Lee. Artificial Intelligence in Finance & Investing: State-Of-The-Art Technologies for Securities Selection and Portfolio Management. Irwin Professional Publishing; Revised Edition (January 1, 1996).
[11] Dajun Wang, Paul J. Fortier, Howard E. Michel, and Theophano Mitsa. T-outlier and a novel dimensionality reduction framework in high dimensional time series financial data. The Second International Conference on Computational Finance and its Applications, June 2006
[12] Dajun Wang, Paul J. Fortier, Howard E. Michel, and Theophano Mitsa. Hierarchical Agglomerative Clustering Based T-outlier Detection. The Sixth IEEE International Conference on Data Mining, Risk Mining Workshop Page(s):731–738
[13] Huanmei Wu, Betty Salzberg, and Donghui Zhang. Online Event-driven Subsequence Matching over Financial Data Streams. ACM SIGMOD International Conference on Management of Data, Pages: 23–34, 2004.
[14] Kenji Yamanishi and Jun-ichi Takeuchi. A Unifying Framework for Detecting Outliers and Change Points from Non-Stationary Time series Data. The eighth ACM SIGKDD International Conference on Knowledge Discovery and Data Mining, Pages: 676–681, 2002.

Feasible estimation of the long term interest rate dynamics by nonlinear techniques

S. Fink[1] & J. Walde[2]
[1]*Treasury Department, Raiffeisenlandesbank Oberoesterreich, Austria*
[2]*Department of Statistics, University of Innsbruck, Austria*

Abstract

Due to the importance of the risk-free capital market interest rate, nearly all large economic and financial institutions deal with the analysis of its future development. Although sometimes advanced econometric methods (VAR, ECM) are used instead of or alongside the standard OLS regression approach, almost all of the work in this field deals with the basic assumption of (multi-variate, multi-equation) linear relationships between the variables. In our paper we try to find out whether nonlinearity can really be neglected. We apply artificial neural networks as a nonlinear modelling tool. Using monthly data from 1960–2005, we forecast the interest rate by means of multi-layer perceptrons (MLP). As a benchmark method we use vector autoregression models dealing with the identical dataset. The obtained results give evidence of the underlying nonlinearity of the problem. The MLP outperform the classical tools with regard to different error measures and especially in capturing the turning points of the interest curve.

Keywords: error correction model, multi-layer perceptrons, interest rate, nonlinear modelling.

1 Introduction

Due to the importance of the risk-free capital market rate, nearly all large economic and financial institutions deal with the analysis of its determinants and future development. In most cases the German 10-year Government Bond, the so-called "Bund", is used as a benchmark for the European capital market. As the futures markets are highly liquid, the most widely used forecasting technique

www.witpress.com, ISSN 1743-3517 (on-line)
doi:10.2495/CF080051

is chart-technical analysis although e.g. Lo et al. show that it only turns out to be of use in the short term [1].

Beside these charting techniques, a wide range of econometric literature focuses on approaches that come up to the demands of scientific rigour. Part of the research focuses exclusively on long-term interest rates [2, 3], while the other part deals with analyzing the structure of the yield curve [4, 5]. The proposed independent variables in these approaches are as heterogeneous as they can be. Nevertheless, they have one thing in common: Although advanced econometric methods are used instead of or alongside standard OLS regressions, almost all the work in this field deals with the basic assumption of linear relationships between the variables. These considerations lead necessarily to the following two essential questions:

- What is the optimal set of independent variables that performs best in determining and forecasting the German government Bond rate?
- Is a linear modelling of the relationships suitable for this kind of problem or is there any additional nonlinear information?

In our work we focus on both steps of long-term interest rate modelling: the question of variable selection (and whether "common knowledge" among market participants can improve results) as well as the methodological question of linear versus nonlinear modelling. The remainder of the paper is organized as follows. In Section 2 interest theories are pictured briefly to get an idea about possible influence variables. We describe the used variable selection process by means of interviewing traders on equity and fixed income trading floors of 15 investment banks. The employed econometric models as well as the artificial neural network are presented together with the obtained results in Section 4. Finally, we summarize the main results and implications of our work.

2 Theory

In the following we try to identify the most common theoretical approaches and determinants for the risk-free Capital market rate.

In the classical capital theory the interest rate is explained by confronting demand for and supply of capital [6]. The interest rate parity [7] assumes integrated international capital (bond) markets where arbitrage will cause elimination of (international) price differences. For this reason foreign interest rate developments can be of influence on the domestic rates. The preferred habitat theory [8] shows that money market investments are a substitute for investments in the bond market. Returns may differ, but when the difference between returns gets out of equilibrium, it may induce capital movements to or from the money market, leading to changing bond prices. The preferred habitat theory acknowledges that investors and borrowers have a preference for a certain maturity (which makes this theory differ from the expectations theory of the term structure), but that changing prices in either the money market or bond market can change the investment or borrowing decisions. Hence movements in the money markets affect the long-term interest rate [9]. Fisher's interest rate theory states that investors want to be compensated for inflation [10]. They add the expected inflation over the investment period to the market clearing real interest rate. Portfolio theory asserts that the difference in asset prices is caused by differences in risk, where it is assumed that investors are risk averse and that they will only invest in higher risk assets when they are being compensated for this [11].

3 Data

To select the relevant independent variables for our problem we conducted a survey. The questionnaire contained all 18 variables proposed by theory. This questionnaire was sent to traders on equity and fixed income trading floors of 15 investment banks in the USA, Great Britain, France, Germany, and Austria. They were asked to select the variables that for them were the key factors influencing long term European government Bond yield. Furthermore they were asked about the sign of the influence and were given the opportunity of proposing additional important variables missing in the given list.

The survey resulted in the following variable set. For all variables we used end-of-month data from 1960/01/31 to 2003/12/31, the expected signs of the influences are in parentheses.

Foreign long-term interest rates (+): Traders focus on the US market as the largest foreign economic zone. As independent variable we use the average yield of the US 10 year treasury bills (USD10Y, source: Bloomberg).

Exchange rate (-) respectively (+): Our survey confirmed the importance of the exchange rate in general and the USD/EUR exchange rate in particular (ERUSDEUR, source: Federal Reserve Bank of St. Louis). In contrast to theory the sign of the exchange rate's influence was suggested to be positive.

Short-term interest rate (+): A positive relation is assumed between the long-term and the short-term interest. Corresponding to the survey's results, we use the European as well as the US short rate. For the European rate we employ the 3-month Frankfurt Interbank Offered rate (FRIBOR) from 1960 to 1998 and the EURIBOR (European Interbank Offered rate) from 1999 to 2003 (EUR3M, source: Bloomberg). The U.S. short rate is represented by the 3-month USD-Libor (USD3M, London Interbank Offered rate).

Business cycle (+): The survey resulted in the U.S. Industrial Production Index to be the most important indicator for the state of the world economy (IPUS, source: Federal Board of Governors).

Inflation rate (+) respectively (–): We use the *Consumer Price Index for All Urban Consumers: All Items* for US inflation (CPIUS, source: U.S. Department of Labor, Bureau of Labor Statistics) and *Consumer Price Index for Germany: All Items* for German Inflation (CPIGER, source: Bloomberg). We did not get a distinct sign of the influence in our survey.

Returns on assets (+): Asset returns are suggested to play an important role for the development of the long-term Bund rate. The following two stock indices were proposed by the survey: the German DAX (DAX) and the S&P 500 (SPX) which are both performance indices (source: Reuters).

As proposed before we used the German government Bond rate as dependent variable, which is the average yield of the German 10-year government bond (GDBR10Y, source: Datastream).

All data is seasonally unadjusted. We have 526 observation units as we loose the first two observations due to data preparation.

4 Specification and estimation results

As first approach we employ an error correction model (ECM). Unit root tests (Augmented Dickey-Fuller test, Phillips-Perron test) give evidence that six out of ten variables (ERUSDEUR, CPIGER, CPIUS, USD10Y, USD3M, GDBR10Y) follow a unit root process. Johansen's cointegration test indicates at a 5% significance level one cointegrating equation. Hence, we estimate the following model: $y_t = m + \alpha_1 y_{t-1} + \beta_{01} x_{t-1}^{(1)} + \beta_{11} x_{t-2}^{(1)} + \beta_{02} x_{t-1}^{(2)} + \beta_{12} x_{t-2}^{(2)} + \ldots + \gamma_1 x_{t-1}^{(6)} + \ldots + u_t$, where $x_{t-1}^{(1)}, \ldots, x_{t-1}^{(5)}$ are $I(1)$ variables ($I(1)$ denotes integrated of order 1), and $x_{t-1}^{(6)}, \ldots, x_{t-1}^{(9)}$ are $I(0)$ variables. In order to capture the entire structure of the residuals an autoregressive term and GARCH(1,1) are used. Neither the Ljung-Box-Q-statistic nor the estimated autocorrelation and partial autocorrelation function indicate any remaining structure in the residuals. AIC is -0.672 and SIC is -0.510. The detailed results for the coefficients and their significance are given in Table 2.

Table 1: Estimation results for the model. In the second column the estimates are listed and in the following column their standard errors. The value of the statistic and the corresponding p-value are shown in columns four and five. Additionally, the estimates for the variance equation are given.

Independent variables	Coefficient	Std. Error	p-value	Independent variables	Coefficient	Std. Error	p-value
$\hat{m}$	0.2037	0.0702	0.0037	USD10Y(-1)	0.0957	0.0335	0.0043
GDBR10Y(-1)	0.9097	0.0200	0.0000	USD10Y(-2)	-0.0917	0.0358	0.0105
ERUSDEUR(-1)	0.2941	0.1384	0.0335	USD3M(-1)	0.0047	0.0280	0.8663
ERUSDEUR(-2)	-0.2617	0.1370	0.0562	USD3M(-2)	0.01891	0.0283	0.5044
CPIGER(-1)	-0.0037	0.0205	0.8581	DAX(-1)	-0.0019	0.0012	0.1230
CPIGER(-2)	0.0256	0.0202	0.2056	IPUS(-1)	0.0058	0.0025	0.0234
CPIUS(-1)	0.0255	0.0240	0.2868	SPX(-1)	-0.0010	0.0016	0.5151
CPIUS(-2)	-0.0250	0.0236	0.2887	EUR3M(-1)	0.0216	0.0085	0.0112
$\hat{\rho}_1$	0.3928	0.0497	0.0000				
Variance Equation							
$\hat{\omega}$	0.0009	0.0004	0.0463				
ARCH: $\hat{\gamma}_1$	0.1512	0.0419	0.0003	GARCH: $\hat{\gamma}_2$	0.8359	0.0450	0.0000

For an easier interpretation we transform the estimated mean equation into the typical error correction type expression:

$$\Delta\hat{y}_t = 0.262\cdot\Delta ERUSDEUR_{t-1} - 0.026\cdot\Delta CPIGER_{t-1} + 0.025\cdot\Delta CPIUS_{t-1} + 0.092\cdot\Delta USD10Y_{t-1}$$
$$-0.019\cdot\Delta USD3M_{t-1} - 0.002\cdot DAX_{t-1} + 0.006\cdot IPUS_{t-1} - 0.001\cdot SPX_{t-1} + 0.022\cdot EUR3M_{t-1}$$
$$-0.090\cdot[y_{t-1} - 2.256 - 0.360\cdot ERUSDEUR_{t-1} - 0.243\cdot CPIGER_{t-1} - 0.006\cdot CPIUS_{t-1}$$
$$-0.044\cdot USD10Y_{t-1} - 0.262\cdot USD3M_{t-1}]$$

The sign of the DAX is unexpectedly negative but it is not significant. ERUSDEUR, EUR3M, and USD10Y show a significant influence on the dependent variable with the expected sign. Additionally, the business cycle variable (IPUS) has a significant influence and is useful for forecasting the yield of the German 10-year government bond.

Figure 1 gives the one period ahead forecast for the out-of-sample period defined before. In addition the 95% confidence interval and the original time series, which lies except one date inside the confidence bands, are plotted.

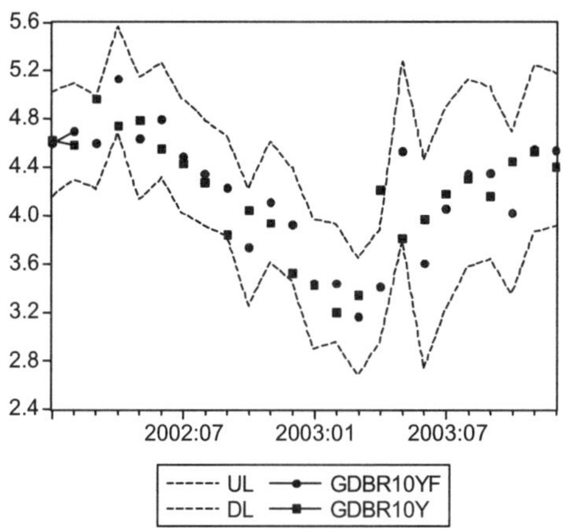

Figure 1: One-period-ahead forecasts (GDBR10YF) by means of the ECM. UL denotes the upper limit of the 95% confidence interval of the estimates and DL the down limit. The original time series (GDBR10Y) is also drawn.

The second modelling approach uses a feedforward, fully connected three layer perceptron (MLP) [12]. Although the objective of this paper is forecasting, we neglect at first the time dependence structure. This implies that the forecast of the yield of the German 10-year government bond by the MLP is solely achieved by means of the independent variables. We analyze if this procedure leads to better forecasts than the more traditional method. We split the data arbitrarily into three samples: a training set for estimating the parameters (70% of the observations), a validation set to control the optimization algorithm with respect to overfitting (20% of the observations), and a generalization set to evaluate the quality of the estimated model. The employed MLP looks like $\hat{y}_s = f\left(\boldsymbol{x}_s, \hat{\boldsymbol{\theta}}\right) = G\left(\sum_{j=1}^{HU} w_j^{(2)} \cdot G\left(\sum_{k=0}^{9} w_{kj}^{(1)} x_{k,s}\right) + w_0\right)$, $G(x) = \frac{1}{1+e^{-x}}$, where HU is the number of hidden units, $w_{..}^{(.)}$ are the weights, $\boldsymbol{x}_s$ is the input vector of the observation units ($x_{s-1}^{(1)},\ldots,x_{s-1}^{(9)}$), $\hat{y}_s = f\left(\boldsymbol{x}_s, \hat{\boldsymbol{\theta}}\right)$ is the network output, $\hat{\boldsymbol{\theta}}$ is the vector of all estimated parameters. For technical reasons, all input variables are transformed to the interval (-1,1) and the output variable to (0,1). The number of hidden units is varied from 1 to 15, for each constellation 50 weight initializations are carried out. The best network with respect to the mean squared error calculated on the validation set is chosen for further analysis. The so obtained optimal network achieves a determination coefficient (R^2) on the training set of 98.35%, an R^2 on the validation set of 97.16%, and an R^2 on the generalization set of 96.77%. AIC is -2.223 and SIC is -1.412, which is significantly better than the previous model.

Mainly we are interested in the forecasting ability. The previously described optimization procedure is done for all 24 networks that have to be calculated for the out-of sample period to get the one-period-ahead forecasts. Figure 2 shows the estimates obtained by the MLP (GDBR10YF) as well as the original time series (GDBR10Y). Additionally the naive forecast ($E\left(y_{t+1} \middle| \Omega_t\right) = \hat{y}_t$, where Ω_t is the set of all available information up to date t) is plotted to allow another kind of evaluation.

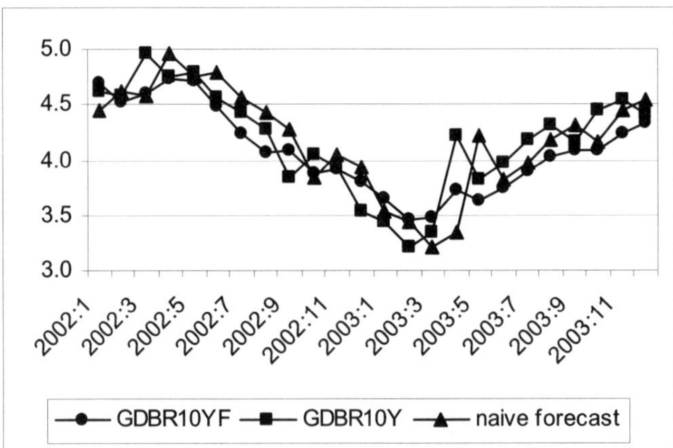

Figure 2: One-period-ahead forecasts (GDBR10YF) by means of the MLP. The original time series (GDBR10YF) is drawn as well as the estimates obtained by the naive forecast method.

The forecast by means of the MLP is quite appropriate, worth mentioning only the information contained in the independent variables is processed nonlinearly. Regarding the mean squared error (MSE, 0.052 versus 0.081), the mean absolute error (MAE, 0.194 versus 0.225), and the mean absolute percentage error (MAPE, 4.742 versus 5.488) the MLP is better than the naive forecast method. This approach is even better than the nonlinear model incorporating the remaining time structure of the residuals. The MLP accounting for the time dependency obtained a MSE of 0.069, a MAE of 0.200, and a MAPE of 4.753. To evaluate the models regarding their forecast abilities we use more forecast error statistics. The root mean squared error (RMSE) and the MAE depend on the scale of the dependent variable. Whereas the MAPE and the Theil inequality coefficient are scale invariant. The Theil inequality coefficient lies between zero and one, where zero indicates a perfect fit. To measure the ability of capturing the turning points, Theil's U_Δ statistic is used.

With respect to the forecast errors Table 2 shows the superiority of the multi layer perceptron, which do not model the time structure. Both MLP approaches do better in predicting the turning points. They are superior to the naive forecast, which obtained a Theil's U_Δ statistic of 1.137.

Table 2: Error measures of the three models.

Error Measures	ECM	MLP	MLP & time structure
RMSE	0.3191	0.2283	0.2636
MAE	0.2459	0.1938	0.2001
MAPE	6.0147	4.7393	4.7525
Theil inequality coefficient	0.0378	0.0275	0.0599
Bias proportion	0.0033	0.1929	0.1418
Variance proportion	0.0142	0.1511	0.0002
Covariance proportion	0.9825	0.6560	0.8580
Theil's U_Δ statistic	1.5768	0.7909	1.0235

5 Discussion and conclusions

As the different partial interest theories offer a wide range of influential variables on the average yield of the German 10-year government bond, we conducted a survey and asked traders on equity and fixed income trading floors of 15 investment banks. By means of the nine selected independent variables, the nonlinear modelling approaches did quite well. The performances in forecasting the two year hold-out sample of the basic structural model and of the error correction model are not distinguishable. The outstanding models are the multi-layer perceptrons that handle the relationships in a nonlinear fashion and therefore they are able to do better forecasts. Especially, the turning points of the interest curve are captured much more precisely by the MLP. This has to be due to a stable nonlinear relationship between the interest rate and the carefully selected independent variables. To be able to get reliable results by nonlinear modelling tools, sufficient data must be available. If this requirement is given and careful optimization techniques are used, this approach enhances the econometric tools for forecasting time series. The additional information can be used to enhance and enlarge the relevant information base for taking decisions. Especially turning point recognition is of practical relevance for both trading and hedging.

References

[1] Lo, A.W., Mamaysky, H. & Wang, J., Foundations of Technical Analysis: Computational Algorithms, Statistical Inference, and Empirical Implementation. *The Journal of Finance*, **55 (4)**, pp. 1705–1765, 2000

[2] Breedon, F., Henry, B. & Williams, G., Long-term real interest rates: Evidence on the global capital market, *Oxford Review of Economic Policy*, **15(2)**, pp. 128–142, 1999

[3] Den Butter, F. A. C. & Jansen, P. W., An empirical analysis of the German long-term interest rate, *University of Amsterdam – Series Research Memoranda*, Research Memorandum 2000–29

[4] Diebold, F. X., Rudebusch, G. D., Boragan Aruoba, S., The Macroeconomy and the Yield Curve: A Nonstructural Analysis, CFS Working Paper Series, Number 2003/31, http://www.ifk-cfs.de/papers/03_31.pdf

[5] Ang, A., Piazzesi, M., A no-arbitrage vector autoregression of term structure dynamics with macroeconomic and latent variables, *Journal of Monetary Economics*, **50 (4)**, pp. 745–787, 2003

[6] Burmeister, E., *Capital Theory and Dynamics*, Cambridge University Press: Cambridge, 1980

[7] Blenman, L.P., Henock, L., Thatcher, J., Interest Rate Parity and the Behavior of the Bid-Ask Spread, *Journal of Financial Research*, **22 (2)**, pp. 189–206, 1999

[8] Mishkin, F. S., *The Economics of Money, Banking and Financial Markets*, 5th edition, Harper Collins: New York, 1997

[9] Riedel, F., Heterogeneous Time Preferences and Humps in the Yield Curve: The Preferred Habitat Theory Revisited, *European Journal of Finance*, **10 (1)**, pp. 3–22, 2004

[10] Phillips, P. C. B., Phillips on Fisher's Equation, *American Journal of Economics and Sociology*, **64 (1)**, pp. 125–168, 2005

[11] Nawrocki, D., Capital Market Theory: Is it relevant to practitioners? *Journal of Financial Planning*, **10 (5)**, pp. 97–103, 1997

[12] Bishop, C. M., *Neural Networks for Pattern Recognition*, Oxford University Press: New York, 1996

Section 2
Derivatives pricing

Derivative pricing as a business grid application using NextGRID technology

A. Basermann, G. A. Kohring & C. Neff
NEC Laboratories Europe,
IT Research Division NEC Europe Ltd, Rathausallee 10,
D-53757 Sankt Augustin, Germany

Abstract

The focus of the option valuation application described in this paper is on complex derivatives like American style options on multiple underlyings. The MPI-parallel and vectorized pricing code developed is based on Monte Carlo and Quasi Monte Carlo simulation methods. Within the European Commission Project NextGRID, whose primary goal is to develop architectural principles for the Next Generation Grid, experiments with derivative pricing scenarios have been performed that test the viability and adequacy of the NextGRID security model as well as the interoperability of NextGRID components. The main benefit of the usage of NextGRID principles and components for the derivative pricing application itself is that it supported the transition from a mere high performance computing Grid application to a business Grid application much better reflecting the functional separation and different levels of expertise of the parties involved. Based on SLAs, it is now possible to make the selection of optimal hardware transparent to the users. The NextGRID security model ensures security and integrity of the data, in a framework that is flexible enough to be adapted to cases where Grid resources are added dynamically.

Keywords: derivative pricing, NextGRID, security, SLAs, business Grid application, performance.

1 Introduction

Both the steadily increasing number of traded financial derivatives and the demand for more and more complex derivatives tailored for special purposes require continuously increasing capacities for the numerical valuation of these

WIT Transactions on Information and Communication Technologies, Vol 41, © 2008 WIT Press
www.witpress.com, ISSN 1743-3517 (on-line)
doi:10.2495/CF080061

financial instruments. The price estimation for these complex products is already demanding, but their constant revaluation within the financial institutions' risk assessment, hedging and portfolio optimization processes can increase the computational resource requirements significantly. Regulation authorities amplify the need for fast and reliable computing capacities by imposing higher standards for availability, system integrity and security on financial institutions. At the same time, financial institutions feel the pressure to cut development times and costs for the introduction of new products and the need to reduce their IT costs. Grid-based solutions will become more and more important in this sector, since they offer a higher utilization of existing resources and offer the additional possibility to increase the computational capacity temporarily by adding external resources in the case of demand peaks.

For the realization of the derivative pricing service discussed in this paper NLE-IT developed a portable Monte Carlo and Quasi-Monte Carlo simulation [1] based pricing toolkit that enables the estimation of derivative prices and sensitivities for European- and American-style options. The parallel simulation toolkit has been tested on a variety of different architectures ranging from NEC SX vector computers to PC Clusters, providing a set of basic random number and low-discrepancy generators, underlying models and product templates [2]. It is designed to be easily extendable to new product templates and underlying models, which can be integrated internally or invoked by the toolkit.

The main requirements for the derivative pricing application in the context of a distributed computing environment are small response times, high service availability, interactive calculation modes for trading purposes, interfaces to sources for market data as well as privacy and integrity of the data.

Within the European Commission Project NextGRID [3], whose primary goal is to develop architectural principles for the Next Generation Grid, use cases with a range of likely financial business scenarios have been composed. NLE-IT's portable derivative pricing code used for the investigations within NextGRID was controlled via an Excel Client on a standard PC. Excel was chosen as interface due to its wide-spread use in financial institutions and its capabilities in pre- and post-processing of the data. Experiments with derivative pricing scenarios have been performed that test the viability and adequacy of the NextGRID security model as well as the interoperability of implementations of NextGRID components on Windows/.NET and on Linux. At the same time, both the performance of available implementations of NextGRID components and potential bottlenecks in NextGRID specifications were examined.

2 NextGRID application architecture

The overall architecture of the derivative pricing application as mapped onto the NextGRID nomenclature is depicted in Figure 1 (cf. [4, 5]). The components coloured green are application independent NextGRID components, while those coloured white are application specific.

As NextGRID takes a business oriented approach to Grid computing, the package groups are geared towards delivering business needs. As can be seen from Figure 1 the packages group components according to their expected use within a business relationship.

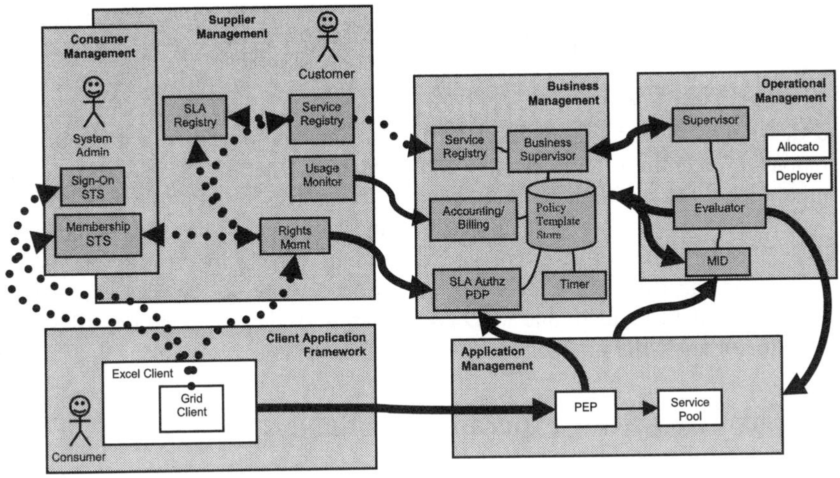

Figure 1: Schematic view of the derivative pricing application's architecture mapped on to the NextGRID nomenclature.

The Supplier Management package is used by customers to manage their relationships with one or more service suppliers. The components in this package allow the customer to keep a local registry of approved services and SLAs (Service Level Agreements), as well as offering the ability to monitor the consumption of resources. Additionally, the Rights Management component allows the customer to inform the service provider as to who in the customer's organization is allowed to use the services on offer; this fine grained resource allocation can be broken down to the level of individual operations on any given service. The components in this package are deployed at the consumer's site.

The Consumer Management package contains components which enable the consumer to control access to the Grid infrastructure to particular members of the consumer's organization.

The client application framework and the application management package contain the application specific components sitting at the consumer and provider sites respectively. While the NextGRID software provides support for these components, they were developed within the scope of this work to the particular demands of this application. In particular, .NET bindings were produced on the application side in order to integrate the Grid client into an Excel worksheet.

The Business Management package is deployed at the service provider's site and enables the provider to manage business relationships with multiple consumers. It contains a service registry detailing the services and their related SLAs which are on offer, as well as components for handling accounting and billing functionality. Since NextGRID provides an SLA driven Grid dynamic, a mapping is established between the terms of the SLA and policies governing how resources are to be allocated and services deployed. These mappings are stored in the Policy Template Store component and provided to the Operational Management component through the Business Supervisor component.

It is the Operational Management package which provides the coupling between the SLAs governing the usage of the service and the services instances themselves. This is an event driven package, in which the MID (Management Information Distribution) component accepts events coming from other packages and distributes them to instances of the Evaluator component. Each Evaluator component examines the events and decides whether to allocate new computational resources and deploy new services corresponding to a given SLA, or whether to de-allocate previously allocated resources. The exact allocation and deployment mechanisms are site dependent. The Supervisors role is to interact with the Business Supervisor and to deploy the policy files associated with SLAs to the Evaluator and MID components. Basically, the policy files tell the Evaluator and MID how to react to particular events.

3 Derivative pricing experiments with NextGRID components

3.1 Security model

This experiment employed the basic NextGRID security model [5] as shown in Figure 2. Not every user in the consumer's organization is known explicitly by the service provider, rather a trust relationship is established between the Consumer Management component and the Business Management component. Through the use of the Rights Management component it is possible for the consumer to assign attributes to each user and instruct the provider how to interpret the attributes for use in making authorization decisions. Using this approach, the provider does not need to keep a list of which users are to be allowed access to the managerial interfaces and which are only to be allowed access to the normal compute interface. This system also allows a manager on the consumer side to decide which SLA any given user is allowed to use when accessing a given service.

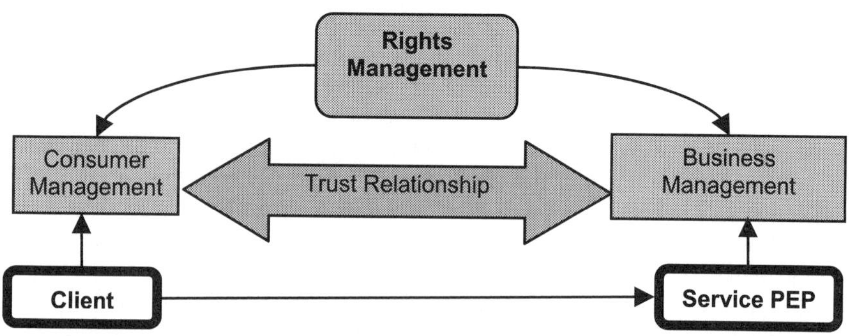

Figure 2: The security model employed for this experiment.

The sequence of events for sending and processing a request is as follows: When the consumer is ready to send a request to the service, the client software first obtains a security token from the Consumer Management component through the NextGRID Endpoint Security infrastructure [5]. This token is attached to the request inside the federation header, which contains information pertaining to the SLA under which the request should be processed along with other billing information, and then sent to the server. At the server side, the federation header is examined, the necessary information is extracted and passed to the Business Management component for verification and validation and only if the Business Management component returns a positive response the request is allowed to proceed to the pricing service for evaluation. The call to the Business Management component is a NextGRID specific feature and represents the main innovation in the security architecture compared with other state-of-the-art frameworks.

3.2 Experiment setup

The physical setup for the derivative pricing experiment depicted in Figure 3 was chosen to be as realistic as possible in that there are firewalls between the user and the service provider; furthermore the application server is protected from the internet gateway machine via a second firewall.

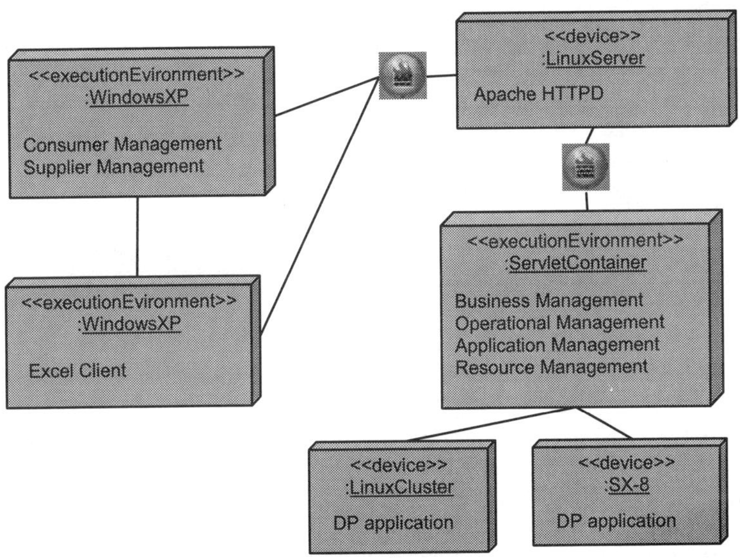

Figure 3: The physical setup for the derivative pricing experiments.

In a more complete scenario there would also be a firewall between the end-users machine running the Excel Client and the machine running the client side Consumer Management services; however, resource limitations for this experiment did not allow an exploration of such a scenario.

There were two compute systems used for the experiments, a Linux cluster consisting of 32 dual AMD Athlon Processors interconnected through Myrinet network and an NEC SX-8 vector computer with 4 processors. Two different compute nodes were used since certain types of models run more efficiently on vector machines while other models are more efficient on scalar machines.

The Excel Client (cf. Figure 4) reflects the setup properly. The interaction with NextGRID components is based completely on .NET (implemented in C#). The client additionally makes use of VBA (Visual Basic for Applications) code serving for pre- and post-processing of the data. A number of callback routines and interfacing objects makes the interaction of the VBA legacy code with the NextGRID components possible. That this worked without problems is an important lesson, since VBA code running in Excel is widely used in financial institutions.

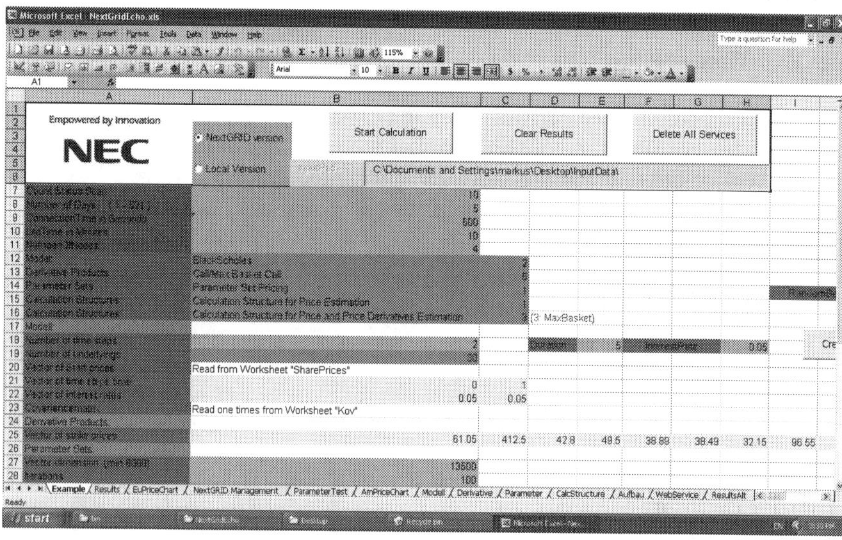

Figure 4: Control sheet of the Excel client.

3.3 SLAs

The first step in creating the new infrastructure involved designing the SLA templates by which the services would be governed. Initially three SLA templates were created, "bronze", "silver" and "gold". The "bronze" and "silver" levels represented relative performance increments on the Linux Cluster, while the "gold" level represented a service running on the SX-8. Later a fourth SLA was added which included a performance model to automatically determine the best computing platform for any given data set.

Regarding the NextGRID SLA schema [5–7], one can distinguish between functional and non-functional terms. The functional terms are mainly guarantees given by the provider covering performance and service availability, while the non-functional terms apply to both parties. The most important performance criterion is the minimum raw computational power to be applied to processing the request, while the most important availability criterion is the daily percentage of up-time. One very important non-functional term concerns IPR (Intellectual Property Rights). The consumer agrees to indemnify the provider in the case where the consumer sends requests containing data for which he/she has not secured the proper permissions and the original data holder takes legal action against the provider. On the other hand, the provider agrees to indemnify the consumer in the case it has not secured the proper license for its pricing algorithms and the proper owner takes legal action against the consumer.

The next step in setting up the experiments involved installing the Business Management and Operational Management packages and configuring the two to work together. Doing so involved the creation of SLA policy files for the MID and Evaluator components (cf. Figure 1). These policy files are distributed by the Supervisor component when the SLA is deployed.

3.4 Service management

The use of the Operational Management package enabled a new approach to managing the application. Instead of using a one-user-one-service technique, a group of service pools was created, with one pool for each of the predefined SLAs. Figure 5 depicts the newly developed service management architecture.

When a new pricing request arrives the SLA under which it should execute is extracted from the message and a request for a corresponding service is made at the "Service Pool". If a suitable service exists and is not busy, then the service, or rather a proxy, providing an interface to the service is returned and the request executes normally. If no suitable service is available, or all services are currently busy executing requests for other users, then a "Service Not Available" response is returned to the "Switchboard". Where upon, the "Switchboard" puts the request on hold, issues a "Waiting" event to the MID component and after a waiting period which is SLA dependent, inquires once again at the "Service Pool" whether or not a suitable service instance is available.

If, when the "Switchboard" inquires after a service supporting a particular SLA, the "Service Pool" is unable to find such a service, it will issue a "Deploy Service" event to the MID. Upon receipt of a "Deploy Service" event, the MID will forward it to the Evaluator component which will trigger an "Action" causing the "Service Manager" to deploy a new service instance operating under the desired SLA. The next time the "Switchboard" inquires whether or not a service is available, the "Service Pool" will return the newly created instance.

Now it can also happen that all service instances are busy, in which case the "Switchboard" will send out repeated "Waiting" events. At some point the waiting time will exceed an SLA dependent threshold, and the next event will then trigger an action causing the "Service Manager" to deploy a new service instance (provided sufficient hardware resources exist).

Finally, it may happen that a particular service instance is idle. After a length of time, an "Idle" event will be sent by the "Service Pool" to the MID. Once the length of the idle period exceeds a given threshold, the next "Idle" event will trigger an action causing the "Service Manager" to retire the idle instance.

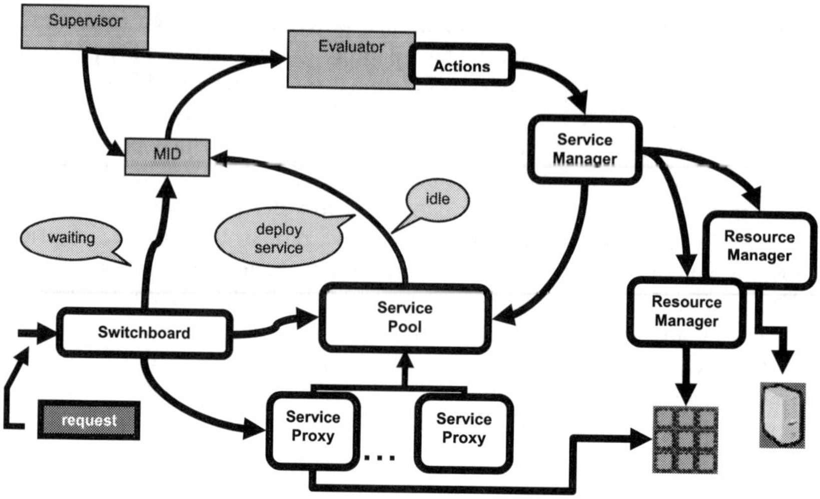

Figure 5: A view of the service management architecture.

3.5 Performance measurements

In [2], the scalability and performance of the MPI-parallel and vectorized derivative pricing code developed was discussed. As an example, Figure 6 shows the scaling behavior of the code for pricing of an American Max. Basket call option (Black Scholes model) on the maximum of five underlying stocks.

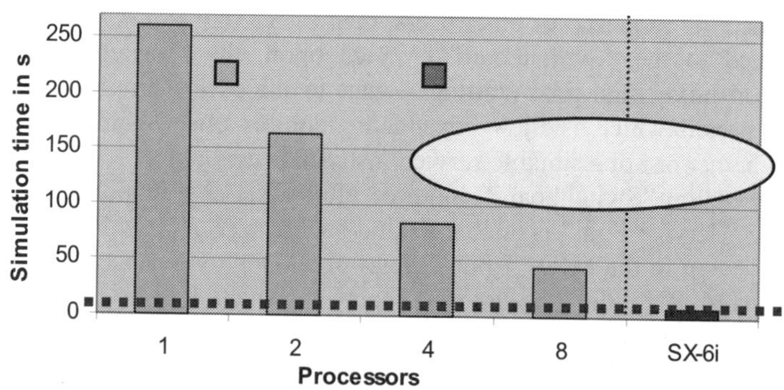

Figure 6: Scalability of the derivative pricing code.

The measurements were performed on a PC cluster with 2-way AMD Athlon 1900+ SMP nodes and on an ultra-compact NEC SX-6i vector processor ("micro-supercomputer"). Beside a good parallel efficiency due to the Monte Carlo approach, an advantageous cache exploitation on RISC processors and a high vectorization degree on vector machines provided an excellent per-processor performance of the code. The latter explains the superior performance of the pricing application on the SX-6i in Figure 6.

One of the important criteria for the application scenarios discussed in this paper was performance in a distributed environment, in particular the penalty paid when accessing the application remotely. Remoting overheads were measured using NextGRID compliant security components and compared to the case where no security was in force. The results are shown in Figure 7.

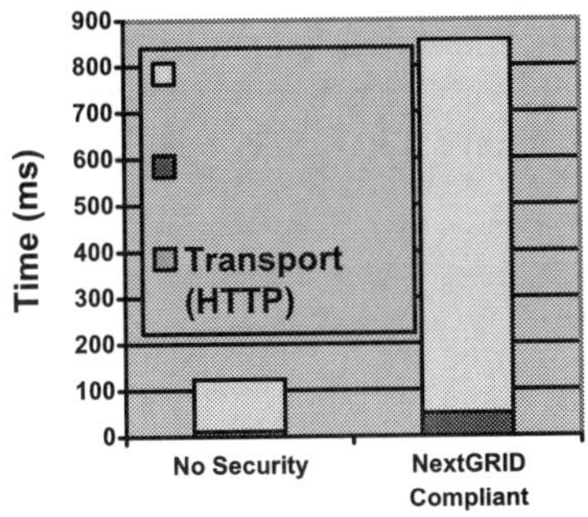

Figure 7: Remoting overheads per request for the derivative pricing service.

The "WS Overhead" is the complete overhead required for processing the Web Services related parts of the message, excluding any time required for the pricing calculation itself. As can be seen, the remoting overheads for using the fully NextGRID compliant security architecture are significant. In many usage scenarios, these overheads are acceptable, however there may be usage scenarios where they would not be. There is still room for optimization in this scenario. For example, if a security context was employed then one could avoid transmitting the SAML (Security Assertion Markup Language) token (which is approximately 18 KB) with every request. Hence, the NextGRID security model could be improved by integration of a more efficient token exchange approach such as that provided by the WS-Secure Conversation specification [8].

4 Conclusions

The Integration of NextGRID components into the derivative Pricing application enabled the transition from an initially purely high performance computing Grid application (with excellent scaling behavior and per-processor performance) to a business Grid application properly reflecting organizational structures.

The NextGRID SLA orientation inspired the implementation of new service levels where, based on a performance model, the optimal platform is selected from the input data. The Grid service can then be utilized by users without the technical background necessary to decide whether a pricing problem would run faster on how many nodes of a PC cluster than on a vector computer or special purpose hardware. For service providers this offers the additional advantage that they can adapt and optimize their resources to the needs documented in the SLAs and make better use of technological advancements. Other service levels may allow access to specific hardware, such that this solution is flexible and can be easily adapted to specific needs in an organization.

Security is of vital importance in financial applications, and even intra-organizational access to data is subject to rigid restrictions controlled by regulation agencies. The NextGRID security model can be mapped to these restrictions, and NextGRID components allow secure implementations keeping the security issues mostly transparent to end users of the Excel Client. The performance of the NextGRID components used for secure transport is sufficient for many time-critical applications (market situations can change within seconds, and options in particular are very sensitive to changes). Approaches such as the use of WS-Secure Conversation could further reduce overheads.

Acknowledgements

This work was partly supported by the European Commission's IST research program under the contract 511563-NextGRID [3]. This paper expresses the authors' opinions and not necessarily those of the European Commission. The Commission is not liable for any use that may be made of the information contained in this document.

References

[1] Boyle, P., Options: A Monte Carlo Approach, *J. of Financial Economics*, **4**, pp. 323–338, 1977.
[2] Schumacher, J, Jaekel, U. & Basermann, A., Parallelization and Vectorization of Simulation Based Option Pricing Methods, *Proc. of ICCSA 03*, Springer, LNCS 2669, pp. 139–147, 2003.
[3] NextGRID, http://www.nextgrid.org/.
[4] Snelling, D., Anjomshoaa, A., Wray, F., Basermann, A., Fischer, M., Surridge, M. & Wieder, P., NextGRID Architectural Concepts, *Proc. of the CoreGRID Symposium in conjunction with the Euro-Par 2007*, Rennes, France, 2007, to appear (http://www.nextgrid.org/download/publications/NextGRID_Architectural_Concepts.pdf) .
[5] Snelling, D., Fischer, M., Basermann, A., Wray, F., Wieder, P., & Surridge, M., NextGRID Vision and Architecture White Paper V5, December 2005 (http://www.nextgrid.org/download/publications/NextGRID_Architecture_White_Paper.pdf).
[6] Mitchell, B. and McKee, P., SLAs A Key Commercial Tool, published in: *Innovation and the Knowledge Economy: Issues, Applications, Case Studies*, eds. P. Cunningham & M. Cunningham, IOS Press Amsterdam, 2005.
[7] Hasselmeyer, P., Koller, B., Schubert, L. & Wieder, P., Towards SLA-Supported Resource Management, *Proc. of HPCC-06*, Lecture Notes in Computer Science, Volume 4208, Springer, Munich, pp. 743–752, 2006.
[8] WS-Secure Conversation 1.3, http://docs.oasis-open.org/ws-sx/ws-secureconversation/ 200512/ws-secureconversation-1.3-os.html.

Valuation of swing options with supplier flexibility – switching and recall features: a methodology note

S. Persad
Hess Corporation, USA

Abstract

This paper presents a method for valuation and risk/sensitivity analysis of swing contracts with switching and/or recall features. Standard swing options allow natural gas customers to exercise a limited number of call features over a period (month) to select the optimal amount of energy to receive each period (day) at a given strike price. More complex versions of these instruments also allow the supplier some flexibility. Two supplier-friendly features are discussed in this paper: (1) Switching features: the supplier must fulfil the buyer's nomination in full, but has a choice of which commodity/delivery location to supply (2) Recall Features: the supplier may recall some of the buyer's nomination amount. This paper offers an algorithm for backward solution. The method draws from Jaillet, Ronn and Tompaidis (2004, Valuation of commodity based swing options. Management Science Vol. 50, Iss. 7, pp. 909–921) by using a forest of trees to represent remaining swing rights, but extends it to a two player (customer and supplier) setting. At each stage the players gather the relevant nodes to which they can transition and engage in a Stackelberg game to determine the optimal action. At each point, the game's outcome is determined employing the game theoretic concept of subgame perfect Nash equilibrium. Because different locations for gas delivery are essentially separate but related markets, the underlying prices to be constructed are two gas locations with a specified correlation. This paper employs Rubenstein's ("Somewhere Over the Rainbow", *RISK* 4 (November 1991), pp. 63–66; "Return to Oz", *RISK* 7 (November 1994), pp. 67–71) pyramid methodology for modelling correlated asset price processes. In addition, we adapt the Hull and White (1994, Numerical Procedures for Implementing Models I: Single Factor Models, Journal of Derivatives Vol 2, pp 37–48) procedure for incorporating drift so that our price pyramid captures the mean reversion feature of natural gas. Finally we make adjustments so that the simulation captures seasonality of natural gas prices.
Keywords: path-dependent option pricing, correlated trinomial tree, lattice, swing options, energy options.

WIT Transactions on Information and Communication Technologies, Vol 41, © 2008 WIT Press
www.witpress.com, ISSN 1743-3517 (on-line)
doi:10.2495/CF080071

1 Introduction

Commonly used in the natural gas market, swing contracts allow customers some flexibility is choosing the delivery time and amount of their gas. They may exercise a limited number of call features to select the optimal amount of energy to receive each period. For an ordinary swing, the valuation becomes a backward induction problem (with multiple states for number of calls remaining).

More complex versions of these instruments also allow the supplier some flexibility. Two supplier-friendly features are discussed in this paper: (1) Switching features: the supplier must fulfil the buyer's nomination in full, but has a choice of which commodity/delivery location to supply (2) Recall Features: the supplier may recall some of the buyer's nomination amount. The first option allows the supplier to take benefit from location or commodity price differentials. The second feature allows the supplier to act optimally under shortages or upward sloping supply curves.

This paper provides the highlights of the full methodology and empirical analysis of this pricing algorithm as is fully detailed in Persad [5].

1.1 The specifics of a swing contract

A vanilla swing contract specifies a strike price (or index), a contract period T, and the length of a subperiod t. The contract specifies that over this contract period (e.g., 30 days), the customer must purchase a given amount M of gas by taking delivery of up to m on some customer-selected subperiods (e.g. a day). The number of subperiods on which a customer can choose to take deliver is T/t. In the contracts the daily maximum, m, is such that $m*T/t > M$ and $m<M$. That is, in order to reach the contractual quantity M, the customer must exercise on less that the available number of subperiods. In this manner, his/her choice of which day to exercise becomes non-trivial. The customer will have c swing rights where $c=M/m$.

A swing contract with switching feature grants the supplier a fixed number of switching rights s, where s is less than or equal to c. That is, the number of switching features is less than the number of swing rights. Each switching right grants the supplier to deliver a substitutable fuel or the same fuel from a different pricing location. For simplicity, we assume that the customer is indifferent between the two fuels. However, the non-trivial Stackelberg game outlined below would easily incorporate a distinction between the two fuels from the customer's point of view.

A swing contract with recall feature allows the supplier to buy back, at a contractually specified price, a certain amount of the daily swing amount if nominated. This is valuable in times of fuel shortages or if the cost of obtaining the supply will increase far beyond the specified strike in the swing contract.

1.2 Previous work

Previous work on swing contracts have been examined by Joskow [6], Jalliet et al [1], Barbieri and Garman [7] , Pilipovic and Wengler [8], and Harrbrucker and Kuhn [9].

1.3 Overview of methodology

The method draws from Jaillet et al [1] by using a forest of trees to represent remaining swing rights, but extends it to a two player (customer and supplier) setting. At each stage the players gather the relevant nodes to which they can transition and engage in a Stackelberg game to determine the optimal action. At each point, the game's outcome is determined employing the game theoretic concept of subgame perfect Nash equilibrium. Because different locations for gas delivery are essentially separate but related markets, the underlying prices to be constructed are two gas locations with a specified correlation. This paper employs Rubenstein's [2, 3] pyramid methodology for modelling correlated asset price processes. In addition, we adapt the Hull and White [4] procedure for incorporating drift so that our price pyramid captures the mean reversion feature of natural gas. Finally we make adjustments so that the simulation captures seasonality of natural gas prices.

2 A correlated process for prices

Because different locations for gas delivery are essentially separate but related markets, the underlying prices to be constructed are two gas locations with a specified correlation. This paper employs Rubenstein's [2, 3] pyramid methodology for modelling correlated asset price processes. In addition, we adapt the Hull and White [4] procedure for incorporating drift so that our price pyramid captures the mean reversion feature of natural gas. Finally we make adjustments so that the simulation captures seasonality of natural gas prices.

We assume that the price processes are Ornstein Uhlenbeck form with correlation rho.

$$dX_t = \alpha_X(\theta_X - X_t)dt + \sigma_X dW_X \tag{1}$$

$$dY_t = \alpha_Y(\theta_Y - Y_t)dt + \sigma_Y dW_Y \tag{2}$$

$$dW_t dW_t = \rho dt \tag{3}$$

To create a lattice, analogous to Rubenstein's pyramid, but with enough depth to capture mean reversion without collapsing the tree, we settle on using a nine point transition. That is, at time from point A in time t, the prices can transition to any of the nodes in the diagram below (including staying the same).

The pair at each node indicates the movement of prices X and Y, where U indicates up, M indicates middle (no move) and D indicates down. The values at each node are given below:

$$(U,D) = \left\{\Delta X, \left(\rho - \sqrt{1-\rho^2}\right)\Delta Y\right\} \tag{3}$$

$$(U,M) = \{\Delta X, \rho\Delta Y\} \tag{4}$$

$$(U,U) = \left\{\Delta X, \left(\rho + \sqrt{1-\rho^2}\right)\Delta Y\right\} \tag{5}$$

$$(M,D) = \left\{0, \left(-\sqrt{1-\rho^2}\right)\Delta Y\right\} \tag{6}$$

$$(M,M) = \{0,0\} \tag{7}$$

$$(M,U) = \left\{0,\left(\sqrt{1-\rho^2}\right)\Delta Y\right\} \tag{8}$$

$$(D,D) = \left\{-\Delta X,-\left(\rho+\sqrt{1-\rho^2}\right)\Delta Y\right\} \tag{9}$$

$$(D,M) = \{-\Delta X,-\rho\Delta Y\} \tag{10}$$

$$(D,U) = \left\{-\Delta X,-\left(\rho-\sqrt{1-\rho^2}\right)\Delta Y\right\} \tag{11}$$

where

$$\Delta X = \sigma_X \sqrt{3/2\,\Delta t} \tag{12}$$

$$\Delta Y = \sigma_Y \sqrt{3/2\,\Delta t} \tag{13}$$

The shape is a parallelogram rather than a square in order to allow the tree to recombine for the changes in the Y price while leaving correlations simple to parameterize. The probabilities of moving to each node are denoted by P(xmove, ymove). We have six natural conditions: two expected values, two means, a correlation and a requirement that the probabilities sum to one. The remaining three conditions are established to ensure that the tree starts off equally likely to move in any direction and to ensure that both prices moving upward is as likely as both prices moving downward and that X increasing and Y decreasing is as likely as Y decreasing and X decreasing. This can be changed by the user to suit the empirical properties of the underlying prices in question.

Now our price simulation looks like a pyramid with today's change (0,0) at the peak. As we move through time we move toward the base of the pyramid. The only distinction is that the pyramid is somewhat skewed as it is the stack of smaller parallelograms. At each time step, the size of the parallelogram is (2t+1) x (2t +1) as dy and dx can have arrived at, at most, t-1 downward steps or t-1 upward steps until time t-1. Because the tree is recombining, we do not need to store the pyramid, but merely the base. Then we can draw the relevant values at each time step by choosing an increasingly larger dimensioned parallelogram.

The next step is to incorporate mean reversion. We follow the method of Hull and White [4] who construct a mean reverting process in a trinomial tree. They establish three branching patterns and then solve for the probabilities in each. Which branching pattern is relevant is determined by whether or not the price has fallen below or risen above thresholds that depend on the mean.

In our model we must consider nine branching patterns: (1) the standard pattern in figure 1, and the following (2) X is too high, (3) X is too low, (4) Y is too high, (5) Y is too low, (6) X is too high and Y is too low, (7) X is too high and Y is too high, (8) X is too low and Y is too low, (9) X is too low and Y is too high. These branching patterns are illustrated in figure 2. Probabilities are solved for using similar conditions to those required in the ordinary branching pattern. In addition we establish threshold values for X and Y so that the probabilities do not become negative. The equations can be solved for the probabilities explicitly (using for example, Matlab's symbolic toolbox) or they can be solved numerically. The full results are provided in an the paper Persad [6]. Now our price processes can be envisioned not as a pyramid, but rather as an obelisk, also decreasing storage used.

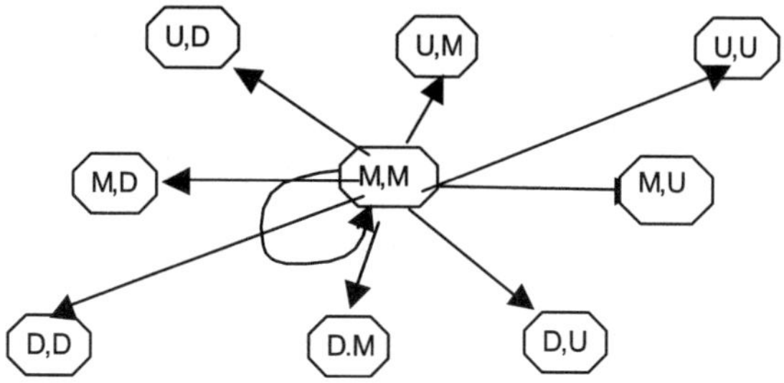

Figure 1: Transition pattern.

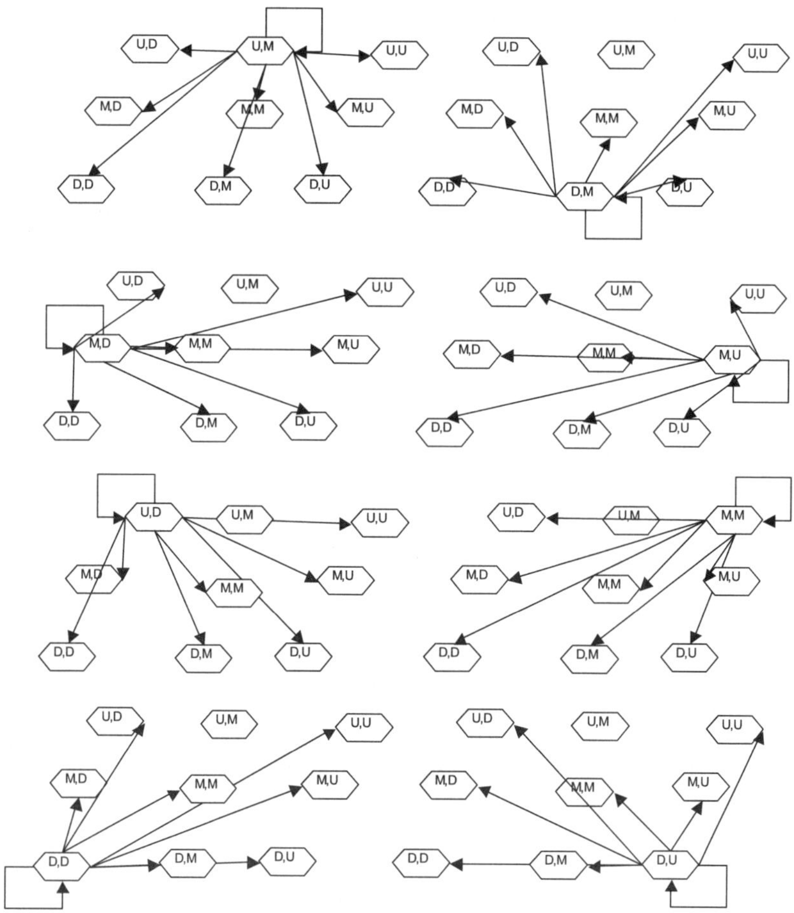

Figure 2: Alternative branching patterns.

Finally we would like to perturb the tree in order to take into account the current market's expectation of prices in the future. In order to do this we adjust the obelisk at each time step so that in expectation we reach the forward price. This methodology is described in detail in Jaillet, et al [1]. At the end of this step, our price process, can be conceptualised as a crooked obelisk that bends one way or the other in the shape of the forward curve.

In order to assess the reasonableness of our price process, the obelisk is traversed for a large number of paths. The calculated probabilities at each time step, create a probability density function (and therefore a cumulative distribution function). We can make random draws from a uniform distribution to see what our next move should be. Doing this for the entire number of timesteps for a large number of paths will produce several simulations which can then be examined to assess whether they possess the desired behaviour. The results are included in the empirical analysis of this methodology, Persad [5].

3 Valuation methodology

The method draws from Jaillet et al [1] by using a forest of trees to represent remaining swing rights, but extends it to a two player (customer and supplier) setting. At each stage the players gather the relevant nodes to which they can transition and engage in a Stackelberg game to determine the optimal action. At each point, the game's outcome is determined employing the game theoretic concept of subgame perfect Nash equilibrium.

For the case of ruthless exercise, the maximum daily amount is transacted for each swing and substitution. Two conditions are sufficient for ruthless exercise (1) if the customer finds the option in the money, he/she will demand the full quantity (demand curve is flat) and (2) in which the supplier can switch fuel but offers any amount up to the maximum daily amount, that the customer demands (supply curve is flat). In the case of ruthless exercise, the equilibrium of the Stackelberg game reduces to the simple expression:

$$\max\left\{0+U_{c,t+1}\left(E_s\right),-\max\left(K-X+U_{s,t+1},\left(E_c+1,E_s\right),K-Y+U_{s,t+1}\left(E_c+1,E_s+1\right)\right)\right\} \tag{14}$$

where Es and Ec denote the number of substitution rights or swing rights used and Us,t and Uc,t denote the utility or payoff to the customer or the supplier at time t.

Some contracts include a recall feature, in which the supplier also has the option to provide less than the maximum daily nomination amount. This arrangement is reasonable when the supplier must deal with shortages or, in the less extreme case, an upward sloping (as opposed to flat) supply curve. Intuitively, the supplier may agree to meet demand to a less than full customer request on a given day if the supply for the first lots fuel comes at a lower unit price than additional lots. This would be the situation if there is a regional shortage or pipeline disruption.

This case allows non-ruthless exercise; the equilibrium may call for transacting less than the maximum daily nomination quantity. The customer and the supplier then each influence the other's decision-making. The customer may then want to wait to exercise a swing right when it is more certain of being fulfilled. The supplier may want to save a recall right against future possible calls.

For each decision node, the optimisation problem involves checking three state spaces for the next period: the customer does not call (and the supplier does not use his/her recall or substitution right), the customer calls and the supplier does not substitute, and the customer calls and the supplier substitutes. In this way, the program does not need to hold the entire future state space in memory at one time. Instead it can just call the ones that are necessary.

4 Results and conclusions

The pricing results can be compared to a number of limiting cases. First, we know that the swing option with switching grants additional flexibility to the supplier. Since this is a zero-sum game, such flexibility must come at the customer's expense. Therefore the swing option with recall feature must trade at a discount to the standard swing option. The standard swing option may, in turn, be viewed as a basket of American options with the additional constraint that the validity (ability to exercise) the option on any given day depends on the number of options exercised in the past. That is, there is a limited number of swing rights strictly less than the number of possible periods of exercise. Therefore the standard swing option should trade at a (severe) discount to a basket of American options. Because American options on are traded and publicly priced, we are able to compare our results to valid market data. This comparison is reported in the empirical examination of this method as reported in Persad [5].

We can also subject the price methodology to competition. An alternative method of valuation would be to use least-squares Monte Carlo of the type proposed by Longstaff and Schwartz [10]. For practical purposes, this method is not favored because the state space (number of price paths x number of customer swing rights x number of supplier recall rights) is large enough to considerably retard computation time. However, it is a valid computational alternative whose merits must also be examined. These comparisons have been performed and are reported in Persad [5].

References

[1] Jaillet, P., Ronn, E., and Tompaidis, S., 2004, Valuation of commodity based swing options. Management Science Vol. 50, Iss. 7, pp. 909–921.

[2] Rubenstein, M. "Somewhere Over the Rainbow", *RISK* 4 (November 1991), pp. 63–66.

[3] Rubenstein, M. "Return to Oz", *RISK* 7 (November 1994), pp. 67–71.

[4] Hull, John C., and Alan White, 1994, Numerical Procedures for Implementing Models I: Single Factor Models, Journal of Derivatives Vol 2, pp 37–48.

[5] Persad, Sandhya, 2008, "Valuation of Swing Options with Supplier Flexibility – Switching and Recall Features: an empirical analysis".

[6] Joskow, 1987, "Contract Duration and Relationship-Specific Investments: Empirical Evidence from Coal Markets, *American Economic Review 77,* pp 168–185.
[7] Barbieri, A. and Garman, M., 1997, "Ups and Downs of Swing" *Energy and Power Risk Management, 2.*
[8] Pilipovic, D and J. Wengler, 1998, "Getting into the Swing," Energy and Power Risk Management, 2.
[9] Haarbrucker, G. and Kuhn, D., 2006, "Valuation of Electricity Swing Options by Multistage Stochastic Programming," Working Paper, Institute for Operations Research and Computational Finance, University of St. Gallen.
[10] FA Longstaff; ES Schwartz, "Valuing American options by simulation: a simple least-squares approach," *The Review of Financial Studies;* Spring 2001; 14, 1; ABI/INFORM Global pg. 113.

A neural network approach to option pricing

F. Mostafa & T. Dillon
DEBI Institute, Curtin University, Australia

Abstract

In this paper the pricing performance of the artificial neural network is compared to the Black-Scholes and the GARCH option-pricing model. The artificial neural network is trained on the implied volatility rather then the option price, which leads to an improved performance when compared to the competing models. The hedging performance of the neural network, GARCH option-pricing model and the Black-Scholes are also analysed.
Keywords: neural networks, option pricing, hedging, implied volatility, GARCH option pricing model.

1 Introduction

Since the publication of the Black-Scholes model in 1973 (Black and Scholes [1]), it remains the most quoted scientific paper in the world. The model made a key contribution to option trading, where investors are able to calculate a fair value of an option contract. This model had its limitations, which stem from the unrealistic assumptions. The Black-Scholes behaviour has been well documented in literature (Henderson [2]). The most interesting stylised fact of the Black-Scholes model that has captured the attention of researches and practitioners alike is the volatility skew (or volatility smile). This stylised fact can be seen when the implied volatility is backed out from the Black-Scholes formula and is plotted with respect to the option moneyness. The graph deviated from a flat line, which is a contradiction to the constant volatility assumption of the Black-Scholes.

Researchers then turned to more sophisticated methods for option valuation using stochastic volatility models (Ritchken and Trevor [3], Peter and Kris [4], Engle and Mustafa [5], Duan [6] and Heston *et al.* [7]). The GARCH option pricing model (GOPM) introduced by Duan [6] is based on a discrete-time

WIT Transactions on Information and Communication Technologies, Vol 41, © 2008 WIT Press
www.witpress.com, ISSN 1743-3517 (on-line)
doi:10.2495/CF080081

model of the economy. The GOPM is derived based on the locally risk-neutralised probability measure where the option value can be calculated as a discounted expected value. In addition, the model allows the underlying asset return to follow a GARCH process (Bollerslev [8]). Consequently, eliminating the assumption of a constant volatility. This is indeed an attractive feature for the GOPM, however the main drawback of the model is that it does not have a closed form solution. Therefore, Monte Carlo simulation is used to optimise the models parameters. Duan and Simonato [9] have introduced empirical martingale simulation that speeds up the Monte Carlo simulation process.

Recently research has also adopted different methods for pricing options, such as neural networks (Karaali *et al.* [10]). The vast majority of neural networks research has been focused on forecasting financial time series (Schittenkopf *et al.* [11], Kaastra and Boyd [12]). Until the late 1990's research on option pricing with neural networks was limited. To date most research compares the performance of neural networks to the Black-Scholes option-pricing model (Meissner and Kawano [13], Amilon [14], Yao *et al.* [15], Tino *et al.* [16] and Bennell and Sutcliffe [17]). Most research demonstrates comparable or slightly better performance of neural networks to the tradition models. However, there has been no real attempt to compare the neural networks to more advanced models such as the GARCH option pricing model (GOPM). In Hanke [18], a neural network was constructed to give an approximate price to GOPM. This was achieved by training the network on different input combinations. Thus, utilising the network output as an approximation to the option pricing formula to overcoming the numerical simulation issues.

The aim of this paper is improve on the neural networks ability to price option out-of-sample by learning the Black-Scholes implied volatility. The implied volatility produced by the neural networks is then used in the Black-Scholes formula to produce the neural network valuation of the option. The performance of the neural networks is then compared to the GARCH Option pricing model and the Black-Scholes based on the pricing and hedging criteria. Section two of this paper examines the competing models. The historical data used in this research is described in section three. The experiential design is illustrated in section four. Sections five and six describe the methods used for the pricing errors and the results achieved. The summary and conclusion are discussed in section seven.

2 Competing models

In this research, we study the out of sample pricing capabilities of different option pricing models. The GARCH option pricing model and the Black-Scholes are compared with two types of neural network designs. The first design is the common approach using the option price as the target output of the network. The second method is to train the neural network directly on the Black-Scholes implied volatility and then using the Black-Scholes formula to derive the theoretical price.

2.1 GARCH Option Pricing Model (GOPM)

The GARCH Option Pricing Model (GOPM) introduced by Duan [6] is based on a discrete-time model of the economy. The value of the index at time t, can be assumed to have the following dynamics,

$$r_t = r_f + \lambda\sigma_t - \frac{1}{2}\sigma_t + \sigma_t\varepsilon_t \tag{1}$$

$$\varepsilon_t \mid \Omega_{t-1} \sim N(0,1)$$

$$\sigma_t^2 = \beta_0 + \beta_1(\varepsilon_{t-1} - \gamma)^2\sigma_{t-1}^2 + \beta_2\sigma_{t-1}^2 \tag{2}$$

Where λ is interpreted as the risk premium. To ensure the variance is positive and stationary the following constraints are applied:

$$\beta_0 > 0$$
$$\beta_1 \geq 0$$
$$B_2 \geq 0$$
$$\beta_1(1+\lambda^2) + \beta_2 < 1$$

The unconditional variance is given by $\beta_0 / (1-\beta_1(1+\lambda^2)-\beta_2)$. This process is reduced to the Black-Scholes homoskedastic lognormal process when β_1=0 and β_2=0.

It has been demonstrated by Duan [6] that under the Local Risk Neutral Valuation Relationship (LRNVR) the conditional variance does not change , however under measure Q the conditional expectation of r_t is the risk free rate r_f.

$$E^Q[\exp(r_t) \mid \Omega_{t-1}] = \exp(r_f) \tag{3}$$

To derive the GOPM, the risk neutral valuation relationship has to be generalized to the LRNVR:

$$\begin{aligned} r_t &= r_f - \frac{1}{2}\sigma_t^{*2} + \sigma_t^*\varepsilon_t^*, \\ \varepsilon_t^* &\sim N(0,1), \end{aligned} \tag{4}$$

$$\sigma_t^{*2} = \beta_0 + \beta_1(\varepsilon_{t-1}^* - \tilde{\gamma})^2\sigma_{t-1}^{*2} + \beta_2\sigma_{t-1}^{*2} \tag{5}$$

By having $\tilde{\gamma} = \lambda + \gamma$, the risk-neutral pricing measure is determined by four parameters, β_0,β_1,β_2 and $\tilde{\gamma}$. Using the above formulation the asset terminal is then calculated at time T

$$S_T = S_t \exp\left(r_f(T-t) - \frac{1}{2}\sum_{i=t+1}^{T}\sigma_i^{*2} + \sum_{i=t+1}^{T}\sigma_i^*\varepsilon_i^* \right) \tag{6}$$

The terminal asset price is then calculated using Monte Carlo Simulation. A set of N random path of residuals $(\varepsilon^*_{t+1,j},\ldots,\varepsilon^*_{T,j})$ are generated with J = 1 to N. The residuals are used to calculate the asset prices $S_{T,j}$. Using the terminal asset price series the option price is then obtained by risk-neutral conditional expectation E^*:

$$C_{GARCH} = \exp(-r_f^*(T-t))E^*\left[\max(S_T - K,0)\right] \tag{7}$$

The final option price is then approximated as follow:

$$C_{GARCH} = \exp(-r_f^*(T-t))\frac{1}{N}\sum_{j=1}^{M}\max(S_{T,j} - K,0) \tag{8}$$

Rather than using standard Monte Carlo simulation, Empirical Martingale Simulation (EMS) is adopted. The EMS method has been shown to accelerate the convergence of the Monte Carlo prices estimates as demonstrated by Duan and Simonato [9].

The Monte Carlo simulation is give by:

$$\begin{aligned} S_t(i) &= S_0\exp[r_f t]Z_t(i) \\ Z_t(i) &= Z_{t-1}(I)\exp[-0.5\sigma_t^2 + \sigma_t\varepsilon_t(i)] \end{aligned} \tag{9}$$

(10)

and for the EMS, $Z_t(i) = \dfrac{Z_{t-1}(i)\exp[-0.5\sigma_t^2 + \sigma_t\varepsilon_t(i)]}{\frac{1}{n}\sum_{i=1}^{n}Z_{t-1}(i)\exp[-0.5\sigma_t^2 + \sigma_t\varepsilon_t(i)]}$

The delta that corresponds to the GOPM is given by Duan [6]:

$$\Delta_t^G = \exp\{-(T-t)r\}E\left[\frac{S_T}{S_t}I(S_T,K)\middle|\phi_t\right] \tag{11}$$

Where $I(S_t,X) = 1$ is $S_t \geq K$ and 0 if $S < K$. Since there is no analytical solution for Δ_t^G the deltas are computed via Monte Carlo simulations.

2.2 The Black-Scholes option pricing model

The Black-Scholes theorem was first published in 1971 (Black and Scholes [1]). It is most widely used model for pricing model. The model states if S(t) is asset price that follows a generalised Wiener Process

$$dS(t) = \mu S(t)dt + \sigma S(t)dz(t) \tag{12}$$

$z(t)$ is a Brownian motion, the interest rate and volatility are constant. Then a call option on the asset, expiring at time T and with strike price K will have value at time t:

$$C(t,T) = S(t)N(d_1) - Ke^{-r(T-t)}N(d_2) \tag{13}$$

where, $d_1 = \dfrac{\ln\left(\dfrac{S(t)}{K}\right) + \left(r + \dfrac{\sigma^2}{2}\right)(T-t)}{\sigma\sqrt{T-t}}$

$$d_2 = \frac{\ln\left(\frac{S(t)}{K}\right) + \left(r - \frac{\sigma^2}{2}\right)(T-t)}{\sigma\sqrt{T-t}} \tag{14}$$

$$N(x) = (2\pi)^{-1/2} \int_{-\infty}^{x} \exp\left(-\frac{z^2}{2}\right) dz \tag{15}$$

N(x) is the cumulative probability distribution for a standard normally distributed variable. The Black-Scholes delta is given by N(d1). Which measures the sensitivity to the underlying instrument.

2.2.1 Implied volatility

The implied volatility is volatility parameter, which equates the market price with the price given by the Black-Scholes formula. The implied volatility, $\sigma_t^{BS}(K,T)$ is a function of K (Strike) and T (time to maturity) (Hull [19]). The two most interesting features of the volatility surface, which have been studied and analysed by researchers, are, the volatility smile (skew) and the term structure and the level of implied volatility changes with time. The volatility smile is a key indicator of unrealistic assumption of constant volatility. Whereas the changes in the implied volatility level with time is seen by the deformation of the volatility surface with time. Therefore, the ability to capture the deformation of the volatility surface will lead to accurate option pricing.

Cont and da Fonseca [20] have expressed mathematically the implied volatility surface as follows:

$$C_{BS}\left(S_t, K, \tau, \sigma_t^{BS}(K,T)\right) = C_t^*(K,T) \tag{16}$$

where $\sigma_t^{BS}(K,T) > 0$

The value of the call option as a function of the volatility is a monotonic mapping from $[0,+\infty[$ to $]0,S_t\text{-}Ke^{-rt}[$. The implied volatility $\sigma_t^{BS}(K,T)$ of a call option with strike K and price maturity of T is dependent on K and T. If K and T are fixed, $\sigma_t^{BS}(K,T)$ can be generalised to follow a stochastic process. For a fixed t the value will depend on the options characteristics such as maturity and strike level K. Eqn. (17) represents the volatility surface at time t.

$$\sigma_t^{BS} : (K,T) \longrightarrow \sigma_t^{BS}(K,T) \tag{17}$$

$$I_t(m,\tau) = \sigma_t^{BS}(mS(t), t+\tau) \tag{18}$$

where m is the moneyness, $I_t(m,\tau)$ is the implied volatility function

The two most important features of this surface are volatility term structure (or volatility smile) and the changes in the volatility levels with time. Thus the evolution in time of this surface will reflect the evolution of market option prices.

2.3 Artificial neural network (ANN)

The ANN consists mainly of an input layer, one more hidden layers and an output layer. The layers are connected via a set off weights. The hidden layer and the output layer consist of individual neurons. The inputs are multiplied by the weights and a bias term is added which then constitutes the input to the activation function. This is then served as the inputs to the proceeding layer. The activation of the output layer is given by,

$$F(x) = G(\sum_{J} w_{ij} H(\sum_{K} w_{jk} x_k + B_k) + B_J) \tag{19}$$

The activation functions of the neurons could be chosen to be linear or non-linear functions. A sum of error-squared function is normally used as the objective function for the training the MLP. So the MLP is trained to minimize this function with respect to the in-sample data.

$$E = \frac{1}{N}\sum_{1}^{N}(t_i - F_i(x))^2 \tag{20}$$

The MLP performance is dependent on the initial values of the weights. To overcome this issue, the neural network is trained 50 times using different initial values for the weights. The weight set that introduces the least error is then adopted.

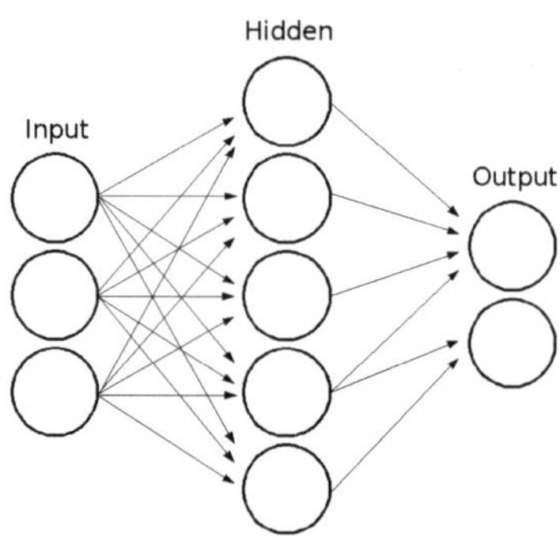

Figure 1: Single layer artificial neural network.

3 The data

The data used in this research consists of European call options on the FTSE 100 index traded at the London International Financial and Options Exchange (LIFFE). The data obtained in this research was obtained from SIRCA (http://www.sirca.org.au/), which covered a two-year period starting from 2/1/2000 and ends on 31/12/2001. The sample made up of 63,094 call options and the daily Index value (adjusted for dividends).

The following constraints were applied to filter the data series, Moneyness (Index/Strike) outside [-1.01,0.9], maturity greater 175 days and less than 7 days and Close price less than five where removed. The data series was then reduced to 26533 options. GB Libor rates were used for the risk free rate inputs to the models.

The parameters for the GOPM and Black-Scholes were estimated on a daily basis. However, when optimising the ANN the data was split into 3 sets: in-sample, validation and out-of-sample. The in-sample set is used as inputs to the ANN thus impacting the weights. The validation set is used to evaluate the error at each epoch. The training of the network is terminated when the error of the validation increases. The out-of-sampled is data set is used for evaluating the ANN model. The hedging analysis was done over 1 month horizon for the month of Feburary-2000.

4 Experimental design

The aim of this research is to investigate the capability of Neural Networks to capture the market volatility dynamics, and hence accurately price call options. The competing models are the GOPM; two Neural Networks trained on the option price (NNp) and implied volatility (NNiv) respectively. The models are then compared based on the out of sample pricing accuracy and the hedging performance.

4.1 GOPM parameters

The GOPM parameters were estimated for each day of the data sample. This was achieved by minimizing the average sum squared error eqn. (21) (Aboura [21], Lehnert [22]) over all options on day t, with parameters form day t-1 as the initial values (Lehar *et al.* [23]).

$$\text{Min } SSE(\Theta) = \sum_{t=1}^{T}\sum_{n=1}^{N}\left(\frac{\left(\hat{C}_{t,n} - C_{t,n}\right)}{C_{t,n}}\right) \tag{21}$$

where $\Theta = \{\beta_0, \beta_1, \beta_2, \lambda\}$

Where $\hat{C}$ and C are the model theoretical price and the actual call price respectively. The number of Monte Carlo simulation was initially set to 15,000. This was sufficient to generate stable estimates. In some case the number of simulation had to be increased to 30,000.

4.2 ANN models and training

ANN has been applied to many option pricing problems. Most researchers focus on training the ANN to estimate the option price directly (Donaldson and Kamstra [24], Meissner and Kawano [13] and Hutchinson *et al.* [25]). In this research, two methods are examined; the first method is commonly used in research where the neural network is training on the option price. The second method the neural network is trained using the Black-Scholes implied volatility as the target output. This method is similar to the one adopted by Duan [26]. The neural network was optimized by varying the number of inputs, length of in sample and validation sets, and the number of hidden unites. The combination that gives the lowest error is chosen. The weight values were initialized randomly. To eliminate the dependency on the initial weight values this process was repeated 50 times.

4.2.1 ANN with pricing options

This approach has been widely studied in literature. This approach was also followed by Bennell and Sutcliffe [17]. The input data was partitioned according the moneyness of the options in-the money (ITM), at-the-money (ATM) and out-of-the-money (OTM). For each set, a different network was used. This method has been proven to improve the pricing capabilities of the ANN (Yao *et al.* [15]). The in-sample and validation set for ATM and ITM were 168 days and 84 respectively. For OTM 64 and 20 days for the in-sample and validation set were used.

The homogeneity hint (Merton [27]) is used to simplify the input parameters (Garcia and Cirano [28]). The Strike and Index can be combined into a single input Index/Strike that is also interpreted as the measure of the option's moneyness. The other inputs used are the option maturity and historical volatility. The target set is the Close price/ Strike. From this point onwards this models will be referred to as NNp.

4.2.2 ANN with implied volatility

In this paper adopt a new methodology is adopted which will allow the neural network to capture the dynamics of the underlying instruments and the changes in the volatility levels through time. To achieve the desired effect the neural network is trained on the Black-Scholes implied volatility. In this exercise, the data set was not partitioned by moneyness, therefore allowing the neural network full visibility of the volatility surface. This approach is a mapping exercise described in eqn. (17).

After experimentation with the different inputs, the following combination was selected for optimal performance. The in sample and validation set were 20 and 5 days respectively, and the output sample was 1 day. The inputs used were moneyness (index/strike), Time to expiry and historical volatility. The target data set was the Black-Scholes implied volatility. Once the training of the ANN is completed, the implied volatility produced by the ANN would be plugged into the Black-Schole formula to obtain an analytical price of the option. The same concept is applied to generating the delta's, where the Black-Scholes delta is used with the implied volatility produced via the neural network. This model would be referred to as NNiv.

5 Performance measure

The first measure of the model performance is its ability to price options out of sample. However, this measure does not give a clear indication of the models ability to generate profits. Therefore, the hedging performance of the model is a much better indication of the models ability to capture the underlying dynamics in the market.

5.1 Pricing accuracy

To analyze the models performance, Relative Pricing Error (PE) and Absolute Relative Pricing Error (APE) were calculated for each model.

$$RPE = \frac{1}{n}\sum_{i=1}^{n}\left(\frac{\hat{C}_i - C_i}{C_i}\right) \tag{22}$$

$$ARPE = \frac{1}{n}\sum_{i=1}^{n}\left|\frac{\hat{C}_i - C_i}{C_i}\right| \tag{23}$$

where $\hat{C}$ and C is the model theoretical call price and the actual call price. The errors are reported against maturity and Moneyness.

5.2 Delta hedging

Most papers consider a hedge portfolio with one unit short in an option, Δ units of the underlying and the rest in a risk free asset (Schittenkopf and Dorffner [29]). In this research a hedge portfolio is constructed in a similar fashion to that adopted by Amilon [14] and Vahamaa [30]. That is we buy that are under priced (where theoretical option price is higher then market price) and sell the options that are overpriced. For under priced options we construct the following portfolio:

We by option $V_0^C = C_0$ and sell index $V_0^I = -I_0\Delta_0$ and put the rest in risk-free asset, $V_0^B = I_0\Delta_0 - V_0^C$. The portfolio is then replicated as follows:

$$V_t^I = -I_t\Delta_t \quad , \quad V_t^C = C_t$$

$$V_t^B = \exp(rt)V_{t-1}^B + I_t(\Delta_t - \Delta_{t-1})$$

The value of the portfolio at time T is given by,

$$V_T = V_T^B + V_T^I + V_T^C \tag{24}$$

Which gives us the absolute hedging error

$$\xi = \exp(rt)|V_T| \tag{25}$$

Where, V_t^B, V_t^I and V_t^C are the amount invested in the risk free asset, index and call option at time t.

6 Results

Below are the estimated mean values of the GOPM parameters.

The risk premium is extracted from the option prices rather than from the index time series. It was found to be a little weak which intern will have minor impact on the option price. The Annual volatility was found to be approx 22.37% which is a close approximation to the historical volatility when estimated on the index prices 20.7%.

Table 1: GOPM average parameters.

β_0	β_1	β_2	γ	$\sqrt{\sigma}$
3.109E-05	1.848E-01	3.184E-01	6.745E-01	22.37%

Table 2: Relative pricing errors for all models.

Moneyness	Model	Time to Maturity			
		LT	MT	ST	TOTAL
DOTM	GOPM	0.021	-0.010	-0.020	-0.009
	NNp	-0.062	-0.047	0.837	0.128
	BLACK-SCHOLES	-0.098	-0.011	0.038	-0.005
	NNiv	0.034	0.114	-0.024	0.073
OTM	GOPM	0.027	-0.007	0.059	0.024
	NNp	-0.145	-0.365	0.269	-0.085
	BLACK-SCHOLES	-0.497	-0.691	-0.901	-0.762
	NNiv	0.005	0.014	0.024	0.017
ATM	GOPM	0.039	0.008	0.030	0.021
	NNp	-0.133	-0.083	0.238	0.044
	BLACK-SCHOLES	-0.272	-0.240	-0.215	-0.232
	NNiv	0.025	0.004	0.007	0.007
ITM	GOPM	0.059	0.013	-0.008	0.007
	NNp	0.063	-0.013	0.142	0.066
	BLACK-SCHOLES	-0.165	-0.084	0.002	-0.049
	NNiv	0.040	0.008	-0.019	-0.002
DITM	GOPM	0.069	0.059	0.044	0.057
	NNp	-0.088	-0.104	0.010	-0.051
	BLACK-SCHOLES	-0.098	-0.011	0.038	-0.005
	NNiv	0.075	-0.002	-0.020	0.004
All	GOPM	*0.045*	*0.018*	*0.042*	*0.030*
	NNp	*-0.109*	*-0.199*	*0.350*	*0.004*
	BLACK-SCHOLES	*-0.584*	*-0.900*	*-0.641*	*-0.767*
	NNiv	*0.022*	*0.043*	*0.009*	*0.027*

The performance measures used for all models are relative pricing error (RPE) and the absolute relative pricing error (ARPE). A positive or negative value of PE indicates overpricing or under pricing of the model respectively. Table (2) shows the RPE for all models. On average, the GOPM and the NNiv overprice call options, whereas the Black-Scholes and NNp under price the options. The NNp tends to over price ST options and under price options in the LT and MT range. The GOPM and NNiv have similar behavior where both models over price options over all maturities. The BLACK-SCHOLES model seems to under prices options over all maturities. In addition, it has the worst miss-pricing performance across all maturity and moneyness.

Table 3: Absolute relative pricing errors for all models.

Moneyness	Model	Time to Maturity			
		LT	MT	ST	TOTAL
DOTM	GOPM	0.179	0.246	0.384	0.267
	NNp	0.590	0.513	1.014	0.625
	BLACK-SCHOLES	0.993	1.815	1.289	1.584
	NNiv	0.167	0.269	0.358	0.273
OTM	GOPM	0.105	0.157	0.272	0.202
	NNp	0.519	0.483	0.711	0.580
	BLACK-SCHOLES	0.502	0.713	0.984	0.809
	NNiv	0.102	0.154	0.262	0.195
ATM	GOPM	0.078	0.100	0.139	0.116
	NNp	0.263	0.212	0.400	0.295
	BLACK-SCHOLES	0.274	0.262	0.277	0.270
	NNiv	0.086	0.094	0.135	0.112
ITM	GOPM	0.082	0.074	0.079	0.077
	NNp	0.154	0.131	0.232	0.181
	BLACK-SCHOLES	0.169	0.120	0.077	0.104
	NNiv	0.081	0.071	0.075	0.074
DITM	GOPM	0.039	0.061	0.050	0.053
	NNp	0.160	0.143	0.151	0.149
	BLACK-SCHOLES	0.099	0.074	0.051	0.069
	NNiv	0.098	0.066	0.058	0.068
All	GOPM	*0.121*	*0.167*	*0.233*	*0.188*
	NNp	*0.491*	*0.440*	*0.674*	*0.528*
	BLACK-SCHOLES	*0.589*	*0.924*	*0.742*	*0.818*
	NNiv	*0.119*	*0.172*	*0.222*	*0.185*

The GOPM and NNiv models over prices LT options across all moneyness. The worst miss pricing performance of the GOPM model has a RPE of 0.069 for LT-DITM contracts. This behavior is also seen for NNiv, where the model has the worst miss pricing for LT-DITM contracts with a RPE of 0.075. For BLACK-SCHOLES model the worst performance for ST-OTM options with a RPE of −0.901 and the NNp has a PE of 0.837 for ST-DOTM contracts.

The APE figures are displayed in table (3). On average the performance of GOPM and NNiv models increase with maturity. Again, the BLACK-SCHOLES model performs the worst on all accounts. On average, the NNiv has a slightly better performance than the GOPM. The GOPM model slightly performs better for MT contracts and the NNiv has a better performance for ST and LT contracts. All models have performed the worst for ST-DOTM contracts. In addition, the GOPM performs the best for LT-DITM whereas the NNiv and BLACK-SCHOLES are at their best for ST-DITM contracts. The NNiv seem to perform best for the MT-ITM contracts.

Table 4: Discounted absolute hedging error.

	Model	LT	MT	ST	Total
ATM	NNiv	0.38	19.56	**15.66**	15.20
	BLACK-SCHOLES	**0.29**	**19.09**	15.74	**15.06**
	GOPM	0.41	22.38	16.33	16.56
ITM	NNiv	0.41	23.37	**27.47**	**22.83**
	BLACK-SCHOLES	**0.31**	**21.99**	29.65	23.22
	GOPM	0.42	25.93	30.62	25.39
OTM	NNiv	0.23	9.91	6.70	7.57
	BLACK-SCHOLES	**0.20**	**9.90**	**5.89**	**7.28**
	GOPM	0.30	12.20	6.52	8.72
Total Nniv		0.33	16.67	17.03	14.90
Total BLACK-SCHOLES		**0.26**	**16.11**	**17.55**	**14.87**
Total GOPM		0.37	19.18	18.27	16.56

NNp will be excluded from the hedging analysis due to the unsatisfactory performance with the option pricing. The rest of the models are compared over 1 month horizon, where delta hedging was performed until the option expiry. Then absolute hedging error eqn. (25) was used as the benchmark statistic for all models. As shown in table (4) the BLACK-SCHOLES and NNiv on average are very close with a difference of 0.03.But the NNiv on average performed better for the ITM options. The GOPM has the worst performance on all accounts. For ATM-ST and ITM-ST options, the NNiv performed better to the reset of the models. In addition, NNiv seem to get very close to the Black-Scholes. For instance, the OTM-MT option, the BLACK-SCHOLES and NNiv were in fact very close with a difference of 0.01. However, the GOPM display far worse performance with big differences when compared to the Black-Scholes. The NNiv was clearly out performed the GOPM on all accounts expected for OTM-ST but with a difference of 0.18.

7 Summary and conclusion

In this research, a new method for pricing options via neural networks is introduced. The neural network was trained using the implied volatility as the target output of the neural network rather then the options price. This method has shown to improve the out-of-sample pricing performance of the neural network. The neural networks performance was also compared to the GOPM and the Black-Scholes. The overall performance of the NNiv was slightly better than GOPM and much better than the Black-Scholes. The improvement in the neural network pricing performance is a result of the neural network ability to capture the underlying volatility structure and volatility levels with time. Which is apparent in its out of sample pricing abilities.

The models were also tested with respect to their hedging performance. The GOPM performed the worst. However, the Black-Scholes on averaged outperformed the others except for the ITM options where NNiv did better. The NNiv did perform better then the Black-Scholes in some categories and in most cases was trailing very closely. However, it did outperform the GOPM. There are a couple of factors that may have affected the outcome of the results. Firstly, the exclusion of options based on moneyness and maturity could have resulted in the loss of significant information. Also, the hedging strategy of keeping the option till maturity could skew the results. The method described in Amilon [14] would have been a better option. In addition, the use of the discounted absolute hedging error alone does not provide enough statistics to evaluate the model performance.

The results presented in this paper are very promising. It has been demonstrated the superiority of the neural networks over the GOPM. In addition, the ability of the neural network to produce an option price instantaneously enables it to be deployed as real time trading tool. An ongoing direction of this research is to extend the current findings to train the neural network on the Black-Scholes delta rather than using the neural networks implied volatility and to examine different types of neural networks such as RBF that may produce improved results.

References

[1] F. Black, and M. Scholes, The Pricing of Options and Corporate Liabilities. The Journal of Political Economy 81 (1973) 637–654.

[2] V. Henderson, The Black Scholes Model.

[3] P. Ritchken, and R. Trevor, Pricing Options under Generalized GARCH and Stochastic Volatility Processes. The Journal of Finance 54 (1999) 377–402.

[4] C. Peter, and J. Kris, Which GARCH Model for Option Valuation? Manage. Sci. 50 (2004) 1204–1221.
[5] R.F. Engle, and C. Mustafa, Implied ARCH Models from Options Prices. Journal of Econometrics 52 (1992) 2.
[6] J.C. Duan, The GARCH Option Pricing Model. Mathematical Finance 5 (1995) 13–32.
[7] S.L. Heston, S. Nandi, and A. Federal Reserve Bank of, A Closed-form GARCH Option Pricing Model, Federal Reserve Bank of Atlanta, 1997.
[8] T.I.M. Bollerslev, Generalized Autoregressive Conditional Heteroskedasticity. ARCH: Selected Readings (1995).
[9] J.C. Duan, and J.G. Simonato, Empirical Martingale Simulation for Asset Prices. Management Science 44 (1998) 1218–1233.
[10] O. Karaali, W. Edelberg, J. Higgins, M. Inc, and I.L. Schaumburg, Modelling volatility derivatives using neural networks. Computational Intelligence for Financial Engineering (CIFEr), 1997., Proceedings of the IEEE/IAFE 1997 (1997) 280–286.
[11] C. Schittenkopf, G. Dorffner, and E.J. Dockner, Forecasting time-dependent conditional densities: a semi non-parametric neural network approach. Journal of Forecasting 19 (2000) 355–374.
[12] I. Kaastra, and M. Boyd, Designing a neural network for forecasting financial and economic time series. Neurocomputing 10 (1996) 215–236.
[13] G. Meissner, and N. Kawano, Capturing the Volatility Smile of Options on High-Tech Stocks-A Combined GARCH-Neural Network Approach. Journal of Economics and Finance 25 (2001) 276–292.
[14] H. Amilon, A neural network versus Black-Scholes: a comparison of pricing and hedging performances. Journal of Forecasting 22 (2003) 317–335.
[15] J. Yao, Y. Li, and C.L. Tan, Option price forecasting using neural networks. Omega 28 (2000) 455–466.
[16] P. Tino, C. Schittenkopf, and G. Dorffner, Financial volatility trading using recurrent neural networks. Neural Networks, IEEE Transactions on 12 (2001) 865–874.
[17] J.A. Bennell, and C. Sutcliffe, Black-Scholes Versus Artificial Neural Networks in Pricing FTSE 100 Options, Dept. of Accounting and Management Science, University of Southampton, 2000.
[18] M. Hanke, Neural Network Approximation of Option Pricing Formulas for Analytically Intractable Option Pricing Models. Journal of Computational Intelligence in Finance 5 (1997) 20–27.
[19] J. Hull, Options, futures, and other derivatives, Prentice Hall Upper Saddle River, NJ, 2003.
[20] R. Cont, and J. da Fonseca, Deformation of implied volatility surfaces: an empirical analysis. Empirical Approaches to Financial Fluctuations (2001).
[21] S. Aboura, GARCH Option Pricing Under Skew. Journal: The ICFAI Journal of Applied Economics November 4 (2005) 78–86.
[22] T. Lehnert, Mandelbrot and the Smile.

[23] A. Lehar, M. Scheicher, and C. Schittenkopf, GARCH vs. stochastic volatility: Option pricing and risk management. Journal of Banking and Finance 26 (2002) 323–345.
[24] R.G. Donaldson, and M. Kamstra, Forecast combining with neural networks. Journal of Forecasting 15 (1996) 49–61.
[25] J.M. Hutchinson, A.W. Lo, and T. Poggio, A Nonparametric Approach to Pricing and Hedging Derivative Securities Via Learning Networks. The Journal of Finance 49 (1994) 851–889.
[26] J.C. Duan, Cracking the smile. Risk 9 (1996) 55–59.
[27] R.C. Merton, Theory of Rational Option Pricing. The Bell Journal of Economics and Management Science 4 (1973) 141–183.
[28] R. Garcia, and Cirano, Pricing and Hedging Derivative Securities with Neural Networks and a Homogeneity Hint, CIRANO, 1998.
[29] C. Schittenkopf, and G. Dorffner, Risk-neutral density extraction from option prices: improved pricing with mixture density networks. Neural Networks, IEEE Transactions on 12 (2001) 716–725.
[30] S. Vahamaa, Delta Hedging with the Smile. Financial Markets and Portfolio Management 18 (2004) 241–255.

A Green's function-based iterative approach to the pricing of American options

M. Y. Melnikov
Labry School of Business and Economics, Cumberland University, USA

Abstract

An iterative semi-analytic procedure is developed for solution of problems arising in the pricing of American options. Introduction of a penalty function reduces the problem to a European options problem with a nonlinear term in the Black-Scholes equation. The approach is based on the use of a Green's function constructed for a terminal-boundary value problem stated for the linear Black-Scholes equation. Different boundary conditions can potentially be treated within this approach. Closed analytic form of Green's functions are obtained by a combination of the methods of Laplace transform and variation of parameters. A numerical experiment reveals high accuracy level attained in computing of solutions of linear problems that arise at each stage of the iterative procedure.
Keywords: American options, Green's function, iterative approach.

1 Introduction

Upon implementing a penalty function approach in the way suggested in [1] and later used in [2], the pricing of American options can be simulated by the following nonlinear terminal-boundary value problem

$$\frac{\partial v(S,t)}{\partial t} + \frac{\sigma^2 S^2}{2}\frac{\partial^2 v(S,t)}{\partial S^2} + rS\frac{\partial v(S,t)}{\partial S} - rv(S,t) + \frac{\varepsilon C}{v(S,t)+\varepsilon - q(S)} = 0 \tag{1}$$

$$v(S,T) = \varphi(S) \tag{2}$$

$$v(S_1,t) = A(t) \quad \text{and} \quad v(S_2,t) = B(t) \tag{3}$$

posed for the two variable function $v(S,t)$ in the rectangular region $\Omega = (S_1 < S < S_2) \times (0 < t < T)$ of the S, t-plane.

WIT Transactions on Information and Communication Technologies, Vol 41, © 2008 WIT Press
www.witpress.com, ISSN 1743-3517 (on-line)
doi:10.2495/CF080091

In the above setting, $v = v(S,t)$ is the price of the derivative product, $\varphi(S)$ is the pay-off function of a given derivative problem at the expiration time T, with S and t being the share price of the underlying asset and time, respectively. The parameters σ, and r represent the volatility of the underlying asset and the risk-free interest rate, while $q(S)$ represents a barrier function. Here, $0 < \varepsilon \ll 1$ and C are a small regularization parameter and is a positive constant, respectively. Note that smoothness is not required for the functions $\varphi(S)$, $A(t)$ and $B(t)$ that specify the terminal and boundary conditions.

By the evident substitution

$$v(S,t) = V(S,t) + \frac{(S_2 - S)A(t) + (S - S_1)B(t)}{S_2 - S_1} \tag{4}$$

the terminal-boundary value problem in (1)–(3) reduces to

$$\frac{\partial V(S,t)}{\partial t} + \frac{\sigma^2 S^2}{2}\frac{\partial^2 V(S,t)}{\partial S^2} + rS\frac{\partial V(S,t)}{\partial S} - rV(S,t) = F(V(S,t),S,t) \tag{5}$$

$$V(S,T) = f(S) \tag{6}$$

$$V(S_1,t) = 0 \quad \text{and} \quad V(S_2,t) = 0 \tag{7}$$

with the homogeneous boundary conditions imposed at $S = S_1$ and $S = S_2$. The right-hand side function $F(V(S,t),S,t)$ in the governing equation (5) is determined by the substitution in (4) as

$$\begin{aligned} F(V(S,t),S,t) = {} & -\varepsilon C(S_2 - S_1)/\{(S_2 - S_1)[V(S,t) + \varepsilon - q(S)] \\ & + (S_2 - S)A(t) + (S - S_1)B(t)\} + \frac{rS}{S_2 - S_1}[A(t) - B(t)] \\ & - \left(\frac{d}{dt} - r\right)\left(\frac{S_2 - S}{S_2 - S_1}A(t) + \frac{S - S_1}{S_2 - S_1}B(t)\right) \end{aligned} \tag{8}$$

while the function $f(S)$ in (6) is defined by the substitution in (4) in terms of the pay-off function $\varphi(S)$ as

$$f(S) = \varphi(S) - \frac{(S_2 - S)A(T) + (S - S_1)B(T)}{S_2 - S_1} \tag{9}$$

A semi-analytic approach, which is proposed in this study to the problem in (5)–(7), is based on the Green's function method. In [3] one can find an effective algorithm developed for the construction of closed analytic representations of Green's functions to a variety of terminal-boundary value problems stated for the Black-Scholes equation. Earlier in [4], we had also investigated the potential of the Green's function method in solving linear terminal-boundary value problems for the Black-Scholes equation.

To make this presentation complete, we construct, in what follows, the Green's function, which is later employed for the solution of the problem in (5)–(7).

2 Construction of Green's function

Consider the terminal-boundary value problem in (6) and (7) stated for the homogeneous Black-Scholes equation

$$\frac{\partial V(S,t)}{\partial t}+\frac{\sigma^2 S^2}{2}\frac{\partial^2 V(S,t)}{\partial S^2}+rS\frac{\partial V(S,t)}{\partial S}-rV(S,t)=0 \tag{10}$$

in Ω. By implementing the standard substitutions

$$x=\ln S \quad \text{and} \quad \tau=\frac{\sigma^2}{2}(T-t) \tag{11}$$

and setting $u(x,\tau)=V(S,t)$, the terminal-boundary value problem in (10), (6) and (7) converts to the following initial-boundary value problem in $u(x,\tau)$

$$\frac{\partial u(x,\tau)}{\partial \tau}=\frac{\partial^2 u(x,\tau)}{\partial x^2}+(c-1)\frac{\partial u(x,\tau)}{\partial x}-cu(x,\tau) \tag{12}$$

$$u(x,0)=f(\exp x) \tag{13}$$

$$u(a,\tau)=0 \quad \text{and} \quad u(b,\tau)=0 \tag{14}$$

stated on the rectangle $\widetilde{\Omega}=(a<x<b)\times(0<\tau<T)$, on which the region Ω maps by the change of variables introduced in (11). The end-values a and b of the variable x are evidently determined in terms of S_1 and S_2 as

$$a=\ln S_1 \quad \text{and} \quad b=\ln S_2$$

while the parameter c is defined in terms of the coefficients of the Black-Scholes equation as $c=2r/\sigma^2$.

Applying the integral Laplace transform

$$U(x;s)=\int_0^\infty \exp(-s\tau)u(x,\tau)d\tau$$

to the setting in (12)–(14), one arrives at the following boundary value problem

$$\frac{d^2U(x;s)}{dx^2}+(c-1)\frac{dU(x;s)}{dx}-(s+c)U(x;s)=-f(\exp x) \tag{15}$$

$$U(a;s)=0, \quad U(b;s)=0 \tag{16}$$

for the transform $U(x;s)$.

In compliance with the method of variation of parameters, the general solution to (15) is found in the form

$$U(x,s)=\int_a^x \frac{\exp\alpha(x-\xi)}{2\omega}[\exp\omega(\xi-x)-\exp\omega(x-\xi)]f(\exp\xi)d\xi$$
$$+\,Q(s)\exp(\alpha+\omega)x+R(s)\exp(\alpha-\omega)x \tag{17}$$

where the parameter ω is introduced as $\omega = (s+\beta)^{1/2}$, while the parameters α and β are defined in terms of c as

$$\alpha = \frac{1-c}{2} \quad \text{and} \quad \beta = \left(\frac{1+c}{2}\right)^2 \tag{18}$$

Satisfaction of the boundary conditions at $x = a$ and $x = b$ yields the system of linear algebraic equations

$$\begin{pmatrix} \exp(\alpha+\omega)a & \exp(\alpha-\omega)a \\ \exp(\alpha+\omega)b & \exp(\alpha-\omega)b \end{pmatrix} \begin{pmatrix} Q(s) \\ R(s) \end{pmatrix} = \begin{pmatrix} 0 \\ \Psi(s) \end{pmatrix} \tag{19}$$

in $Q(s)$ and $R(s)$. Here

$$\Psi(s) = -\int_a^b \frac{1}{2\omega}[\exp(\alpha-\omega)(b-\xi) - \exp(\alpha+\omega)(b-\xi)]f(\exp\xi)d\xi$$

Solving the system in (19), we obtain the functions $Q(s)$ and $R(s)$ as

$$Q(s) = \int_a^b \frac{\exp(\alpha-\omega)a\exp\alpha(b-\xi)}{2\omega[\exp\omega(a-b) - \exp\omega(b-a)]} \times [\exp\omega(\xi-b) - \exp\omega(b-\xi)]f(\exp\xi)d\xi$$

and

$$R(s) = -\int_a^b \frac{\exp(\alpha+\omega)a\exp\alpha(b-\xi)}{2\omega[\exp\omega(a-b) - \exp\omega(b-a)]} \times [\exp\omega(\xi-b) - \exp\omega(b-\xi)]f(\exp\xi)d\xi$$

Upon substituting these in (17), the latter reads as

$$U(x,s) = \int_a^x \frac{\exp\alpha(x-\xi)}{2\omega}[\exp\omega(\xi-x) - \exp\omega(x-\xi)]f(\exp\xi)d\xi + \int_a^b \frac{\exp\alpha(x-\xi)[\exp\omega(x-a) - \exp\omega(a-x)]}{2\omega[\exp\omega(a-b) - \exp\omega(b-a)]} \times [\exp\omega(\xi-b) - \exp\omega(b-\xi)]f(\exp\xi)d\xi$$

which can be expressed in a single-integral form as

$$U(x;s) = \int_a^b \frac{\exp\alpha(x-\xi)}{2\omega[\exp\omega(a-b) - \exp\omega(b-a)]} \times \{\exp\omega[(x+\xi)-(a+b)] + \exp\omega[(a+b)-(x+\xi)] - \exp\omega[|x-\xi|+(a-b)] - \exp\omega[(b-a)-|x-\xi|]\}f(\exp\xi)d\xi$$

Transforming the bracket factor in the denominator as

$$\exp\omega(a-b)-\exp\omega(b-a)=-\exp\omega(b-a)[1-\exp 2\omega(a-b)]$$

we rewrite the above representation for $U(x;s)$ as

$$U(x;s)=-\int_a^b \frac{\exp\alpha(x-\xi)}{2\omega\exp\omega(b-a)[1-\exp 2\omega(a-b)]} \times\{\exp\omega[(x+\xi)-(a+b)]+\exp\omega[(a+b)-(x+\xi)] -\exp\omega[|x-\xi|+(a-b)]-\exp\omega[(b-a)-|x-\xi|]\}f(\exp\xi)d\xi \quad (20)$$

An immediate inverse Laplace transform of the above expression for $U(x;s)$ is problematic if $U(x;s)$ is kept in its current form. Therefore, we adjust it first by representing the factor

$$[1-\exp 2\omega(a-b)]^{-1}$$

in the integrand of (20) as the sum of the geometric series

$$\frac{1}{1-\exp 2\omega(a-b)}=\sum_{n=0}^{\infty}\exp 2n\omega(a-b)$$

whose common ratio $\exp 2\omega(a-b)$ represents a negative exponential function (since $a<b$) and is, therefore, less than one, justifying convergence of the above series. This transforms the expression for $U(x;s)$ in (20) to

$$U(x;s)=\int_a^b \frac{\exp\alpha(x-\xi)}{2\omega}\sum_{n=0}^{\infty}\{\exp\omega[|x-\xi|-2(n+1)(b-a)] +\exp\omega[2(n+1)(a-b)-|x-\xi|] -\exp\omega[2n(a-b)-2b+(x+\xi)] -\exp\omega[2n(a-b)+2a-(x+\xi)]\}f(\exp\xi)d\xi$$

which allows the inverse Laplace transform in the term-by-term fashion. This yields the solution $u(x,\tau)$ to the initial-boundary value problem in (12)–(14) in the form

$$u(x,\tau) = L^{-1}\{U(x,s)\} = \int_a^b \frac{\exp\alpha(x-\xi)\exp(-\beta\tau)}{2\sqrt{\pi\tau}}\sum_{n=0}^{\infty}\left\{\exp\left(-\frac{[|x-\xi|+2(n+1)(a-b)]^2}{4\tau}\right)\right.$$

$$+\exp\left(-\frac{[|x-\xi|-2n(a-b)]^2}{4\tau}\right)-\exp\left(-\frac{[2b-(x+\xi)-2n(a-b)]^2}{4\tau}\right)$$
$$-\exp\left(-\frac{[(x+\xi)-2a-2n(a-b)]^2}{4\tau}\right)\Bigg\}f(\exp\xi)d\xi$$

which converts to a more compact form by rearranging the summation in the above series. This yields

$$u(x,\tau)=\int_a^b \frac{\exp\alpha(x-\xi)\exp(-\beta\tau)}{2\sqrt{\pi\tau}}$$
$$\times\sum_{m=-\infty}^{\infty}\Bigg\{\exp\left(-\frac{[|x-\xi|+2m(a-b)]^2}{4\tau}\right)$$
$$-\exp\left(-\frac{[2b-(x+\xi)-2m(a-b)]^2}{4\tau}\right)\Bigg\}f(\exp\xi)d\xi$$

In compliance with the relations in (11), the solution $V(S,t)$ to the setting in (6), (7) and (10) can be obtained by the backward substitution of the variables x, τ and ξ with S, t and $\widetilde{S}$, respectively. When α and β are replaced, according to (18), with the original parameters r and σ^2 of the Black-Scholes equation, we obtain $V(S,t)$ in the form

$$V(S,t)=\int_{S_1}^{S_2}\frac{1}{\sigma\widetilde{S}\sqrt{2\pi(T-t)}}\exp\left(-\frac{r-\sigma^2/2}{\sigma^2}\ln\frac{S}{\widetilde{S}}-\frac{(r+\sigma^2/2)^2}{2\sigma^2}(T-t)\right)$$
$$\times\sum_{m=-\infty}^{\infty}\Bigg\{\exp\left(-\frac{[\ln(S/\widetilde{S})+2m\ln(S_1/S_2)]^2}{2\sigma^2(T-t)}\right)$$
$$-\exp\left(-\frac{[\ln(S_2^2/S\widetilde{S})-2m\ln(S_1/S_2)]^2}{2\sigma^2(T-t)}\right)\Bigg\}f(\widetilde{S})d\widetilde{S}$$

which can be transformed, by combining the logarithmic components in the series factor. This yields

$$V(S,t)=\int_{S_1}^{S_2}\frac{1}{\sigma\widetilde{S}\sqrt{2\pi(T-t)}}\exp\left(-\frac{r-\sigma^2/2}{\sigma^2}\ln\frac{S}{\widetilde{S}}-\frac{(r+\sigma^2/2)^2}{2\sigma^2}(T-t)\right)$$
$$\times\sum_{m=-\infty}^{\infty}\Bigg\{\exp\left(-\frac{[\ln(SS_1^{2m}/\widetilde{S}S_2^{2m})]^2}{2\sigma^2(T-t)}\right)$$
$$-\exp\left(-\frac{[\ln(S_2^{2(m+1)}/S\widetilde{S}S_1^{2m})]^2}{2\sigma^2(T-t)}\right)\Bigg\}f(\widetilde{S})d\widetilde{S} \tag{21}$$

Thus, the kernel

$$
\begin{aligned}
G(S,t;\widetilde{S}) = {} & \frac{1}{\sigma\widetilde{S}\sqrt{2\pi(T-t)}}\exp\left(-\frac{r-\sigma^2/2}{\sigma^2}\ln\frac{S}{\widetilde{S}}-\frac{(r+\sigma^2/2)^2}{2\sigma^2}(T-t)\right) \\
& \times\sum_{m=-\infty}^{\infty}\left\{\exp\left(-\frac{[\ln(SS_1^{2m}/\widetilde{S}S_2^{2m})]^2}{2\sigma^2(T-t)}\right)\right. \\
& \left.-\exp\left(-\frac{[\ln(S_2^{2(m+1)}/S\widetilde{S}S_1^{2m})]^2}{2\sigma^2(T-t)}\right)\right\}
\end{aligned}
\tag{22}
$$

in the integral form of (21) represents the Green's function to the setting in (6), (7) and (10). The series in this representation converges at a high rate unless the difference $(T-t)$ is significantly small. This implies that, in computing approximate values of $G(S,t;\widetilde{S})$, an accuracy level required for applications can, in most cases, be attained by appropriately truncating the series in (22) to a partial sum.

3 Iterative procedure

A Green's function-based algorithm is proposed for solution of the nonlinear terminal-boundary value problem stated in (5)–(7). At the first stage in the algorithm, the function $V(S,t)$ is broken onto two components

$$V(S,t) = V_1(S,t) + V_2(S,t) \tag{23}$$

where $V_1(S,t)$ represents solution of the following linear problem for the Black-Scholes equation

$$\frac{\partial V_1(S,t)}{\partial t}+\frac{\sigma^2S^2}{2}\frac{\partial^2V_1(S,t)}{\partial S^2}+rS\frac{\partial V_1(S,t)}{\partial S}-rV_1(S,t)=0 \tag{24}$$

$$V_1(S,T) = f(S) \tag{25}$$

$$V_1(S,t) = 0 \quad \text{and} \quad V_1(S,t) = 0 \tag{26}$$

while the second component $V_2(S,t)$ in (23) represents solution to the following nonlinear problem

$$\frac{\partial V_2(S,t)}{\partial t}+\frac{\sigma^2S^2}{2}\frac{\partial^2V_2(S,t)}{\partial S^2}+rS\frac{\partial V_2(S,t)}{\partial S}-rV_2(S,t)=F(V_2(S,t),S,t)$$

$$V_2(S,T) = 0$$

$$V_2(S_1,t) = 0 \quad \text{and} \quad V_2(S_2,t) = 0$$

As to the linear setting in (24)–(26), we express its solution in terms of the Green's function $G(S, t; \widetilde{S})$ derived in (22) as

$$V_1(S,t) = \int_{S_1}^{S_2} G(S,t;\widetilde{S}) f(\widetilde{S}) d\widetilde{S} \tag{27}$$

Evidently, approximate values of the above integral representation can be computed at any point (S, t) in Ω at any accuracy with the aid of standard quadrature formulae. This study brings a solid justification to this assertion.

The function $V_2(S, t)$ can be computed on an iterative basis. We look for it as the limit of a sequence $\{V_2^{(k)}(S, t)\}$ whose components $V_2^{(k)}(S, t)$, $(k = 0, 1, 2, \dots)$ are obtained in compliance with the following iterative scheme

$$\frac{\partial V_2^{(k)}(S,t)}{\partial t} + \frac{\sigma^2 S^2}{2} \frac{\partial^2 V_2^{(k)}(S,t)}{\partial S^2} + rS \frac{\partial V_2^{(k)}(S,t)}{\partial S} - rV_2^{(k)}(S,t)$$
$$= F(V_2^{(k-1)}(S,t), S, t), \quad k = 1, 2, 3, \dots \tag{28}$$

$$V_2^{(k)}(S,T) = 0 \tag{29}$$

$$V_2^{(k)}(S_1,t) = 0 \quad \text{and} \quad V_2^{(k)}(S_2,t) = 0 \tag{30}$$

To run the first loop of the procedure, an appropriate form ought to be chosen for $F(V_2^{(0)}(S, t), S, t)$ in the governing equation of the above setting. The form of $F(0, S, t)$ can, for example, be recommended as an option.

As to the solution $V_2^{(k)}(S, t)$ of the problem in (28)–(30), at each stage $(k = 1, 2, 3, \dots)$ of the iterative procedure, we express it as

$$V_2^{(k)}(S,t) = \int_t^T \int_{S_1}^{S_2} G(S, t-\widetilde{t}, \widetilde{S}) F(V_2^{(k-1)}(\widetilde{S}, \widetilde{t}), \widetilde{S}, \widetilde{t}) d\widetilde{S} d\widetilde{t}, \quad k = 1, 2, 3, \dots \tag{31}$$

in terms of the Green's function $G(S, t; \widetilde{S})$. A standard method of quadratures is also recommended in this case for computing values of $V_2^{(k)}(S, t)$ in Ω.

Convergence of the sequence $\{V_2^{(k)}(S, t)\}$ of successive approximations is yet to be investigated. It depends upon a number of factors one of which is the accuracy level potentially attainable for solutions of those linear problems that arise at each stage of the iterative procedure. The present study focuses on this issue and aims at the creation of a solid reliable background for computing values of the integral representations in (27) and (31). The values of $V_1(S, T/2)$ and $V_2(S, T/2)$ in Tables 1 and 2 were obtained for the following set of initial data: $r = 0.06$, $\sigma = 0.8$, $\varepsilon = 0.1$, $C = 1$, $T = 1$, $S_1 = 1$ and $S_2 = 2$; while the functions $q(S)$, $A(t)$, $B(t)$ and $\varphi(S)$ were defined as

$$q(S) = S, \quad A(t) = 10\exp(-50(t - T/2))^2, \quad B(t) = 20t^3 \sin(\pi t/T)$$

and

$$\varphi(S) = \begin{cases} 320(S - S_1)((S_1 + S_2)/2 - S), & S < (S_1 + S_2)/2 \\ 0, & S > (S_1 + S_2)/2 \end{cases}$$

Table 1: Approximate values $V_1(S, T/2)$ attained in computing (27).

Number of quadrature nodes	S coordinate					
	1.0	1.2	1.4	1.6	1.8	2.0
5	.00000	.30506	.44110	.39510	.22473	.00000
10	.00000	.28983	.41908	.37536	.21352	.00000
15	.00000	.29720	.42975	.38492	.21894	.00000
20	.00000	.29445	.42576	.38135	.21692	.00000

Table 2: Approximate values of $V_2(S, T/2)$ attained in computing (31).

Number of quadrature nodes	S coordinate					
	1.0	1.2	1.4	1.6	1.8	2.0
5	.05325	.03736	.02805	.01930	.00986	.00000
10	.01925	.01738	.01627	.01268	.00686	.00000
15	.04806	.03584	.02795	.01967	.01017	.00000
20	.04120	.03107	.02502	.01798	.00937	.00000

The data in Tables 1 and 2 advise that quite accurate values of the integral representations in (27) and (31) can be obtained by using the standard trapezoidal rule with a limited number of quadrature nodes.

4 Conclusion

A semi-analytic approach has been proposed for pricing of American options. It is based on the Green's function method. The approach is supposed to be effective numerically. The following two factors are behind of this assertion. First, the required Green's function is constructed analytically. Second, numerical differentiation, which would substantially deteriorate the accuracy, is completely avoided with only numerical integration (whose accuracy is easy to control) involved.

References

[1] Zvan, R., Forsyth, P.A. & Vetzal, K.R., Penalty method for American options with stochastic volatility. *Journal of Computational and Applied Mathematics*, **91**, pp. 199–218, 1998.

[2] Khaliq, A.Q.M., Voss, D.A. & Kazmi, S. H. K., A linearly implicit predictor-corrector scheme for pricing American options using a penalty method approach. *Journal of Banking & Finance*, **30**, pp. 489–502, 2006.

[3] Melnikov, Max Y. & Melnikov, Yuri A., Construction of Green's functions for the Black-Scholes equation. *Electronic Journal of Differential Equations*, **153**, pp. 1–14, 2007.

[4] Melnikov, Max Y., Black-Scholes equation: Green's function solution for terminal-boundary value problems. *Proc. of the Int. Conf. on Computational and Mathematical Methods in Science and Engineering*, Chicago, pp. 232–237, 2007.

Section 3
Portfolio management and asset allocation

Hedge fund portfolio selection with modified expected shortfall

K. Boudt[1], B. G. Peterson[2] & P. Carl[3]
[1]*FWO, Flanders and K.U.Leuven, Belgium*
[2]*Diamond Management & Technology Consultants, Chicago, IL, USA*
[3]*Guidance Capital Management, Chicago, IL, USA*

Abstract

Modified Value-at-Risk (VaR) and Expected Shortfall (ES) are recently introduced downside risk estimators based on the Cornish-Fisher expansion for assets such as hedge funds whose returns are non-normally distributed. Modified VaR has been widely implemented as a portfolio selection criterion. We are the first to investigate hedge fund portfolio selection using modified ES as optimality criterion. We show that for the EDHEC hedge fund style indices, the optimal portfolios based on modified ES outperform out-of-sample the EDHEC Fund of Funds index and have better risk characteristics than the equal-weighted and Fund of Funds portfolios.
Keywords: portfolio optimization, modified expected shortfall, non-normal returns.

1 Introduction

It is generally accepted that rational investors should allocate their portfolio optimally according to a return/risk criterion. The most widely studied criteria (minimum variance and maximum Sharpe ratio) are based on the first two portfolio moments. A more general set of positive preferences for odd moments (mean, skewness) and aversion to even moments (variance, kurtosis) is discussed by Scott and Horvath [1]. For largely intuitive reasons, the relationships between the moments themselves are often summarized into risk measures. In the presence of non-normal returns and when investors have a non-quadratic utility function, two issues arise: (i) the choice of risk measure and (ii) the estimator for this risk measure.

WIT Transactions on Information and Communication Technologies, Vol 41, © 2008 WIT Press
www.witpress.com, ISSN 1743-3517 (on-line)
doi:10.2495/CF080101

The literature on portfolio risk measurement seems to agree that, in the presence of non-normal returns and non-quadratic utility functions, a downside risk measure should be used rather than the portfolio variance which gives an equal weight to positive and negative returns. Value-at-Risk (VaR) and Expected Shortfall (ES) are the most popular downside risk predictors. VaR is the negative value of the portfolio return such that lower returns will only occur with at most a preset probability level denoted α, which typically is between 1 and 5 per cent. Expected Shortfall is the negative value of the mean of all return realizations that are below the VaR. More formally, let $F(\cdot)$ and $F^{-1}(\cdot)$ be the distribution and quantile function of the portfolio return r_p and assume that they are continuous. Then VaR and ES with loss probability α are defined as follows:

$$\text{VaR}(\alpha) = -F^{-1}(\alpha) \tag{1}$$

$$\text{ES}(\alpha) = -E_F[r_p | r_p \leq F^{-1}(\alpha)]. \tag{2}$$

When portfolio returns are asymmetric, VaR may no longer be an acceptable risk measure in a portfolio context because it fails to be "subadditive". When VaR is used the risk of the overall portfolio could be higher than the combined risks of the single positions in spite of portfolio diversification effects. Moreover, because VaR is not a convex function of the portfolio weights, mean-VaR portfolio optimization is a difficult programming task. Expected Shortfall, on the contrary, is a coherent risk measure and is a convex function of the portfolio weights (Bertsimas *et al.* [2]). Its widespread implementation on portfolios of non-normal returns has been hampered by the fact that before our paper [3], there was no fast-to-compute estimator for ES that performs well when returns are skewed and heavy tailed.

Regarding the issue of the estimation of portfolio VaR and ES, note first of all in eqns. (1) and (2) that these risk measures are defined as a function of the portfolio return distribution function and that this distribution function is unknown for real time series. Very often, VaR and ES are computed under the hypothetical assumption of normality. The resulting estimators are called Gaussian VaR and ES. It is a stylized fact that the returns on many financial assets are not normally distributed. It follows that methods that take into account the non-normality of the true return distribution will produce more accurate downside risk estimates than Gaussian VaR and ES do. One such very popular methodology relies on using the Cornish-Fisher and Edgeworth expansions to estimate the distribution function as the normal distribution plus some correction terms that account for the skewness and excess kurtosis observed in the data. The resulting estimators are called modified VaR and modified ES. Today modified VaR is, among practitioners, one of the most popular estimators for evaluating the risk of hedge funds and other non-normally distributed assets and has been widely used as a portfolio selection criterion (see e.g. Favre and Galeano [4]). Motivated by the desirable mathematical properties of ES and the widespread interest in modified VaR, we have shown in a recent paper [3] how the Edgeworth and Cornish-Fisher expansions of the density and quantile functions can be used to obtain an estimator for ES, called modified ES, that delivers accurate downside risk estimates even in the presence of non-normal returns. This paper studies the use of modified ES as an objective for the construction of a fund of hedge funds based on the EDHEC hedge fund style indices.

The remainder of the paper is organized as follows. In Section 2 we describe our portfolio optimization strategy, introduce the data and present our methodology for solving the portfolio selection problem. Results are discussed in Section 3. Finally, Section 4 concludes and outlines the implications for further research.

2 Data and methodology

2.1 Data

We apply our portfolio construction techniques to the January 1997–December 2007 monthly return series of the EDHEC hedge fund investment style indices (132 observations). EDHEC style indices are constructed such that the returns on these indices reflect the monthly performance of hedge funds pursuing that particular style. (The EDHEC indices are constructed using PCA factor replication against other published hedge hedge fund indices (HFR, CSFB, etc.) and private databases of hedge fund returns. In this manner, they attempt to correct for the biases of the individual hedge fund index construction methodologies and construct a "meta-index" that is more broadly representative of the actual performance of a particular style.) The monthly return on the EDHEC Fund of Funds index is symbolically representative of the performance of the Fund of Hedge Funds providers. The comparison to the Fund of Funds index here is meant to be illustrative; these are general observations about performance of optimized portfolios and the comparison against the Fund of Funds index is merely intended to provide context.

Table 1 reports the main descriptive statistics for each of these series, which will be of importance for the optimal portfolio allocations. From an investor's perspective, the equity market neutral style index has the best combination of statistical properties: a relatively high Sharpe-ratio, low volatility, positive skewness and a low downside risk as measured by the 95% modified VaR and ES statistics. Clearly, assets with negative skewness should have a higher downside risk than assets with positive skewness and the higher the excess kurtosis, the higher downside risk is for negatively skewed return distributions. In Table 1 we see that modified VaR and ES respect these intuitive conditions for being a reliable downside risk estimate for non-normal returns. Indeed, note that Merger Arbitrage and Relative Value have a similar mean return and standard deviation, but Merger Arbitrage has much more negative skewness and higher kurtosis than Relative Value. Consequently, Merger Arbitrage's modified VaR and ES are higher than Relative Value's modified VaR and ES. Note however that the overall level of modified VaR and ES is determined mostly by the asset's mean and standard deviation, while skewness and excess kurtosis have only a second order impact on modified VaR and ES unless either have extreme values.

Table 1: Descriptive statistics for the 1997–2007 monthly return series of the EDHEC hedge fund style indices.

	Mean	Std.Dev.	Skew.	Exc.Kurt.	mVaR (0.05)	mES (0.05)
Convertible Arbitrage	0.007	0.011	-0.835	1.204	0.014	0.022
CTA Global	0.006	0.026	0.086	-0.208	0.035	0.044
Distressed Securities	0.010	0.015	-1.732	9.778	0.018	0.059
Emerging Markets	0.011	0.036	-1.378	7.098	0.055	0.139
Equity Market Neutral	0.007	0.006	0.279	0.815	0.002	0.005
Event Driven	0.009	0.016	-1.872	9.435	0.021	0.062
Fixed Income Arbitrage	0.005	0.010	-5.036	37.567	0.013	0.013
Global Macro	0.009	0.017	0.922	1.830	0.014	0.018
Long Short Equity	0.009	0.020	-0.005	0.899	0.023	0.034
Merger Arbitrage	0.007	0.011	-1.749	7.252	0.013	0.035
Relative Value	0.008	0.010	-1.046	2.586	0.010	0.020
Fund of Funds	0.008	0.016	0.161	3.226	0.017	0.027

2.2 Portfolio optimization problem

We design our portfolio optimization problem to be a stylized representation of actual practice in the fund of hedge funds world. In our exploratory model, investors are either pure risk minimizers or reward/risk maximizers. They use either the portfolio standard deviation or modified Expected Shortfall as risk measures and take the generalized Sharpe ratio defined as the mean return divided by the risk measure as a reward/risk criterion. We rebalance these portfolios annually, as this is symbolically consistent with the actual longer holding periods and lock-ups common in Funds of Funds. Finally, we impose minimum 2.5% and maximum 35% bound constraints on the portfolio weights to avoid "edge" portfolios. We further consider the equal-weighted portfolio and the EDHEC Fund of Funds index as benchmark portfolios to evaluate the performance of our minimum risk and maximum reward/risk portfolios against.

Hedge fund portfolio selection under these criteria requires the solution to a linearly constrained nonlinear optimization problem. Because many local optima points exist to this problem, we have undertaken the two-step approach of (i) brute-force exploration of the feasible space using a step size of 0.05, where we compute for each possible combination of portfolio weights the value of the objective function and save the ten best solutions; followed by (ii) local optimization of the objective function using the DONLP2 sequential quadratic programming algorithm initialized at the ten best solutions obtained via the grid search of step (i). The solution to the optimization problem is the global optimum of these ten local optima. This is clearly a very greedy optimization method, since it consists in evaluating the optimization criterion for hundreds of thousands of potential portfolios. In Boudt *et al.* [3], we showed that all the optimization criteria can be expressed as analytical and fast-to-compute formulae of multivariate moments, which eases the optimization task somewhat. (The data, functions and figures used in this paper are available in the R package PerformanceAnalytics [5] or directly from the authors.)

The risk and reward/risk criteria need to be estimated. We account for the potential time-variation in the distribution of the hedge fund return series by estimating these criteria on the basis of a rolling three year estimation sample. Since the history of the data set starts on January 1997, we thus dispose of out-of-sample returns of the optimally designed portfolios for the period January 2000–December 2007.

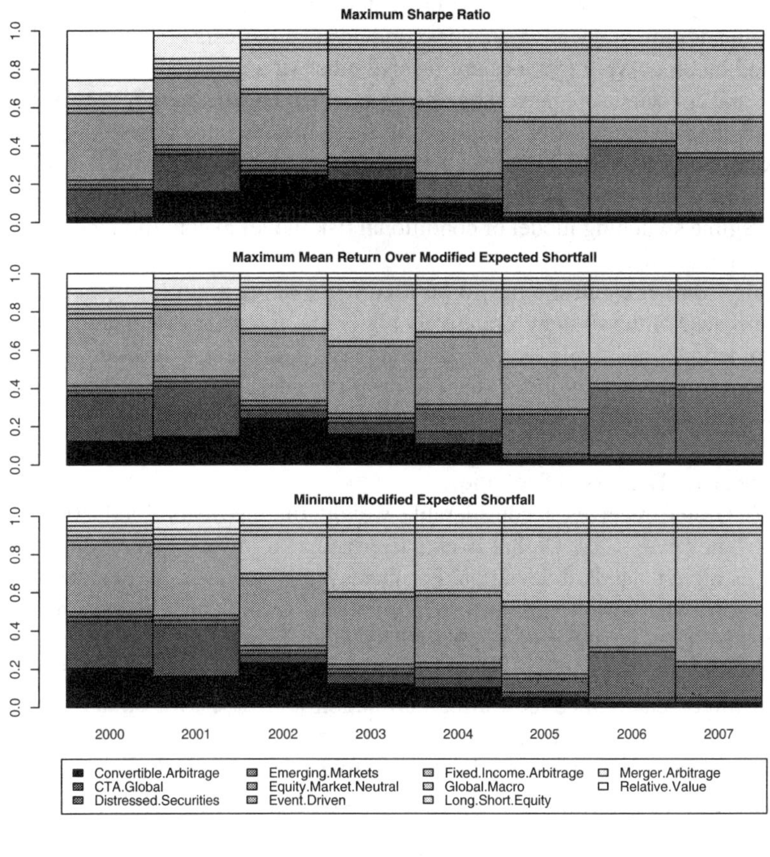

Figure 1: Weight allocations for yearly rebalanced portfolios of EDHEC indices.

3 Results

3.1 Portfolio allocation

The stacked bar weights charts in Figure 1 show that the maximum Sharpe ratio, minimum modified ES, and maximum mean return over modified ES optimization criteria all produce very similar portfolios for the years 2000–2007. Allocations tend to go to low-standard deviation strategies, such as Equity Market Neutral, Convertible Arbitrage and Fixed Income Arbitrage. All three objective functions allocate to CTA global and Convertible Arbitrage at the beginning and then shift into Distressed Securities starting in 2004.

The strategies that receive only a minimum allocation include Emerging Markets, Event Driven, Long-Short Equity, Merger Arbitrage, and Relative Value. For the most part, the omission of these strategies can be explained by their higher standard deviation and (sometimes strongly) negative skewness and positive kurtosis. Where standard deviation may not seem particularly high, such as Long Short Equity, the strategies can be characterized as having lower return to risk ratios, in addition to negative skewness and positive kurtosis.

Fixed Income Arbitrage does not receive much of an allocation in the first two years, and a review of the rolling three-year standard deviation, skewness and kurtosis makes it clear why. The surge in these statistics for this strategy during the Russian crisis and LTCM carry through the analysis until 2001, when that period drops out of the rolling window. In actual practice it may be desirable to use a regime switching model or conditional risk model to condition the moments for use in analysis.

Equity Market Neutral tends to be a cornerstone of portfolios generated like these because of the strategy's relatively high ratio of reward to standard deviation and sometimes positively skewed distributions. The mean return and (positive) skewness to the strategy index seem to drop considerably in 2003, which results in lower allocations in the max SR and min modified ES portfolios. The allocation shrinks somewhat less in the mean return over modified ES portfolio, where it is preferred over Distressed Securities.

CTA Global receives a considerable weight for the years 2000–2001. As a strategy, however, CTA Global is characterized as a lower-Sharpe ratio strategy given its higher standard deviation. For these years, however, the standard deviation is somewhat lower and the correlation of the CTA Global index is near zero or negative (to -0.5) to some indices. The small or even negative correlation is probably the factor explaining the presence of CTA in the portfolios for the first two or three years. Once the rolling correlation level rises, the strategy receives only the minimum allocation.

The most notable difference in the portfolios is a relatively small one. The maximum Sharpe ratio portfolio selects Relative Value in 2000 and Merger Arbitrage in 2001. The objective functions that consider higher moments tend to select near-minimum weights in those strategies during those periods, given their strongly negative skewness and kurtosis measures coming from the crises of

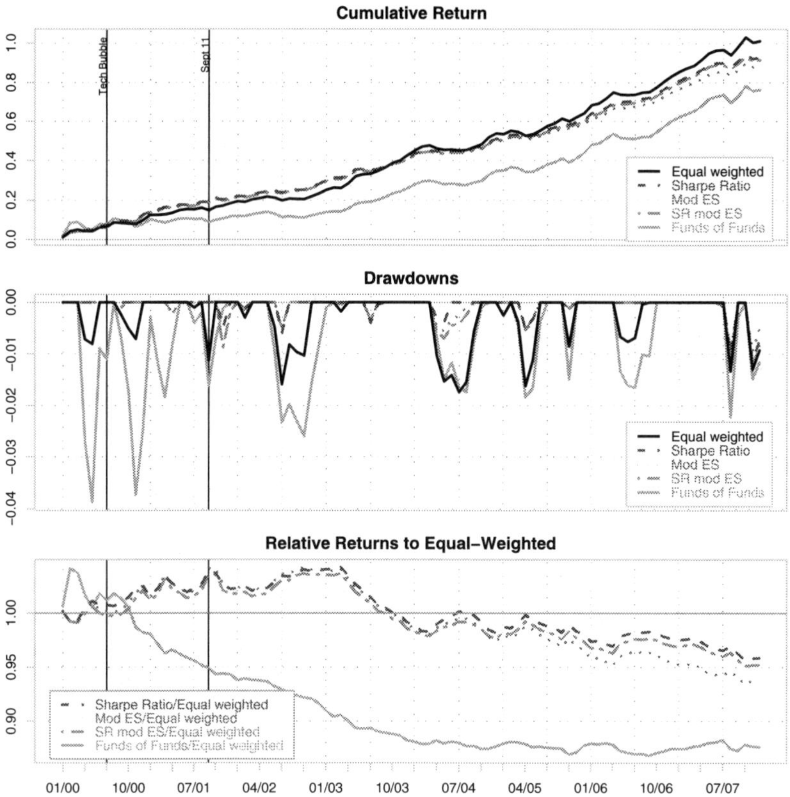

Figure 2: Out-of-sample cumulative portfolio return charts.

1998. Even after the measures of those higher moments fall, however, none of the objective functions allocate to those strategies.

3.2 Portfolio performance

The first panel of Figure 2 shows the cumulative performance of the different portfolios and the EDHEC Fund of Funds index. The portfolios tend to outperform the Fund of Funds index, although the portfolio performance is not shown net of the additional fees that funds of hedge funds charge. Were those fees added, we might see similar performance. It is worth pointing out that the similar allocations we observed above result in very similar performance of the optimized portfolios.

The second panel of Figure 2 shows the portfolios' drawdowns, measured as a percentage of the maximum cumulative return achieved. In this case, we can see that the Fund of Funds index shows drawdowns in 2000 and 2001. Those are modest relative to the equity markets, of course, but are worse than any of the other portfolios. The equal weighted portfolio tends to have the next highest drawdowns. The optimized portfolios tend to have smaller drawdowns than the equal weighted portfolio. The objective functions that consider higher moments do avoid assets with negative skewness that have a higher downside risk, preferring assets with positive skewness. The advantage of considering those higher moments is somewhat unclear here, since the maximum Sharpe ratio (Markowitz) portfolio has also avoided drawdowns by selecting lower standard-deviation strategies. In the presence of non-normal returns, a maximum Sharpe Ratio strategy may not always work, depending on the co-skewness and co-kurtosis of the strategies (which may lead to higher combined *portfolio* variance) and the nature of the drawdown.

The third panel of Figure 2 shows the ratio of the cumulative performance for the monthly returns of the optimized portfolios and the EDHEC Fund of Funds index versus the equal-weighted portfolio. The value of the chart is less important than the slope of the line. If the slope is positive, the optimized portfolio (numerator) is outperforming the equal-weighted one, and vice versa. Note that the relative performance of the optimized portfolios versus the equal-weighted portfolio is very different in the period January 2000–December 2003 from the period January 2004–December 2007. In the first period, the optimized portfolios clearly outperform the equal-weighted portfolio, while in the second period the equal weighted portfolio outperforms the optimized portfolios. Also in the first period, the equal weighted portfolio outperforms the Fund of Funds index. In the second period, performance of the equal-weighted portfolio and Fund of Funds index is very similar (the relative performance line being flat).

The nature of the under- or out-performance to the equal weighted portfolio is instructive. The strategies that are rarely or never selected by the optimizer have been more volatile but have periods of higher performance. Those strategies more frequently selected have lower mean returns but also much lower standard deviation and/or higher (more positive) skewness. During the period following 2003, the rarely selected strategies saw rising mean returns again after their decline in the early part of the decade. Strategies selected saw mean returns remain steady or decline after 2003, with the exception of Distressed Securities.

The “hinge” in relative performance we observe in 2003 might suggest that the broader market conditions that followed provided a positive environment for those lower-Sharpe ratio strategies. The equal-weight portfolio, as it is indifferent to the issues of selection, captures the shift of relative performance. We might speculate that the attributes of high liquidity, low market volatility, and available credit for leverage all combined to help those strategies prevail during that period. Unfortunately for the performance of the optimized portfolios, this information remains outside of their preview.

4 Conclusion

This paper proposed and examined the use of modified Expected Shortfall as a criterion for optimal selection of portfolios of hedge funds and illustrates this approach for the EDHEC hedge fund style indices. Further work will examine portfolio selection in a risk budgeting framework where an explicit maximum risk contribution is specified for each portfolio component, or where the component contributions are minimized as much as possible. Additional works should examine whether different utility functions are called for in a fund of hedge funds context when optimizing individual style portfolios versus optimizing weightings across styles.

References

[1] Scott, R.C. & Horvath, P.A., On the direction of preference for moments of higher order than the variance. *Journal of Finance*, **35(4)**, pp. 915–919, 1980.
[2] Bertsimas, D., Lauprete, G.J. & Samarov, A., Shortfall as a risk measure: Properties, optimization and applications. *Journal of Economic Dynamics and Control*, **28(7)**, pp. 1353–1381, 2004.
[3] Boudt, K., Peterson, B.G. & Croux, C., Estimation and decomposition of downside risk for portfolios with non-normal returns. *Working paper*, 2007.
[4] Favre, L. & Galeano, J.A., Mean-modified value-at-risk optimization with hedge funds. *Journal of Alternative Investment*, **5(2)**, pp. 2–21, 2002.
[5] Carl, P. & Peterson, B.G., PerformanceAnalytics: Econometric tools for performance and risk analysis, 2008. R package version 0.9.7.

Portfolio rankings with skewness and kurtosis

M. Di Pierro[1] & J. Mosevich[2]
[1]*DePaul University, School of Computer Science,*
243 S. Wabash Avenue, Chicago, IL 60604, USA
[2]*DePaul University, College of Commerce, 1 E. Jackson,*
Chicago, IL 60604, USA

Abstract

In this paper we discuss the issue of portfolio ranking for a rational risk averse investor with and without the option to buy a risk free asset. We find that in the former case the use of Sharpe, Omega, Sortino, and Kappa rankings are all justified although they follow from different definitions. We also find that for portfolios with Gaussian distributed returns these rankings, as well as the Stutzer ranking, are equivalent to each other.

Finally we prove that without a risk free asset all the above rankings are incompatible with being a rational risk averse investor and a different ranking is required. We propose an exact analytical formula as well as an approximate formula for practical use.
Keywords: portfolio ranking, skewness, kurtosis, Omega, non-Gaussian disributions.

1 Introduction

In this paper we discuss the issue of portfolio ranking and selection. We will concentrate on selecting one portfolio among a finite set of portfolios, where each portfolio is characterized by its own distribution of returns $p(x)$. This distribution may be inferred from past performances and assumed to be persistent, or it may be derived by some model of future performances.

We distinguish two main cases:

CASE #1 An amount A must be invested and it can be distributed between a risk free asset (that pays a risk free rate r) and the selected portfolio.

CASE #2 An amount A must be invested exclusively in the selected portfolio.

WIT Transactions on Information and Communication Technologies, Vol 41, © 2008 WIT Press
www.witpress.com, ISSN 1743-3517 (on-line)
doi:10.2495/CF080111

The two problems are apparently similar but they are conceptually different and therefore have different solutions. In this paper we wish to clarify the difference between the two, discuss ranking schemes in both cases, and propose a theoretically sound ranking scheme for the second case in the presence of distributions that exhibit arbitrary skewness and kurtosis.

We conclude that in case #2, and in presence of skewness and kurtosis, a rational investor using the CARA utility function should select that portfolio with higher value of

$$\mu - \frac{m\sigma^2}{2} + \frac{m^2\sigma^3 S}{6} - \frac{m^3\sigma^4(K-3)}{720} \tag{1}$$

where μ is the average return of the portfolio, σ is the standard deviation, S is the skewness, K is the kurtosis, and m is the CARA subjective risk aversion parameter.

Eq. (1) extends a previous conclusion by Levy and Markowitz [16] by taking into considerations the effects of skewness and kurtosis. Our formula provides a simple practical way to select one out of many mutually exclusive portfolios.

In this paper we discuss only the issue of portfolio selection, not portfolio construction. For a review, we refer the reader to the work of Ortobelli *et al.* [1].

In this analysis, we will always identify a portfolio with its distribution of returns p since we are not interested in the composition of the portfolios.

2 Portfolio selection

In this section we discuss similarities and differences between CASE #1 and #2.

The main similarity between the two cases is that they both require subjective choice. In Utility Theory [3, 4], this is the choice of a utility function $U(x)$ and its parameters. $U(x)$ is a function that takes as input a possible return x from an investment and outputs a number that represents the investor's degree of satisfaction associated with a return x.

In neoclassical economics, an investor is defined "rational" if

- the investor has a utility function $U(x)$
- the investor acts in order to maximize $U(x)$
- $U(x)$ is monotonic increasing (higher return is preferred to lower return).

A common choice for the utility function is $U_{CARA}(x) \equiv -e^{-mx}$ which is known as the "Constant Absolute Risk Averse" utility function. m is the risk aversion parameter and it is of the order 1.

We call a rational investor with a CARA utility function a "rational risk averse investor" or, more simply, "investor".

The investor will rank a portfolio p by weighting the utility of a return x with the probability of that return $p(x)$, thus he would use the ranking function

$$R_U(p) \stackrel{def}{=} \int_{-\infty}^{+\infty} U(x)p(x)\mathrm{d}x \tag{2}$$

or an equivalent function.

Two rankings function, R_1 and R_2, are equivalent if and only if they produce the same ranking, i.e. if there is a monotonic function h that maps $R_2(p)$ into $R_1(p)$ for every p. We will indicate the equivalence of two ranking functions with $R_1 \sim R_2$.

2.1 CASE #1: with risk free asset

In CASE #1 our investor can choose to invest part of the funds A into a risk free asset, for example a US Threasury-bill. This means that given any two portfolios p_1 and p_2 characterized by an average return and risk (standard deviation) μ_1, σ_1 and μ_2, σ_2 if

$$\frac{\mu_1 - r}{\sigma_1} > \frac{\mu_2 - r}{\sigma_2} \tag{3}$$

then the investor should never choose p_2 over p_1. This is because the investor can invest a fraction $\alpha = \sigma_2/\sigma_1$ of the total funds A into portfolio p_1 and a fraction $(1-\alpha)$ into the risk free asset and obtain a new combined portfolio with the same risk as portfolio p_2 but a higher return, given by [6]

$$\mu' = (1-\alpha)r + \alpha\mu_1 > \mu_2 \tag{4}$$

Hence portfolio p_1 is always preferable to portfolio p_2.

If one applies this argument to every portfolio in the set, one finds that our investor should invest part of the funds A into the portfolio p with the largest value of

$$R_{\text{Sharpe}}(p) \stackrel{def}{=} \frac{\mu - r}{\sigma} \tag{5}$$

This is the well known Sharpe ratio or Sharpe ranking function [7] [6].

The value of α is then determined by maximizing the utility function U. If the expected returns of the portfolios have a Gaussian distribution then

$$\alpha = \alpha \text{ that maximizes} \int U(\alpha x + (1-\alpha)r)p(x)\mathrm{d}x = \frac{\sqrt{\mu/r}}{m\sigma} \tag{6}$$

If the return of the portfolios is not Gaussian distributed, the first equality in eq. (6) remains true, while the second equality is only an approximation since the integral must be performed numerically.

Similarly, if one adopts a definition of risk other than standard deviation of returns the argument that led to the R_{Sharpe} measure remains valid, but σ must be consistently replaced with the new measure of risk. For example, if one chooses to measure risk as the downside risk only

$$\sigma_n^- \stackrel{def}{=} \left[\int_{-\infty}^{r} p(x)(r-x)^n \mathrm{d}x\right]^{\frac{1}{n}} \tag{7}$$

then σ is replaced by σ_n^-, and the Sharpe ranking function is replaced by the Kappa ranking function [11]

$$R_{\text{Kappa-}n}(p) \stackrel{def}{=} \frac{\mu - r}{\sigma_n^-} \quad (8)$$

The Kappa ranking function above is the Sortino and Van Der Meer [8] Sortino and Price [9] Sortino and Forsey [10] ranking function when $n = 2$ and it is equivalent to the Omega [12] ranking function when $n = 1$. A different ranking scheme has been proposed by the Stutzer [14]. For a theoretical analysis of "good" vs "bad" risk measures we refer the reader to the work of Artzner *et al.* [15].

We show in the last section that these rankings are all equivalent to the Sharpe if returns are Gaussian. If returns are not Gaussian, Sharpe, Sortino, Kappa, and Omega, are not equivalent because they follow from different definitions of risk.

2.2 CASE #2: without risk free asset, the wrong way

In CASE #2, our investor has to choose a portfolio and invest the entire available funds in it, hence the argument presented at the beginning of the previous section does not apply. The reason behind the use of the Sharpe ranking (or the Sortino ranking) falls apart as pointed out by Sharpe himself [6].

In this subsection we answer two questions:

- Is the use of the Sharpe ranking (or any of the other rankings) however justified?
- If not, what is an appropriate ranking scheme that leads to the correct choice for a rational risk averse investor?

Let's examine first the Sharpe ranking function and assume that portfolio returns are Gaussian distributed. An explicit computation shows that, for every Gaussian portfolio p

$$R_{U_{naive}}(p) \sim R_{Sharpe}(p) \quad (9)$$

where

$$U_{naive}(x) \stackrel{def}{=} \begin{Bmatrix} -1 & (\text{if } x < 0) \\ +1 & (\text{if } x \geq 0) \end{Bmatrix} \quad (10)$$

and the monotonic mapping function between the two rankings is

$$h(y) = \text{erf}(y/\sqrt{2}) \quad (11)$$

Therefore, an investor who ranks portfolios using the Sharpe function in CASE #2 is implicitly adopting the utility function in eq. (10). The problem here is that eq. (10) is not a risk averse utility function. This function says that a positive return $x > 0$ (gain) has a utility $+1$ and a negative return $x < 0$ (loss) has a utility -1. This investor does not think that a 20% return is better than a 10% return, or that a loss of 100% is worse than a loss of 1%. The investor that uses the Sharpe ranking function for CASE #2 is not a rational risk averse investor.

Under the assumption of Gaussian returns Sortino, Omega, Stutzer and Kappa rankings are all equivalent (as proven in the last section), therefore the use of any of these rankings, in the case considered here, is not consistent with being risk averse.

Returns of real portfolios are, generally, non Gaussian distributed but, if a ranking function works for a general distribution, it must work for Gaussian returns too. Since this is not true for Sharpe, Sortino, Omega, Stutzer, nor Kappa, these ranking schemes should not be used in the CASE #2.

2.3 CASE #2: without risk free asset, the right way

Our investor, a rational risk averse investor, would use the CARA utility function to make choices and would rank portfolios using eq. (2) with U being U_{CARA}. In the last section we prove that $R_{U_{CARA}}$ is equivalent to R_* where

$$R_*(p) \stackrel{def}{=} -\log(-R_{U_{CARA}}(p))/m \qquad (12)$$

$$= \mu - \frac{m\sigma^2}{2} + \frac{m^2\sigma^3 S}{6} - \frac{m^3\sigma^4(K-3)}{720} + O(m^4\sigma^5) \qquad (13)$$

and

- μ is the average return of portfolio p,
- σ is the standard deviation of portfolio p,
- S is the skewness,
- K is the kurtosis ($K - 3$ is the reduced kurtosis)
- m is a parameter of the order of 1, that measures the risk aversion of our investor,
- $O(m^4\sigma^5)$ is the order of terms that are ignored.

Notice that a positive skewness is good while a positive reduced kurtosis is bad because it results in fatter tails for fixed σ.

For Gaussian distributed returns the formula in eq. (12) reduces to

$$R_*(p) = \mu - \frac{m\sigma^2}{2} \qquad (14)$$

and it is exact.

Note that the ranking 14 was originally proposed by Levy and Markowitz [16]. Our approximated formula, eq. (13) extends that result in the case of non-Gaussian returns.

We conclude that a rational risk averse investor who has to choose one portfolio among many and has to invest all funds in the selected portfolio, should make its choice based on the ranking function in eq. (12). This is a general result and it does not make any assumption on the distribution of the returns of the portfolios.

3 Practical considerations

Our conclusions have an immediate practical applicability in CASE #2, i.e. when the investor has to choose one and only one of mutually exclusive portfolios (or investment alternatives) according only to past performance.

Here is an outline of the decision algorithm

- For each portfolio k collect the historical returns r_{kt} (return for portfolio k at time t) and measure

$$\mu_k = (1/N)\sum_t r_{kt}$$

$$\sigma_k = (1/N)\sum_t (r_{kt} - \mu_k)^2$$

$$S_k = (1/N)\sum_t (r_{kt} - \mu_k)^3/\sigma_k^3$$

$$K_k = (1/N)\sum_t (r_{kt} - \mu_k)^4/\sigma_k^4$$

  (where N is the number of available data points)
- For each portfolio compute

$$Rank_k = \mu_k - \frac{m\sigma_k^2}{2} + \frac{m^2\sigma_k^3 S_k}{6} - \frac{m^3\sigma_k^4(K_k - 3)}{720} \tag{15}$$

- Sort the portfolios according to $Rank_k$ and select the one with the highest rank.

If $S_k = 0$ and $K_k = 0$ our rank is equivalent to the formula proposed by Levy and Markowitz [16].

Notice that the rank depends on whether on the time-scale of our analysis via our choice of returns r, which can be daily returns, weekly returns, monthly returns, etc. For a fixed skewness and kurtosis, their relative contribution to the rank increases with the size of the time-scale. In any case, because of the 1/720 factor, the relative contribution of kurtosis is generally very small.

4 Proofs

4.1 Equivalence of ranking schemes for Gaussian distributions

In this section we prove that if $p(x)$ is a Gaussian distribution with mean μ and standard deviation σ, then the Sharpe, Sortino, Omega, Stutzer and Kappa ranking functions are equivalent [5].

Two rankings, R_1 and R_2, are equivalent if and only if, for any two portfolios p_1 and p_2, $R_1(p_1) < R_1(p_2)$ implies $R_2(p_1) < R_2(p_2)$ and vice versa. This can only occur if there is a monotonic increasing function h such that, for any portfolio p, $R_2(p) = h(R_1(p))$.

Kappa Proof:

$$R_{Kappa-n}(p) \stackrel{def}{=} \frac{\mu - r}{[\int_{-\infty}^{r}(r-x)^n p(x)\mathrm{d}x]^{\frac{1}{n}}} = h(R_{Sharpe}(p)) \tag{16}$$

and

$$h(y) = \frac{\pi^{\frac{1}{2n}} 2^{\frac{2-n}{2n}} e^{\frac{y^2}{2n}} y}{[\Gamma(\frac{1+n}{2})_1 F_1(\frac{1+n}{2}, \frac{1}{2}, \frac{y^2}{2}) - \sqrt{2}\Gamma(1+\frac{n}{2}) 1F_1(1+\frac{n}{2}, \frac{3}{2}, \frac{y^2}{2})]^{\frac{1}{n}}} \tag{17}$$

(Γ is Euler's Gamma function and ${}_1F_1$ is an Hypergeometric function).

Omega Proof:

$$R_{\text{Omega}}(p) \stackrel{def}{=} \frac{\int_r^{\infty}(1 - F_p(x))\mathrm{d}x}{\int_{-\infty}^{r} F_p(x)\mathrm{d}x} = R_{\text{Kappa-1}}(p) \tag{18}$$

(here F_p is the cumulative distribution function associated to p).

Sortino Proof:

$$R_{\text{Sortino}}(p) \stackrel{def}{=} \frac{\mu - r}{[\int_{-\infty}^{r}(r-x)^2 p(x)\mathrm{d}x]^{\frac{1}{2}}} = R_{\text{Kappa-2}}(p) \tag{19}$$

Stutzer Proof:

$$R_{\text{Stutzer}}(p) \stackrel{def}{=} \lim_{T\to\infty} \frac{-\log F_p(rT)}{T} = h(R_{\text{Sharpe}}(p)) \tag{20}$$

R_{Stutzer} is well defined only for portfolios with positive Sharpe ratio, and

$$h(y) = y^2/2 \text{ (for } y > 0 \text{ only)} \tag{21}$$

4.2 Equivalence of rankings skemes in presence of skewness and kurtosis

In this section we prove that $R_{U_{CARA}}$ is equivalent to R_*.

Consider a portfolio characterized by a distribution of returns p. Let μ, σ, S, K be the average, standard deviation, skewness and kurtosis of p.

$$R_{U_{CARA}}(p) \stackrel{def}{=} \int_{-\infty}^{\infty} -e^{-mx} p(x)\mathrm{d}x = \int_{-\infty}^{\infty} -e^{-mx} \widetilde{p}((x-\mu)/\sigma)\mathrm{d}x \tag{22}$$

where $\widetilde{p}(y) = p(\sigma y + \mu)\sigma$. With the change of variable $y = (x - \mu)/\sigma$ and a Taylor series expansion in y of the exponential we obtain

$$\begin{aligned} R_{U_{CARA}}(p_i) &= -e^{-m\mu} \sum_{i=0} \frac{(-m\sigma)^i}{i!} \int_{-\infty}^{\infty} y^i \widetilde{p}(y)\mathrm{d}y \\ &= -e^{-m\mu} e^{\log(1+\frac{m^2\sigma^2}{2} - \frac{m^3\sigma^3 S}{3!} + \frac{m^4\sigma^4(K-3)}{6!} + O(m^4\sigma^5))} \\ &= h(R_*(p)) \end{aligned} \tag{23}$$

where $h(y) = -e^{-my}$ is monotonic increasing function in y, and

$$R_*(p) \stackrel{def}{=} -\log(-R_{U_{CARA}}(p))/m \tag{24}$$

$$-\mu - \frac{m\sigma^2}{2} + \frac{m^2\sigma^3 S}{6} - \frac{m^3\sigma^4(K-3)}{720} + O(m^4\sigma^5) \tag{25}$$

Hence the two ranking functions $R_*(p)$ and $R_{U_{CARA}}(p)$ are equivalent. This is a general result and no assumption about the distribution p has been made.

In the special case of p Gaussian, we are able to perform the integration analytically without need for a Taylor expansion and we find that the following exact relation holds [16],

$$R_*(p) = \mu - \frac{m\sigma^2}{2} \tag{26}$$

5 Conclusions

In this paper we discuss the issue of portfolio selection for a rational risk averse investor. We consider two cases: the investor is free to distribute funds between the selected portfolio and a risk free asset; and the case when the investor has to invest all funds in the selected portfolio.

In the first case we find that Sharpe, Omega, Sortino, and Kappa provide valid ranking schemes, although they follow from different definitions of risk, σ, σ_1^-, σ_2^- and σ_n^- respectively. We also find that, in the Gaussian case, Sharpe, Omega, Sortino, Kappa, and Stutzer rankings are all equivalent. In the non-Gaussian case these rankings are not equivalent [15, 1].

In the second case we find that, contrary to what is sometimes claimed, the use of any of the above ranking schemes does not correspond to being a rational risk averse investor. In fact, we prove that a rational risk averse investor (compatible with the choice of the CARA utility function) would choose a portfolio according to the ranking function in eq. (1), which takes into account the skewness of the portfolio, S, and its kurtosis, K. Our formula, eq. (1), extends a result originally due to Levy and Markowitz [16] in the case of non-Gaussian returns.

References

[1] S. Ortobelli, S. T. Rachev, S. Stoyanov, F. Fabozzi, and A. Biglova, "The Proper Use of Risk Measures in Portfolio Theory", International Journal of Theoretical and Applied Finance, Dec 2005.

[2] P. A. Horvath and R. C. Scott, "On the direction of preference for moments of higher order than variance", Journal of Finance 35, 1980, pp. 915–919.

[3] Neumann, John von and Morgenstern, Oskar, Theory of Games and Economic Behavior. Princeton, NJ. Princeton University Press. 1944 sec.ed. 1947.

[4] Nash Jr., John F. The Bargaining Problem. Econometrica 18:155 1950.

[5] M. Di Pierro and J. Mosevich, "On Ranking Schemes and Portfolio Selection", published in "Hedge Funds and Investment Management", I. Nelken Ed., Butterworth-Heinemann publisher.
[6] W. F. Sharpe, "Capital asset prices: A theory of market equilibrium under conditions of risk", Journal of Finance, 1964, 19(3), pp. 425–442.
[7] H. M. Markowitz, "Portfolio Selection", Journal of Finance 1952, 7 (1), pp. 77–91.
[8] F. A. Sortino and R. Van Der Meer, "Downside Risk", Journal of Portfolio Management, 1991, v17(4), 27–32.
[9] F. A. Sortino and L. N. Price, "Performance Measurement In A Downside Risk Framework", Journal of Investing, 1994, v3(3), 59–64.
[10] F. A. Sortino and H. J. Forsey, "On The Use And Misuse Of Downside Risk", Journal of Portfolio Management, 1996, v22(2,Winter), 35–42.
[11] P. D. Kaplan and J. A. Knowles, "Kappa: A Generalized Downside Risk-Adjusted Performance Measure", Journal of Performance Measurement, Vol. 8, #3 - Spring 2004.
[12] H. Kazemi, T. Schneeweis and R. Gupta, "Omega as Performance Measure" CISDM 2003 Proceedings.
[13] F. A. Sortino, "From Alpha to Omega", in Managing Downside Risk in Financial Markets, F. A. Sortino and S. E. Satchell, eds., Reed Educational and Professional Publishing Ltd., 2001.
[14] M. Stutzer, "A Portfolio Performance Index", Financial Analysts Journal, Vol. 56, May–June 2000.
[15] P. Artzner, F. Delbaen, J. M. Heath, and D. Eber, "Coherent measures of Risk", Mathematical Finance 9, 2000, pp. 203–228.
[16] H. Levy and H. Markowitz, "Approximating expected utility by a function of mean and variance", American Economic Review 69, 1979, pp. 308–317.

Active portfolios: diversification across trading strategies

C. Murray
Goldman Sachs and Co., New York, USA

Abstract

Several characteristics of a firm and its past return have been shown to be useful in predicting future returns, leading to long-short trading strategies with positive expected return using no invested capital. I develop the idea of active portfolios, which treat these long-short strategies as investable assets. I show that, since the returns from these long-short strategies are largely uncorrelated, active portfolios which make simultaneous bets on several long-short strategies have Sharpe ratios several times that of the market and extremely attractive return characteristics. I argue that this is because the diversification achievable in active portfolios exceeds that attainable through traditional sources of diversification.

Keywords: long-short trading strategies, value, momentum, diversification.

1 Introduction

Researchers have found a large number of long-short trading strategies that earn significant return with no invested capital. These strategies can be roughly categorized as momentum [5, 11], value [3, 8, 9, 12], firm size [6, 8] and reversal on a long [2, 7] and short [10, 13] time scale. These strategies sort stocks by one of the above criteria every month, then go long a portfolio of stocks that strongly exhibit that criteria and short a portfolio that weakly exhibit it. The return is the spread between the two portfolios. Different studies have used different samples, methodologies, and time periods to find different return spreads from these trading strategies, but a large amount of research supports the view that the above strategies have positive expected return.

I look at the performance of "active" portfolios, which treat long-short trading strategies as investable assets and which follow several strategies at once. They are "active" because the trading strategies turn over some of their capital every

WIT Transactions on Information and Communication Technologies, Vol 41, © 2008 WIT Press
www.witpress.com, ISSN 1743-3517 (on-line)
doi:10.2495/CF080121

month, even if the portfolio doesn't adjust how much capital is allocated to each strategy. Just as holding many uncorrelated assets in a traditional portfolio can reduce the portfolio's variance, an active portfolio will benefit by following multiple trading strategies if their returns are uncorrelated. If all the trading strategies earn a return via exposure to one or two common underlying factors (such as a market factor or firm distress factor), then the diversification achievable in an active portfolio will not be significant. However, if the returns to the strategies are not driven by common factor exposures, an active portfolio may achieve a higher risk-adjusted return than any single strategy.

This paper's goal is to see how trading strategies interact in an active portfolio. While research like Asness [4] looks forming a trading strategy by jointly conditioning on two different variables, this paper looks at how trading strategies interact in portfolios. I find that, due to their low correlations, extremely high Sharpe ratios are achievable with active portfolios, and active portfolios don't have any alternative risk characteristics that would justify their high return.

2 Data and methodology

The data for zero-cost trading strategies are monthly returns from January 1956 through December 2005. All data are taken from Professor Kenneth French's Data Library, which has monthly returns for decile portfolios sorted on various criteria. I use monthly return series for equal-weight decile portfolios sorted on firm size, book-to-market, past return over the last 12 months, excluding last month (PAST(12,2)), and past return over the last 60 months, excluding the most recent year (PAST(60,13)). From this I create five zero-cost trading strategy return series that will be the components of active portfolios. **MKT** is the return of the CRSP value-weighted market portfolio minus the one month treasury rate.

HML is the return of a strategy that goes long the highest decile book-to-market portfolio and short the lowest decile book-to-market portfolio. **SMB** is the return achieved going long the smallest market capitalization decile and short the largest market capitalization decile. **MOM** is long the decile with the highest PAST(12,2) and short the decile with the lowest PAST(12,2).

REV is long the decile with the lowest value of PAST(60,13) and short the decile highest value. A one-month reversal strategy, which was by far the most profitable, was ruled out due to high turnover. Results including this strategy are available from the author upon request.

2.1 Trading strategies

Summary statistics for the five trading strategies are shown in Table 1. Note that all the returns shown are zero-cost returns: they are return spreads from a long minus a short position (or in the case of the market, the return of the market minus the T-bill rate). An investor following these strategies would also earn a cash return, which isn't included. The long-short trading strategies have monthly volatilities generally of the same magnitude of the long-short market return, but the trading strategies tend to have higher returns and Sharpe ratios. More importantly, Table 1 shows that the return series from the trading strategies are largely uncorrelated, with an average correlation of 0.00 to two significant digits. This is what will offer the great diversification benefits in an active portfolio.

Table 1: Trading strategies return properties.

	MKT	SMB	HML	MOM	REV
Monthly Mean Excess Return	0.50%	0.56%	1.10%	1.22%	1.01%
Geometric Mean Excess Return	0.40%	0.44%	1.02%	1.03%	0.90%
Monthly Volatility	4.33%	5.09%	4.11%	5.75%	4.08%
Sharpe Ratio	0.33	0.30	0.91	0.66	0.81
Adjusted Sharpe Ratio	0.31	0.26	0.81	0.72	0.71

Correlations	MKT	SMB	HML	MOM	REV
MKT	1.00	0.05	-0.41	-0.09	-0.09
SMB		1.00	0.18	-0.41	0.68
HML			1.00	-0.04	0.50
MOM				1.00	-0.36
REV					1.00

Table 2 looks at higher order risk characteristics of the trading strategies (again based on monthly returns). This indicates that mean-variance analysis may understate the trading strategy risk relative to the market because of the trading strategies higher kurtosis, indicating a larger probability of extreme movements, and higher autocorrelation, which leads to higher annual variance than we'd expect by naively annualizing monthly variance.

Table 2: Higher-order risk.

	MKT	SMB	HML	MOM	REV
Skewness	-0.50	0.99	0.26	-2.79	2.14
Kurtosis	4.94	6.33	6.21	27.49	15.32
ACF(1)	0.07	0.16	0.12	-0.10	0.14
% negative	41%	50%	38%	32%	44%

Autocorrelation is especially high for the SMB and HML strategies. It's well known that value strategies can have long periods of low returns [3], and the returns to the SMB strategy have been lower in the later part of the sample period than in the earlier part, leading to autocorrelation. The SMB strategies mean return declined from 0.84% per month in the first half of the sample to 0.28% in the second half. The *adjusted Sharpe ratio* calculated in Table 1 recalculates the annualized variance to take account of this return continuation by modeling returns as an auto-regressive model. The trading strategies' adjusted Sharpe ratios are slightly lower than their raw Sharpe ratios, but still generally higher than that of the market. Individually, the four active trading strategies (HML,SMB,MOM, and REV) seem to perform better than the market, but combining trading strategies can provide even better returns.

3 Active portfolios

To see how trading strategies interact, I construct four kinds of active portfolios, each of which invests some of its capital in all of the trading strategies. An ***equal-weight active portfolio*** invests an equal amount in all trading strategies and rebalances annually. At the end of every year the magnitude of the bet on each strategy is adjusted so they are all equal again. A ***leveraged active portfolio*** is the same as the equal-weight active portfolio, but it uses leverage so that the monthly volatility of the active portfolio is the same as the average monthly volatility of the individual strategies (4.67% per month). The intuition is that an investor willing to engage in long-short strategies is willing to accept trading-strategy levels of volatility, so this portfolio delivers as much return as it can for that level of volatility, while maintaining equal bets in all the strategies.

An annually-rebalanced mean-variance ***optimized active portfolio*** uses foreknowledge of the trading strategies' variance-covariance structure and returns to select portfolio weights to maximize the Sharpe ratio. The annually-rebalanced optimized ***minimum-variance active portfolio*** similarly minimizes the variance.

The two optimized portfolios are simply for demonstration: an investor without foreknowledge of the strategies' future return and covariance structure could not have constructed these portfolios, and any investor who does have such foreknowledge needn't read journals to be successful!

Table 3: Active portfolio properties.

Portfolio	Equal Weight	Equal Weight Levered	Optimized	Min. Var.
Leverage	1	2.005	1	1
Monthly Mean Excess Return	0.91%	1.88%	0.95%	0.87%
Geometric Mean Excess Return	0.88%	1.77%	0.93%	0.85%
Monthly Volatility	2.21%	4.67%	2.04%	1.93%
Volatility Reduction	53%	0%	56%	59%
Annualized Sharpe Ratio:	1.45	1.45	1.66	1.60
Adjusted Sharpe Ratio	1.24	1.26	1.57	1.43
Higher order moments and time series properties of active portfolios				
Skewness	0.69	0.37	-0.81	-0.53
Kurtosis	7.98	8.01	13.22	9.36
ACF(1)	0.17	0.15	0.06	0.12

The return properties of these active portfolios are shown in Table 3. The non-leveraged portfolios all have similar returns of just less than 1% per month, but the diversification in active portfolios drives the volatility below half the average volatility of the individual trading strategies. This reduction in volatility gives the active portfolios their extremely high Sharpe ratios. Optimization isn't required, since even the equal-weight active portfolio has superb performance, with a Sharpe ratio (1.45) and adjusted Sharpe ratio (1.24) roughly four times that of the market. The leveraged portfolio has returns of nearly 2% per month with market-like levels of volatility. Since all returns shown are zero-cost returns, the active portfolios short some subset of stocks, use the proceeds of the short sale to buy a long position, and then deposit the original capital in an interest-bearing account (some of which will be put up as margin). All returns shown ignore transaction and margin costs (which would reduce reported returns) but also ignore the cash return from the interest bearing account.

4 Measures of diversification

The high Sharpe ratios reported in the previous section come almost entirely from the fact that huge volatility reduction is achievable by investing in several trading strategies at once. Spreading an investment across just five trading strategies resulted in volatility 53% below that of the average trading strategy and 49% below the market's volatility. Since international diversification is often held up as an example of how spreading an investment in different places can benefit investors, I compare the volatility reduction in active portfolios to that in portfolios of MSCI developed country and regional indexes. All country and regional index returns are gross US dollar returns minus the US risk-free rate. Table 4 shows the basic properties of the regional index returns, the correlation across regional indexes, and each index's correlation with the MSCI world index.

Table 4: Regional index excess return properties: 1970–2005.

Returns				
	Nordic	Europe	N. America	Pacific
Monthly Mean Excess Return	0.82%	0.56%	0.50%	0.58%
Geometric Mean Excess Return	0.65%	0.44%	0.40%	0.40%
Monthly Volatility	5.86%	4.83%	4.39%	6.01%
Sharpe Ratio	0.40	0.32	0.32	0.24
ACF(1)	0.07	0.04	0.02	0.12
Correlations				
	Nordic	Europe	N. America	Pacific
Nordic	1.00	0.73	0.57	0.47
Europe		1.00	0.64	0.55
N. America			1.00	0.39
Pacific				1.00
World Index Correlation	0.70	0.83	0.87	0.73

Comparing Table 1 with Table 4, it's clear that the regional indices' ***individual*** return properties aren't that different from the trading strategy returns: the regional indexes have only slightly lower mean returns than the trading strategies with similar levels of volatility. However, the regional returns are far more correlated than the trading strategy returns, and all are tremendously correlated with the world index. The regional indexes have an average correlation of 55% with each other and almost 80% with the MSCI world index. Table 5 shows that the huge reduction in volatility reaped by building active portfolios of trading strategies doesn't occur when building portfolios of regional indexes. The equal-weight regional index portfolio only achieves a volatility reduction of 19% (versus the average regional index volatility), and even the optimized portfolios don't achieve a substantial increase in return or decrease in variance versus the individual regional indexes themselves. Because of this, the portfolios of regional strategies don't achieve substantially higher Sharpe ratios than the individual regional indexes, and the benefits of diversification are limited.

Table 5: Regional index portfolio properties: 1970–2005.

Portfolio	Equal Weight	Equal Weight Levered	Optimized	Min. Var.
Leverage	1.00	1.23	1.00	1.00
Monthly Mean Excess Return	0.63%	0.77%	0.69%	0.53%
Geometric Mean Excess Return	0.53%	0.63%	0.59%	0.45%
Monthly Volatility	4.29%	5.27%	4.58%	4.02%
Volatility Reduction	19%	0%	13%	24%
Annualized Sharpe Ratio	0.44	0.43	0.46	0.40
ACF(1)	0.11	0.11	0.10	0.09

Table 6: Country index portfolio properties: 1970–2005.

Portfolio	Equal Weight	Equal Weight Levered	Optimized	Min. Var.
Leverage	1.00	1.48	1.00	1.00
Monthly Mean Excess Return	0.73%	1.11%	0.99%	0.55%
Geometric Mean Excess Return	0.63%	0.88%	0.86%	0.48%
Monthly Volatility	4.49%	6.62%	5.13%	3.81%
Volatility Reduction	32%	0%	23%	42%
Annualized Sharpe Ratio	0.50	0.48	0.61	0.45
ACF(1)	0.10	0.11	0.06	0.08
Adjusted Sharpe Ratio	0.46	0.44	0.58	0.42

Table 6 looks at portfolios constructed from MSCI country indexes for 14 developed countries. The country indexes are for Japan, Singapore, the USA, Australia, the U.K., Honk Kong, Switzerland, Germany, Canada, Norway, Denmark, Belgium, Sweden, and Spain. The average monthly excess return among the 14 countries over the sample period was 0.71% per year, with average monthly volatility of 6.62% and an average annualized Sharpe ratio of 0.265. Table 6 shows returns to portfolios of country indexes. Diversifying across all 14 countries in an equal-weight portfolio gives a slightly higher Sharpe ratio (0.5) than diversifying across regional indexes, but not by much. The volatility reduction is only 32% across countries (versus the average country's volatility of 6.62% per month), while an active portfolio with just 5 trading strategies reduces the volatility by 53% (versus the average trading strategy volatility of 4.67%). The optimized country portfolio is a little better but still can't match the volatility reduction of the equal-weight active portfolio. The levels of diversification achieved in active portfolios simply cannot be matched with traditional diversification.

5 Robustness checks

Figure 1 examines the consistency of active portfolio returns over five-year sub-periods between 1956 and 2005. The line shows the capital market line, using the market's average excess return and volatility over the entire period. The circles and X's are the returns and volatilities achieved by the equal weight unleveraged active portfolio over each sub-period. Sub-periods in the beginning of the sample are marked with circles while later ones are marked with X's. Figure 1 makes it clear that equal-weight active portfolios strongly dominate the return-variance outcomes achievable in the market, and these results haven't been decreasing.

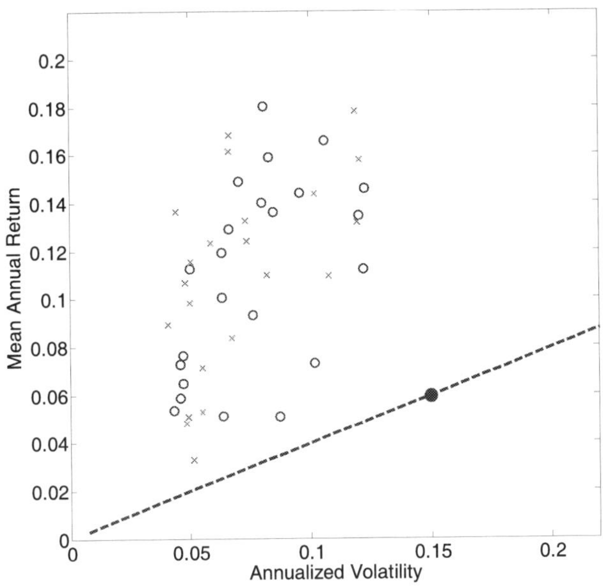

Figure 1: Mean annual excess return of the equal-weight active portfolio over every 5-year sub-period from 1956 to 2005.

6 Conclusion

I showed that diversification, one of the most basic tenants of investing, is extremely effective for non-traditional sources of return. Active portfolios which combine multiple long-short trading strategies achieve significant variance reduction, much more so than portfolios which spread an equity investment across countries or regions. This reduction in variance leads to extremely high Sharpe ratios for active portfolios.

I'd like to thank Kenneth French and MSCI for the use of data and Geoff Gordon and John O'Brien for helpful comments.

References

[1] Arshanapalli, Coggin, and Doukas. Multifactor Asset Pricing Analysis of International Value Investment Strategies. *Journal of Portfolio Management* **24,** pp. 10–23,1998.

[2] Asness, C. Variables that Explain Stock Returns. PhD Thesis, University of Chicago, 1994.

[3] Asness, C, Friedman, J., Krail, R. and Liew J. Style Timing: Value vs Growth. *Journal of Portfolio Management*, **26**. pp 50–60, 2000.

[4] Asness, C. The Interaction of Value and Momentum Strategies. *Financial Analysts Journal*. pp. 29–36 1997.

[5] Asness, C., Liew, J, and Stevens, R. Parallels between the cross-sectional predictability of stock and country returns. *Journal of Portfolio Management* **23** pp. 79–87, 1997.

[6] Banz, R. The Relationship between return and the market value of common stocks *Journal of Financial Economics*, **6** pp. 103–126, 1981.

[7] De Bondt, W. and Thaler, R. Does the Stock Market Overreact? *The Journal of Finance*, **40** pp.793–805, 1985.

[8] Fama, E. and French, K. The Cross-Section of Expected Stock Returns. *The Journal of Finance*, **47** pp. 427–465, 1992.

[9] Fama, E. and French, K. Multifactor Explanations of Asset Pricing Anomalies. *The Journal of Finance*, **51** pp. 55-84, 1996.

[10] Jegadeesh, N. Evidence of predictable behavior of security returns. *The Journal of Finance* **45** pp. 881–898, 1990.

[11] Jegadeesh, N. and Titman, S. Returns to Buying Winners and Selling Losers: Implications for Stock market Efficiency. *Journal of Finance*, **48**, pp. 65–91, 1993

[12] Lakonishok, J., Shleifer, A., and Vishny, R. Contrarian Investment, extrapolation, and Risk. *The Journal of Finance* **49**, pp. 1541–1578, 1994.

[13] Lehmann, B. Fads, Martingales, and Market Efficiency. *Quarterly Journal of Economics* **105** pp.1–28, 1990.

Discovery of multi-component portfolio strategies with continuous tuning to the changing market micro-regimes using input-dependent boosting

V. V. Gavrishchaka[1], O. V. Barinova[2], A. P. Vezhnevets[2] & M. A. Monina[3]
[1]*Alexandra Investment Management, New York, NY, USA*
[2]*Moscow State University, Dept. of Computational Mathematics and Cybernetics, Graphics and Media Lab, Moscow, Russian Federation*
[3]*Moscow State University of Instrument Engineering and Computer Science, Moscow, Russian Federation*

Abstract

Recently proposed boosting-based optimization offers a generic framework for the discovery of compact and interpretable portfolios of complimentary trading strategies with stable (non-resonant) performance over a wide range of market regimes and robust generalization abilities. Inherent complexity control allows the framework to work with very large pools of heterogeneous base strategies with well-established properties. However, in its current version, the framework outputs a collection of dynamic strategies with fixed parameters and constant weights defining capital allocations. This excludes any adaptive regime adjustment or switching on the portfolio level for additional profitability from regime-specific patterns. In this work we extend boosting-based optimization framework by including capability to discover portfolio strategies with continuous and adiabatically smooth adjustment to the current market micro-regime. Such regime adaptivity is naturally provided by the input-dependent boosting. The proposed generalization preserves clarity and interpretability of the original framework since the dynamic base strategies of the multi-component portfolio and their optimal parameters remain fixed. However, the weights of the base strategies are adaptively varied in time according to the implicit rule discovered by boosting. Operational details of the new framework and encouraging results are illustrated using real market data. More rigorous theoretical foundation for the general concept of the boosting-based optimization is also outlined.

Keywords: adaptive boosting, ensemble learning, regime switching, trading strategies, portfolio optimisation.

WIT Transactions on Information and Communication Technologies, Vol 41, © 2008 WIT Press
www.witpress.com, ISSN 1743-3517 (on-line)
doi:10.2495/CF080131

1 Introduction

One of the most pronounced challenges in financial markets modeling and forecasting is nonstationarity of the individual time series and co-dependency relations. Usually it is very difficult or practically impossible to find a single global model based on observable and well-defined variables with desired performance in all market regimes. However, with certain degree of simplification such complex nonstationary dynamics can be approximated as switching between different regimes of market dynamics where each such regime is relatively simple and easy to describe by its own parsimonious model. More generally, one can introduce additional non-observable (hidden) state variables to represent market regimes and dynamical transitions between them.

Intuitively, timely switching or smooth transition between different regimes in such structured models could significantly improve modeling and forecasting of the nonstationary time series. More importantly, this may help to create dynamic trading strategies that consistently exploit regime-specific market patterns. However, although introduction of the hidden variables in the simplified econometric models [1] could lead to better prediction accuracy and overall explanatory power, the usefulness of such models for the discovery of the realistic trading strategies is often very limited. Moreover, potential of model improvement through the introduction of the finer structure of the market regimes (states) is also very limited since adequate model estimation is possible only when historical training data contains enough transitions between different regimes which is often not the case in most financial applications.

Certain simplifications, a priory assumptions and other drawbacks of the typical econometric models can be alleviated using dynamic machine learning approaches. For example, recurrent neural networks (NN) maintain an adaptive internal memory of past inputs that allows implicit regime adjustment or switching and do not require any specific assumptions about hidden state variables and mechanisms of regime transition [2–4]. However, training procedures for such NNs are often significantly more complex and less stable compared to already standard feed-forward NNs such as multi-layer perceptron (MLP) that are not dynamic [2,4]. Moreover, complex dynamic NNs lack interpretability and operational stability control that are very important requirements in financial applications.

Both statistical and machine learning forecasting models are trained using objectives that are not directly relevant to the trading strategy which limits usefulness of such models even when formal forecasting performance measures are reasonable [5]. Technical trading strategies, directly optimized to achieve desirable profit/loss (PL) distributions, usually have more practical value than pure forecasting models mentioned above. However, single trading strategy with reasonable complexity (to ensure out-of-sample performance) still cannot warranty stability across different market regimes.

Many modern automatic systems for systematic trading offer an option for the dynamic capital reallocation among different strategies using explicit user-specified rule that may be a function of the most recent PL time series generated by each strategy and other factors. The goal of such approach is to alleviate limitations of the single trading strategy that may be profitable only in certain market regimes while maintaining simplicity and interpretability of such portfolio of trading strategies. However, these systems do not provide any generic and theoretically-sound frameworks capable to discover such regime-adjusted portfolio strategies with stable performance over wide range of market regimes. For example, usage of resonance strategies tuned to the specific market regimes and simplified empirical switching between different strategies could be very unstable since it requires a very accurate timing which is difficult to achieve in most modern markets.

Recently proposed boosting-based optimization provides a generic framework for the discovery of portfolios of trading strategies with stable (non-resonant) performance over wide range of market regimes using intelligent combination of the complimentary, low-complexity base strategies with well-known properties [6–8]. This framework offers practical solutions for many problems encountered in other approaches. However, in its current version, the framework outputs a collection of dynamic strategies with fixed parameters and constant weights defining capital allocations. This excludes any adaptive regime adjustment or switching on the portfolio level for additional profitability from regime-specific patterns. In this work we extend boosting-based optimization framework by including capability to discover portfolio strategies with continuous and adiabatically smooth adjustment to the current market micro-regime. In many practical settings, the proposed framework could resolve or alleviate limitations of other approaches used for discovery of the regime-adjusted portfolio strategies.

2 Limitations of the existing regime-switching and regime-adjusted models

A flexible and generic approach to incorporate multiple interchanging regimes or states is to use models with hidden variables, i.e., auxiliary variables that are not directly observable [9]. A well-known example of such a framework is hidden Markov models (HMM) that are successfully used alone or in combination with other statistical or machine learning algorithms in speech recognition systems [10], bioinformatics [11], and other applications. Examples of hidden variable models used in financial econometrics include regime-switching models, the GARCH family of models, and credit risk models, where hidden variables are used to represent different economic/market regimes, volatility, and credit worthiness, respectively [1].

One of the widely used types of models with hidden variables is a linear state-space model that can be written in the following way [1]:

$$\begin{aligned} y_\tau &= Az_\tau + Bx_\tau + \varepsilon_\tau \\ z_{\tau+1} &= Cz_\tau + Dx_\tau + \eta_\tau \end{aligned} \qquad (1)$$

Here x_τ, y_τ, and z_τ are the vectors of deterministic inputs, observable outputs, and latent (nonobservable) state variables, respectively. Observation and transition equation white noise are given by ε_τ and η_τ. Observation matrix, input matrix of the observation equation, transition matrix, and input matrix to the transition equation are given by A, B, C, and D.

A typical maximum likelihood (ML) based estimation for (1) would require approximate calculation of the nonobservable states z, which enters corresponding likelihood expression together with observable variables. Kalman filter [12] is usually used to provide optimal estimation of the state variables. Originally, Kalman filter was designed as an adaptive filter that provide optimal estimation and forecasting of the "true" states of the dynamical system from the multi-dimensional noisy observations in engineering applications. The filter is initialized with the initial conditions and computations are carried out recursively to the desired time, i.e. full historical information is used to make current estimation and forecasting.

The intuitive notion of the "states of the market" (e.g. bull, bear, and side markets) is well known to market practitioners. From a modeling perspective, this implies that different models and strategies should be used in different market states. If we add rules that prescribe the switching from one model (or set of models) to another one when market state changes, we arrive at the regime-switching model [1,13].

A broad class of regime-switching models are the Markov-switching vector autoregressive models (MS-VAR) [1,14]. Markov-switching model is a VAR model whose coefficients are driven by a Markov chain:

$$y_\tau = \mu(s) + \left(\sum_{i=1}^{p} A_i(s) L^i \right) y_\tau + \varepsilon_\tau(s), \tag{2}$$

where the matrices $A_i(s)$ are the coefficients of the process at lag i in state s and the noise terms $\varepsilon_\tau(s)$ are independent normal variables. The process is driven by a k-states Markov chain. A Markov chain is a discrete variable which can assume at each instant one of k possible values with transition probabilities:

$$P(s_\tau = i \mid s_{\tau-1} = j) = p_{ij} \tag{3}$$

The realized state s determines the coefficients and the vector of the intercepts of the process at each moment, so that the innovation term of the process is distributed as a mixture of Gaussian distributions. The state variable that could be used to represent market regime is a hidden factor. Due to the state (regime) switching MS-VAR becomes a nonlinear model even though it is based on linear components.

ML-based estimation of the MS-VAR model is presently the mostly widely used approach [1]. Similar to space-state model (1) and other models with hidden variables, one writes a likelihood function that depends on both observables and hidden variables. In the case of linear state-space models (1), Kalman filter is naturally applicable and used to estimate values of hidden variables (states). However, in nonlinear MS-VAR models, Expectation-Maximization (EM) algorithm is used instead. The algorithm is an optimization procedure for finding the maximum of log-likelihood functions in the presence of missing or hidden variables [15]. The idea of EM algorithm is to iterate between the estimate of the best parameters given the missing (hidden) data and the estimate of the missing (hidden) data given the best estimate of parameters.

The obvious limitation of econometric models with hidden state variables mentioned above is the usage of the simplified and pre-specified functional forms as in (1) and (2), (3). Compared to similar econometric models without hidden variables, the requirements for the data sample size will grow much faster with the model complexity increase. For example, even for simple regime-switching model given by (2)–(3), the increase of the regime number beyond 2 or 3 could make adequate estimation of the model unrealistic since the available training data would not have enough transitions between different regimes to ensure reasonable out-of-sample performance. Moreover, even when formal forecasting performance measures are reasonable for explanatory purposes or large-scale risk management applications, the direct usefulness of the econometric-type models to trading strategies may often be limited due to the difference in objectives [5].

Machine learning approaches offer significantly more flexibility in many different applications including modeling of the non-stationary or multi-regime time series. However, the well-known feed-forward NNs such as widely used MLP with standard back-propagation training algorithm may be used to perform nonlinear prediction only on stationary time series. It is done by using delayed vector of inputs as follows:

$$y_\tau = F(x_{\tau-1}, x_{\tau-2}, \ldots, x_{\tau-p}) \tag{4}$$

Here F is a general functional dependence that NN will try to approximate when p delayed input variables will be presented at the input and one output variable will be generated at the NN output. The adequate choice of the lag space could be a difficult problem-dependent task. However, after the lag space is chosen, it remains constant. This limits NN's adaptivity and makes it a static model which can describe only stationary time series.

To make NN dynamic it must be given an "internal" memory [16]. To accomplish this and to retain simplicity of the feed-forward architecture, one can introduce time delays into the synaptic structure of the NN and to adjust their values during the learning phase. Such time delays are also neurobiologically motivated. One of such practical models where MLP with synapses represented by a finite-duration impulse response (FIR) filter was introduced by Wan [3]. The efficient training procedure called temporal back-propagation was also proposed for such FIR MLP [2,3]. One of the examples when effectiveness of the FIR MLP was demonstrated is the winning of the time series prediction competition [17].

A more general dynamic model denoted as a recurrent NN is obtained when the connectivity of the feed-forward network is extended to include feedback connections from the outputs of the units back to their inputs [2,4]. The most general recurrent NN is obtained if the output from every unit in the NN is fed back to the inputs of all units. The advantage of the recurrent NNs compared to the feed-forward NNs is due to an internal memory of past inputs introduced by the feedback connections. This internal memory is adaptive, i.e., during training it may be adapted to encompass those previous inputs which are relevant to the current problem. Such adaptive memory may completely relieve the user from specifying a lag space, since a fully recurrent NN is able to work entirely from its own internal memory, created from only a single external input [4]:

$$y_\tau = F(x_{\tau-1}) \tag{5}$$

However, despite their advantages recurrent NNs have not gained popularity similar to that of feed-forward NNs. Generally, it is more difficult to handle recurrent NNs in practice. In particular it has been found that training using widely accepted algorithms (e.g., gradient descent method and its extensions) is not sufficiently "powerful" to train recurrent NNs [4]. The problem could be in slow convergence or in complete failure to provide practically acceptable solution.

Even when training challenges are resolved, the remaining common problems with NNs and similar black-box machine learning models are poor interpretability and occasional instable behavior which is hard to control and predict. Although these drawbacks are especially undesirable in financial applications, the high noise-to-signal ratio in financial time series enhances probability of unstable behavior of such models.

One of the machine learning approaches to compensate for deficiency of the individual models is to combine several models to form a committee [18,19]. Committee can compensate limitations of the individual models due to both incomplete data and specifics of the algorithms (e.g., multiple local minima in the NN error surface). A number of different ensemble learning techniques to build optimal committees have been proposed over the years in different research communities [e.g., 6 and references therein]. The most relevant framework of this type in the context of the regime-switching or regime-adjusted models is mixture of expert (ME) model [20].

The probabilistic form of ME model can be written as [18]

$$p(y \mid x) = \sum_{t=1}^{T} \pi_t(x) p_t(y \mid x) \tag{6}$$

Here mixing coefficients $\pi_t(x)$ are known as gating functions and the individual component densities $p_t(y|x)$ are called experts. This terminology is due to the fact that different components can model the distribution in different regions of input space (they are "experts" at making predictions in their own regions), and the gating functions determine which components are dominant in which region. If the experts are linear (regression or classification) models, then the whole model can be fitted efficiently using the EM algorithm. An even more flexible model is obtained by using a multilevel gating function to give the hierarchical mixture of experts (HME) model [18]. This model can be imagined as a mixture distribution in which each component in the mixture is itself a mixture distribution.

More complex machine learning models can be used as components in both ME and HME frameworks. For example, NNs can be used as experts as well as gating functions [2]. However, increasing complexity of the models could often lead to practical problems in training of such multi-component system and to poor out-of-sample performance and instability. Thus, it is highly desirable to have committee of the well-understood and low-complexity expert models that consistently demonstrate acceptable combined performance.

Adaptive boosting is a powerful ensemble learning algorithm that combines many desirable features [21,22,19]. Many ensemble learning algorithms including "random sample" techniques like bagging can reduce only variance part of the model error, i.e. they make a combined model more stable. Boosting, on the other hand, can reduce both bias and variance parts of the model error. It means that one can start with simple model ("rule of thumb") with low accuracy and produce committee with much higher accuracy. Therefore, boosting can be applied to the pool of the well-understood low-complexity models to produce qualitatively different but interpretable combined model with significantly higher accuracy and stability [6–8]. Moreover, boosting tries to maximize margin to ensure good out-of-sample performance, i.e. it is a large-margin classifier [21,22,19].

In our previous works [6–8] we propose a boosting-based optimization framework for the discovery of the stable portfolios of trading strategies from the low-complexity base strategies. It was argued that boosting for classification can be used as a basis for such stage-wise optimization framework. The final output of the boosting-based optimization is a collection S of complimentary base trading strategies BS_i with optimal parameter vectors p_i and combination weights w_i that specify capital allocation for each strategy [7,8]:

$$S \to \{[w_1, BS_1(p_1)], \ldots, [w_T, BS_T(p_T)]\} \tag{7}$$

We have shown empirically [7,8] that boosting-based optimization can generate portfolios (7) with stable performance over wide range of market regimes while using just well-known technical base strategies. However, in its current version, the framework outputs a collection of dynamic strategies (7) with fixed parameters $\boldsymbol{p}$ and constant weights $\boldsymbol{w}$. This excludes any adaptive regime adjustment or switching on the portfolio level for additional profitability from regime-specific patterns. Many modern automatic systems for systematic trading offer an option for the dynamic capital reallocation among different strategies in (7) using explicit user-specified rule. However, these systems do not provide any generic and theoretically-sound frameworks capable to discover regime-adjusted portfolio strategies with stable performance over wide range of market regimes. Switching-rule specification based just on the semi-quantitative discretional arguments could often lead to the unreliable trading system.

In this work we extend boosting-based optimization framework by including capability to discover portfolio strategies (7) where weights $\boldsymbol{w}$ are continuously adjusted by the implicit rule discovered by the input-dependent boosting. In the next two sections we summarize our previous results on the boosting-based optimization as well as provide more formal theoretical foundation for the framework. After that we introduce extended framework based on the input-dependent boosting [23] and present regime-adjusted trading strategy obtained from the new framework using real-market data.

3 Boosting-based optimization: discovery of the regime-independent portfolio strategies

As described in our previous works [6–8], boosting for optimization could be based on different boosting frameworks. However, the generalized AdaBoost algorithm for classification [21,22] could be a reasonable choice in many applications due to its simplicity, comprehensive theoretical foundation, and proven robust performance in a large number of realistic classification problems.

For our purposes it is sufficient to describe boosting algorithm only for two-class classification problem, where classifier outputs either +1 or -1. Generalized AdaBoost for two-class classification consists of the following steps [22]:

$$w_n^1 = 1/N \tag{8.1}$$

$$\varepsilon_t = \sum_{n=1}^{N} \left(w_n^t I(-y_n h_t(x_n)) \right) \tag{8.2}$$

$$\gamma_t = \sum_{n=1}^{N} \left(w_n^t y_n h_t(x_n) \right) \tag{8.3}$$

$$\alpha_t = \frac{1}{2} \ln\left(\frac{1+\gamma_t}{1-\gamma_t} \right) - \frac{1}{2} \ln\left(\frac{1+\rho}{1-\rho} \right) \tag{8.4}$$

$$w_n^{t+1} = w_n^t \exp\left(-\alpha_t y_n h_t(x_n) \right) / Z_t \tag{8.5}$$

$$H(x) = \sum_{t=1}^{T} \alpha_t h_t(x) / \sum_{t=1}^{T} \alpha_t \tag{8.6}$$

Here N is a number of training data points, x_n is a model/classifier input set of the n-th data point and y_n is the corresponding class label (i.e., -1 or +1), $I(z) = 0$ for $z<0$ and $I(z)=1$ otherwise, T is a number of boosting iterations, w_n^t is a weight of the n-th data point at t-th iteration, Z_t is weight normalization constant at t-th iteration, $h_t(x_n)$->[-1; +1] is the best base hypothesis/model at t-th iteration, ρ is a margin control parameter, and $H(x)$ is a final weighted linear combination of the base hypotheses.

Boosting starts with equal and normalized weights for all training data (step (8.1)). A base classifier $h_t(x)$ is trained using weighted error function ε_t (step (8.2)). If a pool of several types of base classifiers is used, then each of them is trained and the best one (according to error function) is chosen at the current iteration. The training data weights for the next iteration are computed in steps (8.3)–(8.5).

According to (8.5), at each boosting iteration, data points misclassified by the current best model (i.e., $y_n h_t(x_n) < 0$) are penalized by the weight increase for the next iteration. In subsequent iterations, AdaBoost constructs progressively more difficult learning problems that are focused on hard-to-classify patterns. This process is controlled by the weighted error function (8.2).

Steps (8.2)-(8.5) are repeated at each iteration until stop criteria $\gamma_t < \rho$ (i.e., $\varepsilon_t >= 1/2(1-\rho)$) or $\gamma_t = 1$ (i.e., $\varepsilon_t = 0$) occurs. Step (8.6) represents the final combined (boosted) model that is ready to use. The model classifies unknown sample as class +1 when $H(x) > 0$ and as -1 otherwise.

Portfolio strategy discovery is a direct optimization rather than classification problem. However, it was argued [6–8] that for a large class of objective functions, boosting for classification (8.1) – (8.6) can be efficiently used as a basis for the framework that could be labeled as "boosting for optimization" or "boosting-based optimization".

One of the natural and robust objectives for the trading strategy optimization is to require returns (r) generated by the strategy on a chosen time horizon (τ) to be above certain conservative threshold (r_c). By calculating strategy returns on a series of intervals of length τ shifted with a step $\Delta\tau$ and encoding them as +1 (for $r >= r_c$) and -1 (for $r < r_c$), one obtains symbolically encoded distribution of strategy returns.

Contrary to the classification problems, here the purpose is not to minimize classification error, but rather to minimize the number of -1 samples, i.e., number of subcritical returns. This can still be considered as classification problem with potentially uneven sample number between two classes. The described objective can be incorporated into the boosting operation (8.1) – (8.6) by considering output -1 as misclassification. In such setting, boosting (8.1) – (8.6) provides a framework for optimization, where minimization objection function is a "miss rate", i.e., number of -1 samples divided by the total number of samples. The objective function can be generalized to include any complex condition with combination of different objectives for profit maximization and risk minimization.

In the case of trading strategy optimization, the final usage of boosting output is different from the classical case of boosting for classification. Instead of using weighted linear combination (8.6) of the base models as a final model for classification, one uses boosting weights to construct portfolio of strategies. The initial capital is distributed among different base strategies in amounts according to the weights ($\alpha_t/\Sigma\alpha_t$) obtained from boosting which are already normalized.

As discussed in [6-8], boosting can be used to discover the optimal combination of different dynamic trading strategies for a single financial instrument as well as the simultaneous combination of trading strategies and different instruments. In both cases, boosting steps (8.1) – (8.6) are applied to a pool of base strategies $\{BS_i(\boldsymbol{p}_i)\}$, where $\boldsymbol{p}_i$ is a vector of adjustable parameters for strategy BS_i. However, in the first case all base strategies are applied to a time series of a single financial instrument FI_0, while set $\{BS_i\}\mathrm{x}\{FI_j\}$ of all possible pairs of strategies BS_i and instruments FI_j should be used in the latter case.

According to error function (8.2), if the objective is to maximize the number of supercritical returns on the shifted intervals, the following optimization problems are solved for all base strategies $BS_i(\boldsymbol{p}_i)$ and financial instruments FI_j at each boosting iteration:

$$\min_{p_i}\left[\sum_{n=1}^{N} w_n^{(t)}\, I\left(r_c - r_n^{\tau}\left(BS_i(p_i), FI_j\right)\right)\right] \tag{9}$$

Here, r_n^{τ} is a return produced by the strategy $BS_i(p_i)$ applied to the instrument FI_j over n-th shifted interval of length τ and r_c is a chosen threshold value. Often linear function ~ $(r_c - r_n)$ is better choice for $z<0$ compared to standard step-function I. Based on the results of these minimization procedures for all (i,j) pairs, the best pair "strategy-instrument" of the current iteration is added to the portfolio. This procedure was also generalized to allow simultaneous discovery of new synthetic instruments expressed as multiple spreads between base instruments and dynamic trading strategies for such spreads [8].

The AdaBoost algorithm given by (8.1) – (8.6) is one of the classical versions and it was described as an example suitable for boosting-based optimization in all our previous works. However, a slightly different version is both more natural and more convenient for the extension to the input-dependent boosting [23]. For simplicity, we will omit the margin parameter ρ in all the following formulations. The other standard AdaBoost formulation given in [23], results in a different weight update procedure. Instead of (8.5) one applies:

$$w_n^T = \frac{e^{-H_{T-1}(x_n)y_n}}{\sum_{j=1}^{N} e^{-H_{T-1}(x_j)y_j}} \tag{10}$$

Expression for α is given by the following form equivalent to (8.4) with omitted margin parameter:

$$\alpha_T = \frac{1}{2}\ln\left(\frac{\sum_{n=1}^{N} w_n^T I(h_T(x_n), y_n)}{\sum_{n=1}^{N} w_n^T I(-h_T(x_n), y_n)}\right) = \frac{1}{2}\ln\left(\frac{1-\varepsilon_T}{\varepsilon_T}\right) \tag{11}$$

As mentioned in our previous publications [6–8], boosting also allows natural and easy incorporation of other ensemble learning techniques on the inside and outside levels for further improvement of the accuracy and stability. For example, at each boosting iteration, instead of choosing a single best model, one can choose mini-ensemble of models using other ensemble learning techniques. In the simplest case, this could be an equal weight mini-ensemble of several comparable best models. One can also use boosting in the HME-like framework by building portfolio of portfolios.

As summarized in this section, it is quite intuitive to use boosting for classification as a basis for the boosting-based optimization framework. However, to better understand basic features of the boosting-based optimization and its possible generalizations and limitations, it is still useful to outline formal theoretical foundation for the framework. A short version of such foundation is presented in the next section.

4 Theoretical foundation for boosting-based optimization

Portfolio strategy discovery is a direct optimization rather than classification problem. However, several formal arguments presented in this section should clearly demonstrate that boosting for classification can be naturally generalized for the framework of boosting-based optimization as was suggested in our previous papers [6–8].

One of the operational interpretations of the boosting algorithm shows that boosting fits an additive logistic regression model by a stage-wise optimization of expected exponential loss [24]:

$$\mathrm{E}e^{-yF(x)} \to \min \tag{12}$$

One of the motivations for such choice of the loss function is that exponential loss is an upper bound on the classification error [25]:

$$P[yF(x) < 0] < \mathrm{E}e^{-yF(x)} \tag{13}$$

This kind of upper bound can be generalized for any event A:

$$P[A] \le \mathrm{E}e^{-(2I_A - 1)|F(x)|}, \tag{14}$$

where $I_A=1$ if A takes place and $I_A=0$ otherwise. In the case of standard classification problem event A describes a misclassification, i.e. classification error.

In the case of multi-component portfolio strategy optimization let us consider an event "return of a combined strategy S is lower than a threshold r_c", i.e. $r(S(x))<r_c$. Then inequality (14) can be written as

$$P[r(S(x)) < r_c] \le \mathrm{E}e^{-\left(2I_{[r(S(x))<r_c]}-1\right)\left|r(S(x))-r_c\right|} \tag{15}$$

Looking at the right part of inequality (15) we can see that optimization task can be reduced to classification task in a way proposed in [6–8]. Thus, we get a generalization of boosting framework for optimization tasks, where instead of minimizing classification error we are trying to minimize a number of intervals where $[r(S(x))<r_c]$. Minimization of $P[r(S(x))<r_c]$ is equivalent to the maximization of $P[r(S(x))>=r_c]$.

Boosting is known to demonstrate stable generalization abilities measured by its performance on out-of-sample data. Standard Vapnik-Chernovenkis (VC) analysis [26] of boosting bounds generalization loss by empirical risk (here $\hat{\Pr}[\bullet]$ denotes empirical probability measured on the training set) and a term dependent on VC-dimension of weak learner and number of boosting iterations [27]:

$$P[H(x) \ne y] \le \hat{\Pr}[H(x) \ne y] + \tilde{O}\left(\sqrt{\frac{Td}{m}}\right) \tag{16}$$

where d is the VC-dimension (capacity) of weak learner, m is the size of the training set, and T is the number of weak classifiers in the committee. However, this bound could often contradict with practical experience, which shows that boosting can decrease its test error even when empirical risk is already zero.

The best explanation of boosting generalization capabilities so far is margin theory [28]. Margin theory provides an upper generalization bound independent of number of iterations made by boosting. This bound suggests that boosting may not overfit even if ran for many rounds. For any θ:

$$P[H(x) \neq y] \leq \hat{\Pr}[\text{margin}(x,y) \leq \theta] + \tilde{O}\left(\sqrt{\frac{d}{m\theta^2}}\right), \tag{17}$$

where margin is

$$\text{margin}(x,y) = \frac{y\sum_t \alpha_t h_t(x)}{\sum_t \alpha_t}. \tag{18}$$

Margin is the measure of confidence of a boosted predictor in its decision. It is positive if the decision is correct and negative otherwise. Theory states that for better generalization one should increase the margins of training samples.

In the context of the trading strategy boosting margin can be reformulated as

$$\text{margin}(r_n^\tau) = \frac{\sum_t \alpha_t I\left(r_c - r_n^\tau\left(BS_t(p_t), FI_t\right)\right)}{\sum_t \alpha_t} \tag{19}$$

In such interpretation we want to maximize the confidence of our boosted strategy for over each of n shifted intervals of length τ. In order to strictly apply theory for strategy boosting, some additional statements should be proven (e.g., finite capacity of base strategies – analogous to VC-dimension). Although the rigorous proof is out of scope of this paper, the usage of the low-complexity base strategies should not violate these assumptions in most practical settings.

Under some conditions on a weak learner, it was proven that boosting is a regularized search for a maximum margin solution [29]. That means that in the limit, the boosted committee may have a maximum possible lower margin. Recent studies of boosting suggest that one may expect overfitting in case of increasing VC-dimension of weak learner through iterations [30], or in the case of the overlapping class distributions [31]. However, usage of the low-complexity base strategies should be able to alleviate these problems in most practical applications.

5 Optimization framework based on input-dependent boosting: Discovery of the regime-adjusted portfolio strategies

Majority of the known boosting algorithms including classical AdaBoost assume that the combination weights α_t are fixed constants and therefore do not take particular input patterns into consideration. Application of such algorithms as a basis for the boosting-based optimization allows discovering portfolio strategies with fixed weights, i.e., fixed capital allocations among the individual strategies. This excludes any dynamic regime-adjustment to exploit regime-specific patterns for further increase of the portfolio strategy profitability.

However, several input-dependent boosting algorithms have been recently proposed [23,32,33]. One of these algorithms (called WeightBoost) [23] seems to be the most appealing practical choice due to its close relation to the original AdaBoost and flexibility to vary the form and degree of the regime adjustment.

WeightBoost not only introduces input dependency but also provides practical regularization mechanism that helps to avoid overfitting problems that boosting may encounter in applications with high level of noise.

The original motivation of this input-dependent boosting algorithm [23] is to alleviate two limitations of the classical AdaBoost and its extensions. One is constant combination weights that prevent from using full potential of the base models in the regimes of their expertise. The other problem is potential overfitting in high-noise cases that requires introduction of the practical and efficient regularization. However, most of the previously proposed regularization algorithms are unsuccessful or only partially successful either due to the high computational cost or lack of strong empirical results of improvement.

The following inductive form of the boosted classifier is used in AdaBoost derivation and its input-dependent extension given in [23]

$$H(x) = H_{T-1}(x) + \alpha_T h_T(x) \tag{20}$$

The potential overfitting problem of AdaBoost can be implied from the weight updating function (10). If there are some noisy data patterns that are difficult to classify correctly by the base classifier(s), the value of $-H_{T-1}(x_i)y_i$ for those data points will accumulate linearly (since $H(x)$ is a linear combination of base classifiers) and the corresponding weights will grow exponentially. Therefore, the particular sampling procedure within the AdaBoost algorithm will overemphasize the noisy training data points and may lead to poor generalization.

Since the potential overfitting is caused by the accumulation of errors within the function $H_{T-1}(x)$, one way to avoid this is to modify the expression form for $H_{T-1}(x)$. Instead of constant combination coefficients α_t, we can make them input dependent, i.e.

$$H_T(x) = \sum_{t=1}^{T} \alpha_t e^{-|\beta H_{t-1}(x)|} h_t(x) \tag{21}$$

Compared to (20), the above expression replaces the weighting constant α_t with $\alpha_t exp(-|\beta\ H_{t-1}(x)|)$. More interestingly, it can be shown that when α_t is bounded by some fixed constant, the value of $H_T(x)$ in (21) will increase at most logarithmically with respect to the number of iterations T and the weight of each data pattern will grow at most polynomial with the number of iterations. Therefore, the problem of overemphasizing noisy data patterns will be alleviated substantially compared to the classical AdaBoost.

As pointed out before the other important problem with AdaBoost is fixed combination coefficients. According to AdaBoost, each base classifier (model) $h_t(x)$ is trained intentionally on the data patterns that either misclassified or weakly classified by previous classifiers (models) $H_{t-1}(x)$. Therefore, every base classifier $h_t(x)$ should be appropriate only for a subset of input patterns. However, in the prediction phase, the opinion of the base classifier $h_t(x)$ will always be weighted by the same number α_t no matter what test examples are.

On the contrary, in the new form of $H_T(x)$ given by (21), introduction of the instance-dependent factor $exp(-|\beta H_{t-1}(x)|)$ offers a tradeoff between the opinion of the base classifier $h_t(x)$ and that of the previously built meta-classifier $H_{t-1}(x)$. Since the value of $H_{t-1}(x)$ indicates its confidence on classifying the instance x, the factor $exp(-|\beta H_{t-1}(x)|)$ forces to consider the opinion of $h_t(x)$ seriously only when combination of the previous classifiers $H_{t-1}(x)$ is not confident about its decision. This implies that introduction of the input-dependent factor makes the base classifier $h_t(x)$ to be consistent between the training phase and the prediction phase, i.e., $h_t(x)$ is used for prediction of the particular type of input patterns that it has been trained on.

It is clear from (21) that the extent of the input-dependency can be conveniently controlled by factor β. When β goes to zero, we recover original AdaBoost algorithm. By varying β one can go from small weight modulations (mild regime adjustment) in almost stationary meta-model (small β) to the more regime-switching type of meta-model (large β). The optimal choice of β is determined by the properties that user expects from the meta-model and stability of its out-of-sample performance.

Finally, one needs to obtain a learning procedure that is able to minimize the exponential cost function with the new combination form given by (21). As shown by Jin et al [23], by following standard procedures for AdaBoost derivation, one obtains the new expression for the data weight modification at each boosting iteration:

$$w_n^T = \frac{e^{-H_{T-1}(x_n)y_n - |\beta H_{T-1}(x_n)|}}{\sum_{j=1}^{N} e^{-H_{T-1}(x_j)y_j - |\beta H_{T-1}(x_j)|}} \tag{22}$$

All other relevant expressions given by (8.1) – (8.5) remain the same, while the new combination form is given by (21). Using similar arguments one can obtain learning procedure for an arbitrary bounded regularizer $f(x)$ instead of $exp(-|\beta H_{t-1}(x)|)$ used above [23].

The described input-dependent WeightBoost algorithm consistently outperforms classical AdaBoost algorithm in many typical classification tasks [23]. However to adapt this input-dependent boosting for classification to the boosting-based optimization framework capable to discover regime-adjusted portfolio strategies, additional assumptions should be made. In the standard classification task one can run each base model for a given test data sample to compute each input-dependent combination weight according to (21). After that the output of the combined model (21) can be readily obtained. However, we do not know the base strategies performance (i.e., return) on the tested interval τ in advance and cannot compute input-dependent weights (capital allocations) before running the portfolio of strategies. Therefore, one should use information on the base strategies performance from previous intervals.

A natural way is to use return information on the most recent interval τ^* which could be different from τ used in the objective function (9) in the training phase. The interval τ^* is another parameter that can be varied to achieve specific objectives. For example, for aggressive local regime-switching strategies one can use short period τ^*, while for a slow (adiabatic) regime-adjustment of the already stable portfolio one can use larger τ^*. The final choice of τ^* is empirically determined by the strategy performance.

For some portfolio strategies, time variation of the capital allocations among individual strategies could introduce additional operational challenges. For example, for daily or other low-frequency trading strategies one would need to rebalance existing positions even when individual strategies do not generate new entry or exit signals since weight distribution changes according to latest performance of the base strategies. However, all these technical issues can be resolved for each type of portfolio strategy.

Intraday strategies with no overnight positions introduce the least number of operational challenges in the application of the regime-adjusted portfolio strategies obtained from input-dependent boosting. Indeed, if there are no intraday weight adjustments, all new capital allocations for the next day are computed using already existed performance data from the current day and chosen number of previous days. The example of such strategy is considered in the next section as an illustration of the new framework application to the real-market problem.

6 Application example

Intraday trading strategies with no overnight positions is very important type of strategies in modern markets where many other strategies operating on lower frequency (i.e. daily) could often fail on a short-term horizon (e.g. several months). In addition, operational challenges imposed by the input-dependent boosting framework are minimal in this case. Here we use one of such strategies to illustrate application of the new framework.

The detailed empirical comparison of the previously studied boosting-based optimization with constant weights and new framework with adjustable weights is beyond the scope of this paper. Instead, using real example we summarize the features of the new framework that have been already found very useful in practical market applications. The presented results are mostly relevant to the strategies with slow (adiabatic) and limited-amplitude adjustments of the weights (capital allocations) which are the main focus of our current research. More aggressive, regime-switching strategies that can be profitable even in the cases where stable portfolio strategy with constant capital allocations cannot be found will be discussed elsewhere.

We apply boosting-based optimization to the single financial instrument and the pool of the typical momentum (trend-following) strategies operating on 5min intraday bars. Each base strategy is based on the two types of entry indicators and two types of trailing stop exits that combine risk management and profit-taking capabilities. Since each base strategy is restricted to only one side of entry (i.e., long-only or short-only) and number of entry trades allowed during the trade day is varied from 1 to 3, the pool consists of 24 individual base strategies where parameters of the entry and exit rules are available for optimization.

The entry indicators considered in this application are double exponential cross-up and relative strength index (RSI) [34]. Double exponential indicator consists of two exponential moving averages (EMA) of the 5min bars with 2 parameters each (smoothing constant and averaging period). When price crosses up both EMAs, entry signal for long position is generated (cross-down signals short position). RSI entry rule have two parameters: period and threshold. When price crosses up the RSI threshold the long entry signal is generated (cross-down signals for short position).

Long (short) position is closed when 5min bar closing price fells below $c_{max}[1-\Delta\sigma(m)]$ (jumps above $c_{min}[1+\Delta\sigma(m)]$). Here $c_{max}(c_{min})$ is a maximum (minimum) closing prices with respect to present bar, $\sigma(m)$ is volatility measure computed using m last bars, and parameter Δ controls trailing stop width. Parkinson volatility measure [35] was used in our case. Trailing stops based on global and local (i.e., the most recent) maximum (minimum) calculations used for the exit price level can demonstrate complimentary performance. In this example, both exit types have been used with parameters Δ and m available for optimization.

In the presented example we considered 7 years (1750 days) of historical intraday data for the Russell-2000 (ticker: RUT) small-cap index ending on 2008/02/01. Only 800 days ending on 2007/01/31 are used for training. All other data after (more than 1 year) and before (~3 years) the training period is used to demonstrate out-of-sample stability of the discovered portfolio strategies. The search is restricted to the strategies operating on the last 30 bars of each trading day. Assuming realistic fees of 0.5c per share and stop loss slippage of 5c for IWM which is RUT-based tradable ETF with price ratio 1:10, we used 5c and 50c for RUT index itself. For clear and conservative demonstration of the daily profit-loss (PL) time series no reinvestment was used, i.e., each trading day was started with the same amount of trading capital. Both fixed-weight and input-dependent boosting optimization was restricted to total of 7 iterations. At each boosting iteration, base strategies were optimized using global simulated annealing optimizer [36].

The best portfolio strategies, discovered using fixed-weight boosting (8.1) – (8.6) with the objective function (9) and different parameters τ and r_c, often demonstrate comparable global performance and the variability of the local performance is also quite limited. When we apply input-dependent boosting and vary parameter β that controls regime-adjustment, the immediate result is increased diversity of the obtained portfolio strategies. The discovered regime-adjusted portfolio strategies may not always demonstrate overwhelming global superiority in comparison to the portfolio strategies obtained with fixed-weight boosting. However, as expected, they can demonstrate significantly superior performance in certain regimes and different mechanisms of profit generation.

For example, applying the fixed-weight boosting to the momentum strategies operating on broad market indexes, including Russell-2000, one often finds only portfolio strategies where almost all capital (>90%) allocated to long-only base strategies. This may introduce occasional undesirable effects (e.g., daily draw-downs) in certain local regimes. However, we find that input-dependent boosting with even small values of β is capable to discover much more diverse portfolio strategies including those where capital allocation to long and short strategies is either more uniform or oscillates between long and short dominating portfolios which improves performance in certain market regimes.

These results are illustrated in figure 1 where we plot PL time series of the typical portfolio strategy obtained using fixed-weight boosting (solid line), input-dependent boosting (dashed line), and benchmark buy-and-hold long strategy (dotted line). These solutions are obtained using the following objective function and boosting parameters: τ=15days, r_c=0.2% (for fixed-weight boosting) and $\tau=\tau^*$=15days, r_c=0.1%, β=2 (for input-dependent boosting). It is clear that although global performance of the two portfolio strategies is comparable, the regime-adjusted strategy demonstrates significant advantage in certain regimes. Both boosting strategies show very stable out-of-sample performance and are consistently superior to buy-and-hold strategy.

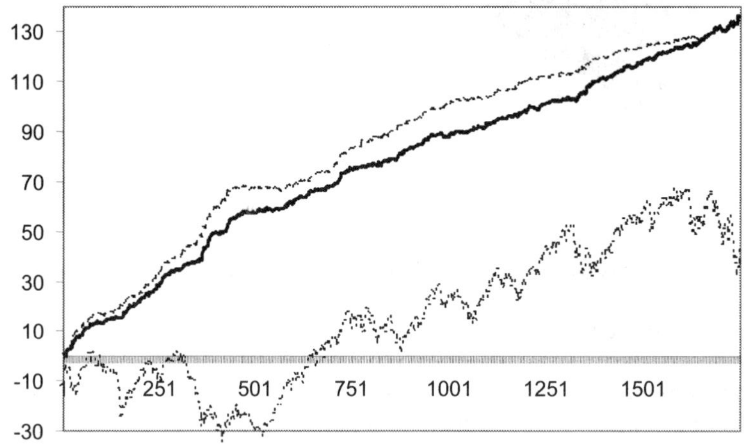

Figure 1: PL(%) vs days.

However, even more important is the ability of the input-dependent boosting to find much greater variety of the portfolio strategies without any additional efforts such as empirical search for more complex objective functions or any other non-generic and problem specific approaches. For example, long-short bias ratio of the regime-adjusted portfolio strategy presented in figure 1 varies from ~0.75 long bias to ~0.7 short bias in different regimes, while the fixed weight portfolio strategy is long-only at all times. The significant reduction of the correlation between these two portfolio strategies is clear from figure 2 where each point represent daily returns of the fixed-weight (horizontal axis) and adjusted-weight (vertical axis) boosted strategies. The ability to generate more diverse portfolio strategies would allow building more stable portfolios of portfolios using HME or similar frameworks. Additionally, using portfolio-level intraday profit-taking or stop losses, more specific return-risk profiles could be achieved. Initial diversity of the boosted strategies will provide a practical advantage in this task. Finally, we found that input-dependent boosting is much more powerful compared to fixed-weight boosting when one searches for some specific hard-to-discover strategies, e.g. short-only hedging strategy that minimally interferes with the original long strategy.

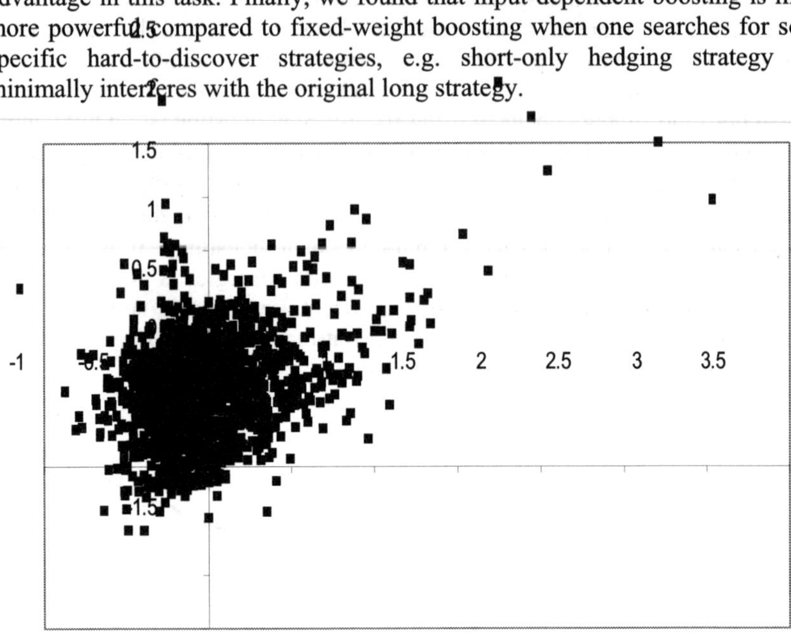

Figure 2: Daily returns(%) (fixed vs adjusted weights).

7 Conclusions

Limitations of the existing regime-switching and regime-adjusted models and modelling frameworks for financial applications have been outlined. Recently proposed boosting-based optimization has been extended to allow discovering of the regime-switching and regime-adjusted portfolio strategies. A formal theoretical foundation for the boosting-based optimization in general has also been outlined. Operation of the new framework was illustrated using real-market example of the intraday trading strategy.

References

[1] Fabozzi, F.J., Financial modelling of the equity market: From CAPM to cointegration, Wiley, 2006.

[2] Haykin, S., Neural networks: A comprehensive foundation, Macmillian College Publishing Company, 1994.

[3] Wan, E.A., Finite impulse response neural networks with applications in time series prediction, PhD Dissertation, Stanford University, 1993.

[4] Pedersen, M.W., Optimization of the recurrent neural networks for time series modelling, PhD Thesis, Technical University of Denmark, 1997.

[5] Gavrishchaka, V.V. & Bykov, V., Market-neutral portfolio of trading strategies as universal indicator of market micro-regimes: From rare-event forecasting to single-example learning of emerging patterns, in proceedings of Second International Conference on Innovative Computing, Information and Control (ICICIC 2007).

[6] Gavrishchaka, V.V., Boosting-based frameworks in financial modeling: Application to symbolic volatility forecasting, Advances in Econometrics, **20B**, p. 123, 2006.

[7] Gavrishchaka, V.V., Boosting-based framework for portfolio strategy discovery and optimization, New Mathematics and Natural Computation, **2**, p. 315, 2006

[8] Gavrishchaka, V.V., Discovery of multi-spread portfolio strategies for weakly-cointegrated instruments using boosting-based optimization, in JCIS-CIEF Proceedings, 2006.

[9] Cappe, O., Moulines, E., Ryden, T., Inference in hidden Markov models, Springer Series in Statistics, Springer, 2005.

[10] Rabiner, L.R., A tutorial on hidden Markov models and selected applications in speech recognition, Proc. IEEE, 77, 257–286, 1989.

[11] Baldi, P. & Brunak, S., Bioinformatics: The machine learning approach, MIT Press, 2001.

[12] Kalman, R.E., A new approach for linear filtering and prediction problems, Transactions of the ASME-Journal of Basic Engineering **82**, Series D, pp.35-45, 1960.

[13] Hamilton, J.D., A new approach to the economic analysis of the nonstationary time series and the business cycle, Econometrica, Econometric Society, 57(2), pp. 357–384, 1989.

[14] Zivot, E. & Wang, J., Modeling financial time series with S-Plus, Springer, 2003.

[15] Dempster, A.P., Laird, N.M. & Rubin, D.B., Maximum-likelihood from incomplete data via the EM algorithm, Journal Royal Statistical Society Series 39, pp. 1–38, 1977.

[16] Elman, J.L., Finding structure in time, Cognitive Science, 14, pp. 179–211, 1990.

[17] Wan, E.A., Time series prediction by using a connectionist network with internal delay lines, in Time series prediction: Forecasting the future and understanding the past (A.S. Weigend and N.A. Gershenfeld, eds.), pp. 195–217, Reading, MA: Addison-Wesley, 1994.

[18] Bishop, C.M., Pattern recognition and machine learning, Springer, 2006.

[19] Hastie, T., Tibshirani, R. & Friedman, J., The Elements of Statistical Learning: Data Mining, Inference, and Prediction, Springer, 2001.

[20] Jacobs, R.A., Jordan, M.I., Nowlan, S.J. & Hinton, G.E., Adaptive mixtures of local experts, Neural Computation, 3(1), pp. 79–87, 1991.

[21] Schapire, R.E., The design and analysis of efficient learning algorithms, PhD thesis, MIT Press, 1992.

[22] Ratsch, G., Robust boosting via convex optimization: Theory and applications, PhD thesis, Potsdam University, 2001.

[23] Jin, R., Liu, Y., Si, L., Carbonell, J. & Hauptmann A.G., A new boosting algorithm using input-dependent regularizer, Proc. of the 20th International Conference on Machine Learning (ICML-2003), Washington DC, 2003.
[24] Friedman, J.H., Hastie, T. & Tibshirani, R., Additive logistic regression: A statistical view of boosting, Annals of Statistics, 28, 2000.
[25] Schapire, R.E. & Singer, Y., Improved boosting using confidence-rated predictions, Machine Learning, 37(3), 1999.
[26] Vapnik, V., Statistical learning theory, Wiley, 1998.
[27] Freund, Y., & Schapire, R. E., A decision-theoretic generalization of online learning and an application to boosting, Journal of Computer and System Sciences, 55, pp. 119–139, 1997.
[28] Schapire, R. E., Freund, Y., Bartlett, P., & Lee, W. S., Boosting the margin: A new explanation for the effectiveness of voting methods, The Annals of Statistics, 26, pp. 1651–1686, 1998.
[29] Rudin, C., Daubechies, I. & Schapire, R.E., The Dynamics of AdaBoost: Cyclic Behavior and Convergence of Margins, Journal of Machine Learning Research, December 2004.
[30] Reyzin, L. & Schapire, R.E., How boosting the margin can also boost classifier complexity, In Proceedings of the 23rd International Conference on Machine Learning, 2006.
[31] Vezhnevets, A. & Barinova, O., Avoiding Boosting Overfitting by Removing 'Confusing Samples', European Conference on Machine Learning (ECML) - 2007, Warsaw, Poland, 2007.
[32] Altincay, H., A dempster-shafer theoretic framework for boosting based ensemble design, Pattern Anal. Applic., 8, pp. 287–302, 2005.
[33] Vetrov, D. & Kropotov, D., Data dependent classifier fusion for construction of stable effective algorithms, Proc. of the 17th International Conference on Pattern Recognition (ICPR-04), 2004.
[34] Katz, J.O. & McCormick, D.L., The encyclopaedia of trading strategies, McGraw-Hill, 2000.
[35] Li, K. & Weinbaum, D., The empirical performance of the alternative extreme value volatility estimators, Working Paper, Stern School of Business, New York, 2000.
[36] Press, W.H., Teukolsky, S.A., Vetterling, W.T. & Flannery, B.P., Numerical Recipes in C: The Art of Scientific Computing, Cambridge University Press, 1992.

Section 4
Market analysis, dynamics and simulation

Day-of-the-week effect in some of the Gulf Cooperation Council (GCC) stock markets

A. M. Al-Barrak
Finance Department, King Faisal University, Saudi Arabia

Abstract

This paper examines the day-of-the-week effects in some of the Gulf Cooperation Council (GCC) stock markets namely the Saudi Stock Market, the Kuwaiti Stock Exchange, and the Dubai Financial Market. The empirical research was conducted using the variances (ANOVA) test to find if there were significant differences between the daily returns in these markets from January 2002 to December 2005. Results obtained indicate the significant presence of the day of the week effect on the Kuwaiti Stock Exchange (KSE), the highest return is observed on Saturday and the lowest return is observed on Sunday.
Keywords: day-of-the-week effect, Gulf cooperation council stock market.

1 Introduction

French (1980) originally observed that stock returns are higher than average on the last trading day of the week and lower than average on the first. Since then, a great number of researchers have attempted to explain and examine what has come to be known as the "weekend" or "day-of-the-week" effect. Now, it is well documented in the finance literature that the weekend or the day-of-the-week could affect the performance of the stock market. Most of these researches have documented that the average return on Friday is abnormally high, and the average return on Monday is abnormally low (Agrawal and Tandon [1], and Mills and Coutts [15]). Jaffe and Westerfield [10] and Keim and Stambaugh [12] say that this anomalous empirical finding is one of the most puzzling phenomena in finance.

In this paper, we extend the determination of the day-of-the-week effect existing in a sample of three Gulf Cooperation Council (GCC) stock markets,

WIT Transactions on Information and Communication Technologies, Vol 41, © 2008 WIT Press
www.witpress.com, ISSN 1743-3517 (on-line)
doi:10.2495/CF080141

namely the Saudi Stock Market, the Kuwaiti Stock Exchange, and the Dubai Financial Market.

The remainder of the paper is structured as follows. Section 2 is an overview of the GCC stock markets. Section 3 summarises a literature review of the issue and discusses related topics. Section 4 outlines the data used and the methodology that is applied. Section 5 presents the findings and Section 6 is the conclusion.

2 Overview of the GCC stock markets

2.1 The Saudi Stock Market (SSM)

The Saudi Stock Market (SSM) is relatively young in age compared to the markets in developed countries. Based on Standard and Poor's Emerging Markets Data Base (EMDB), The SSM is classified as an emerging market belonging to the Middle East and North Africa region. An unofficial stock market began in 1934, when the Arabian Automobile Company was created as the first joint stock company in the Kingdom. The number of joint stock companies increased to a total of five by 1954. By 1964, the total had reached 17, with an issued capital of 29.9 million shares and a value of SR 2,955 million. In May 2007, the number of listed joint stock companies in the Kingdom was 93 in the SSM. Market activities, however, remained largely unregulated until 1985, when the Saudi Arabian Monetary Authority (SAMA) exclusively authorised 12 domestic commercial banks to act as brokers. Electronic trading and settlement systems were implemented in 1988. On 16th June 2003, the Saudi Capital Market Authority (CMA) was established to regulate and develop the Saudi Arabian capital markets and issue the required rules and regulations for the implementation of the provisions of the Capital Market Law aimed at creating an appropriate investment environment. In 2006, the Saudi Government allowed foreigners resident in Saudi Arabia to invest directly in the Kingdom's stock market. Trading days in the SSM were from Saturday to Thursday. However, in June 2006, the CMA reduced the trading days to five, from Saturday to Wednesday.

2.2 The Kuwait Stock Exchange (KSE)

The history of Kuwaiti public share holding companies had its origin in the 1950s. The process started with public subscription in 1952 to the shares of the National Bank of Kuwait (NBK) followed in 1954 by the Kuwaiti National Cinema Company (KSC). An Amiri Decree was issued on 14 August 1983 concerning the reorganisation of the Exchange as an independent financial institution. Following the Iraqi invasion of Kuwait in August 1990, trading in the KSE was interrupted for 28 months, which reduced the number of listed companies from 54 to 28. Securities trading became more efficient in 1995 with the implementation of an electronic trading and settlement system. The Kuwaiti Securities Market signed, on December 25 1996, a cross-listing agreement with the Bahrain and Oman Stock Exchanges. Other GCC nationals were granted market access in 2000. Non-GCC investors are not allowed to invest directly in the Kuwaiti stock market but may subscribe to overseas based mutual funds trading in Kuwaiti securities. The Waad Future Financial Investment Service, the first equity futures market in the Arab world, was launched in 1996, for a limited number of stocks (Bley and Chen [2]). On July 2006, 172 companies were listed on the KSE. Trading days in KSE are from Saturday to Wednesday.

2.3 The Dubai Financial Market (DFM)

Dealing in stocks in the United Arab Emirates (UAE) goes back to the early sixties of the past century, when the government established several joint-stock companies. The Dubai Financial Market was established on 26th March 2000 as a public organisation having independent legal personality. In its early stages, the market played the role of a secondary market for the exchange of stocks issued by joint stock companies, as well as the exchange of bonds issued by the Government of the United Arab Emirates, any of the local government entities, public organisations and institutions within the government, and investment units issued by local investment funds or any other local or foreign financial instrument acceptable to the market. The number of listed securities in the DFM was 30 in July 2006. Trading days in the DFM are from Saturday to Thursday.

Table 1: GCC stock market characteristics (December 2005).

Characteristics	SSM	KSE	DFM
Stock trading began	1934	1952	1989
Current market system established	1985	1983	2000
Electronic trading since	1988	1995	2000
Number of companies listed	81	173	30
Market capitalization (US $ bn)	431	115	114
Length of settlement procedure (days)	Real time	1	2
Trading days	From Saturday to Wednesday	From Saturday to Wednesday	From Sunday to Thursday

3 Literature review

As noted above, the presence of the day of the week effect in stock market returns has been widely documented in the finance literature. In the USA market, French [5] observed consistently lower returns for Monday. In fact, the mean returns for Monday were negative for 20 years during 1952-1977. Moreover, Gibbons and Hess [6], Lakonishok and Levi [14], Keim and Stambaugh [12],

Rogalski [16], Harris [7], and Smirlock and Starts [19] also discovered extensive evidence of the day-of-the-week effect in the USA.

In addition, studies have been conducted on some of the European exchanges. These studies showed that the day-of-the-week effect varied between countries and time periods. Board and Sutcliffe [3] and Hawawini [8] documented in their researches that there was some evidence of the day-of-the-week effect in the London, French, and Finnish Stock Exchanges. In general, it seems to be the case that Mondays and Tuesdays provided lower returns, while the other three days of the week provided higher returns. Condoyanni et al [4] found that returns inform the Greek Stock Exchange were negative on Tuesdays and Wednesdays. In addition, the findings of Savva et al [18] indicate that the day-of-the-week effect is present in either intercept or autocorrelation terms (or both) in the mean equation for the UK, France, Italy, Spain, and Swiss stock markets, but not from Germany and the USA. However, Santesneses [17] did not find a day-of-the-week effect in the Spanish Stock Exchange, nor did Jennergren and Sorensen [11] for the Danish markets.

Regarding the Asian stock exchanges, Kim et al [13] analysed the day-of-the-week effects in the Thailand and Korea stock markets for the period January 1980 – December 1988. The findings of the study did not follow the pattern of high or positive returns on the last trading day and low or negative returns at the start of the trading week. Also, testing for the weekend-effect did not produce any evidence. Wong et al [20] extended study of the day-of the week effect to the stock markets of Hong Kong, Taiwan, Thailand, Singapore, and Malaysia for the period from January 1975 to May 1988. It was found that the day-of-the week effect is present in all markets except Taiwan. Lastly, Hui [9] investigated the day to day behaviour of stock market returns for the USA, Japan, Hong Kong, South Korea, Singapore, and Taiwan. The result showed that Hong Kong, Taiwan and Singapore follow the general pattern of higher average stock returns on the last trading day of the week and lower than average returns on the first, but the mature markets of the USA and Japan and the relatively new Korean stock market do not confirm to the same pattern.

4 Data and methodology

There are seven GCC stock markets, namely the Bahrain, Abu Dhabi, Dubai, Kuwait, Oman, Qatar, and Saudi Arabia stock markets. However, this study covers only three of them: SMM, KSE, and DFM. The reason for selecting these three stock markets is that they are the largest stock markets in term of market capital, volume traded, and shares traded. The data for selected stock markets were obtained from their official websites.

The daily return of each stock index is computed as follows:

$$R_t = (P_t - P_{t-1}) / P_{t-1}$$

Where R_t daily return, P_t and P_{t-1} are the closing prices of the index are period t and $t-1$, respectively.

To examine the day-of-the week effect of the three different stock indices, an analysis of variances (ANOVA) test was used to find if there were significant

differences between the independent variables. A parametric test, 1-way ANOVA, was employed because the data conforms to an ordinal scale and because of the sample size. The test was used with a significant level of 5%, so the null hypothesis is rejected if the result of the test is less than 5%. The hypotheses in this study are as follows:
H_0 = No difference exists in the returns across the days of the week.
H_1 = A difference exists in the returns across the days of the week.

5 Empirical results

The objective of this empirical test was to determine whether the three GCC stock markets tend to exhibit a day-of-the-week effect. Firstly, descriptive statistics were compiled by day of the week for each stock market, shown in Table 2. Table 2 illustrates the mean return and standard deviation for every day of the week for the three GCC stock markets. From Table 2, the lowest return happened on Sunday for the SSM (-0.0003) and KSE (0.0002), and on Wednesday for DFM (-0.0001). Interestingly, KSE recorded positive returns for all days of the week, unlike SSM and DFM. Regarding the volatility, measured by the standard deviations, the most volatile day in SSM was Saturday (0.0152), as it was also for KSE (0.0094). For DFM, Tuesday (0.0500) was the most volatile.

Table 2: Means, and standard deviations (SD), of GCC stock markets.

Days	SSM		KSE		DFM	
	Mean	SD	Mean	SD	Mean	SD
Saturday	0.0018	0.0152	0.0032	0.0094	0.0030	0.0139
Sunday	-0.0003	0.0099	0.0002	0.0081	0.0015	0.0136
Monday	0.0013	0.0116	0.0022	0.0081	0.0022	0.0183
Tuesday	0.0019	0.0122	0.0014	0.0082	0.0042	0.0500
Wednesday	0.0026	0.0126	0.0024	0.0072	-0.0001	0.0316
Thursday	0.0028	0.0079	-------	-------	0.0033	0.0120

Table 3 demonstrates the result of the 1-way ANOVA test of day-of-the-week effects on returns differences in GCC stock markets, using SPSS. The values of the F-test and P-value are insignificant at the 5% level for all the markets except KSE (0.004 p-value). Comparing the mean returns of KSE (Table 2), Saturday has a mean score of 0.0032, Sunday a mean score of 0.0002, Monday a mean score of 0.0022, Tuesday a mean score of 0.0014, and Wednesday a mean score of 0.0024.

To make further investigation into the mean differences in KSE, the LSD Multiple Comparisons test was implemented. Comparing the mean returns of KSE by using LSD Multiple Comparisons at the 0.05 level, as shown in Table 4, Saturday is significantly different from Sunday and Tuesday; Sunday is significantly different from all days except Tuesday; Monday and Wednesday are significantly different from Sunday; Tuesday is significantly different from Saturday.

Table 3: One-way ANOVA result of day-of-the-week effects on returns differences in GCC stock markets.

Stock markets	**F-test**	**P-value**	**Null hypothesis**
SSM	1.789	0.112	Do not reject
KSE	3.885	**0.004**	Reject
DFM	0.636	0.672	Do not reject

Bold and underlined figures refer to a 5% significant difference.

Table 4: LSD Multiple Comparisons results.

(I) D_KSM	**(J) D_KSM**	**Mean Difference (I-J)**	**Sig.**
Saturday	**Sunday**	0.0029783	**0.000**
	Monday	0.0010374	0.202
	Tuesday	0.0018015	**0.027**
	Wednesday	0.0007631	0.348
Sunday	**Saturday**	-0.0029783	**0.000**
	Monday	-0.0019409	**0.017**
	Tuesday	-0.0011768	0.148
	Wednesday	-0.0022151	**0.006**
Monday	Saturday	-0.0010374	0.202
	Sunday	0.0019409	**0.017**
	Tuesday	0.0007641	0.348
	Wednesday	-0.0002743	0.736
Tuesday	**Saturday**	-0.0018015	**0.027**
	Sunday	0.0011768	0.148
	Monday	-0.0007641	0.348
	Wednesday	-0.0010383	0.202
Wednesday	Saturday	-0.0007631	0.348
	Sunday	0.0022151	**0.006**
	Monday	0.0002743	0.736
	Tuesday	0.0010383	0.202

Bold and underlined figures refer to a 5% significant difference.

6 Conclusion

This paper provides a study of the day-of-the-week-effect in three Gulf Cooperation Council emerging stock markets using the one-way ANOVA test. The day-of-the-week effect on both the mean and standard deviation (volatility) of stock returns are studied in this paper. Daily stock returns during January 2002 to December 2005 from Saudi Arabia, Kuwait, and Dubai were applied in the empirical work. The results obtained indicate a significant presence of the day-of-the-week effect in the Kuwait Stock Exchange only. This confirms the notion that the day-of-the-week effect is not just features of the stock markets of the United States and other developed countries but of emerging markets.

References

[1] Agrawal, A. and Tandon, K. Anomalies or illusions? Evidence from stock markets in eighteen countries, Journal of International Money and Finance, 13, pp. 83–106, 1994

[2] Bley, J. and Kim Heng Chen, Gulf Cooperation Council (GCC) stock markets: the dawn of a new era, Globe Finance Journal, Forthcoming, 2006

[3] Board, J. L. C. and Sutcliffe, C. M. S., The Weekend Effect in UK stock market returns. Journal of Business Finance and Accounting, 15, pp. 119–213, 1998

[4] Condoyanni, L., O'Hanlon, J., and Ward C. W. R., An investigation of daily seasonality in the Greek equity market, in: Guimaraes, R., Kingsman, B., and Taylor, S., editors. Reappraisal of the efficiency of financial markets. NATO ASI Series, vol. F54. Berlin: pp. 229–57, 1989

[5] French, K. R., Stock returns and the week-end effect, Journal of Financial Economics, 8, pp. 56–59, 1980

[6] Gibbons, M. and Hess, P., Day of the week effect and asset returns, Journal of Business, 54, pp. 579–596, 1981

[7] Harris, L., An examination of the robustness of the week-end effect, Journal of Financial and Quantitative Analysis, 24, pp. 133–156, 1986

[8] Hawawini, G., Market efficiency and equity pricing: international evidence and implications for global investing. University of Pennsylvania. Working Paper, 1998

[9] Hui, Tak-Kee, Day-of-the-week effects in US and Asia–Pacific stock markets during the Asian financial crisis: a non-parametric approach. Omega, 33, 277–282, 2005

[10] Jaffe, J. and Westerfield, R., The week-end effect in common stock returns: the international evidence, Journal of Finance, 40, pp. 237–44, 1985

[11] Jennergren, P. and Sorensen, B., Random walks and anomalies on the Copenhagen Stock Exchange in the 1890s, in: Guimaraes, R., Kingsman, B., and Taylor, S., editors. Reappraisal of the efficiency of financial markets. NATO ASI Series Vol. FS4, Berlin: pp. 261–282, 1989

[12] Keim, D. and Stambaugh, R., A further investigation of the weekend effect in stock returns, Journal of Finance, 39, pp. 819–35, 1984

[13] Kim, D. J. et al., A comparative analysis of anomalies and daily returns in emerging Asian stock markets. Western Decision Science Institute, Working Paper, 1998

[14] Lakonishok, J. and Levi, M., Weekend effects on stock returns, a note, Journal of Finance, 37, pp. 883–889, 1982

[15] Mills, T. and Coutts, J., Calendar effect in the London Stock Exchange FT-SE indices, European Journal of Finance, 1, pp. 79–93, 1995

[16] Rogalski, R., New findings regarding day of the week returns over trading and non-trading periods. Journal of Finance, 39, pp. 1603–1614, 1984

[17] Santesneses, M., An investigation of the Spanish stock market seasonalities. Journal of Business Finance and Accounting, 13, pp. 267–276, 1986

[18] Savva, C., Osborn, D. R. and Gill, L., The day of the week effect: evidence from six European stock markets and the US. University of Manchester. Working paper, 2006

[19] Smirlock, M. and Starts, L., Day-of-the-week and intraday effects in stock returns, Journal of Financial Economics, 17, pp. 197–210, 1986

[20] Wong, K. A., Hui, T. K., and Chan, C. Y., Day-of-the-week effects: evidence from developing stock markets. Applied Financial Economics, 2, pp. 49–56, 1992

Looking for short term signals in stock market data

A. Bocharov
Microsoft Corp., Redmond, USA

Abstract

This paper offers a method for generating discrimination criteria that can be used to identify strong patterns in stock market data. More effective criteria are necessary as short-term trades are often driven by noise rather than valid market signals - a viewpoint known as the "noisy trader" model of the stock market. To demonstrate why traditional technical analysis falls short, we applied the standard methods to a synthetic market generated by a random walk. Although the market data is engineered to be pure noise, technical analysis "discovers" strong features such as accumulation/distribution patterns, upward and downward trends, support and resistance levels. These secondary features represent noise in the technical indicators.

By comparing the performance of these indicators between a real market and the synthetic noise market, real signals can be identified. We select a subset of technical indicators {T} such that each indicator T in this subset has a mesokurtic (usually, near-normal) distribution across the synthetic noise market. It turns out that many of the common measures (e.g. accumulation, relative strength, moving average trend direction) are mesokurtic for the noise market, but have strongly leptokurtic distributions across the actual stock market. We propose a method for using the kurtosis of such indicators T to separate the noise from the real signal in the indicators. Specifically, having obtained a mesokurtic baseline that corresponds to noise, we use the empirical real market distribution for indicator T to compute discrimination thresholds beyond which a value of T should be considered a strong signal.

The strong signal concept is validated using historical price/volume data for the Standard & Poor's 1500 (S&P 1500) set of stocks.

Keywords: market analysis, kurtosis risk, random walk, technical analysis.

WIT Transactions on Information and Communication Technologies, Vol 41, © 2008 WIT Press
www.witpress.com, ISSN 1743-3517 (on-line)
doi:10.2495/CF080151

1 Introduction

This paper proposes conceptually simple methods for assessing the predictive power of certain stock market technical indicators and for locating ranges of values in which the indicator values are statistically significant. To accomplish this, we apply statistical analysis to answer the following question: what is the relative likelihood that the observed value of a technical indicator could not be explained by a noisy random walk market model? The analysis is based on the empirical observation that certain indicators are strongly leptokurtic across the actual market and generate numerous outlying values that are highly unlikely under random market hypothesis.

The idea of using leptokurtic distributions for describing capital markets' statistics is not entirely new. Bollerslev and Hodrick [1] explored the fat tailed distributions of stock price returns in conjunction with the market efficiency hypothesis. (See also discussions in [2] and [3]). Fischer [4] proposed the use of generalized secant hyperbolic distribution to describe asset returns. Underestimating the kurtosis of the actual asset distributions poses multiple risks, whereby the term "kurtosis risk" has been coined. The notion has been summarized by Mandelbrot and Hudson in [5]. Recently Kitt and Kalda published an outline of Leptokurtic portfolio theory [6] that relies of returns' kurtosis for minimization of portfolio drawdown risk.

This research takes the above ideas in a different perspective. First, we apply the analysis across the market breadth (for a market of Standard & Poor's 1500 [9] size) instead along the price/volume time series. Second, it is extended to a number of technical indicators. We posit the normality (it is an easy pun to say that the real market is "abnormal", but the irony of it is that its "normal" part maybe indistinguishable from noise) of the random market using the following time/breadth equivalence principle: an indicator that is normally distributed along a random walk should be also normally distributed across the broad market snapshot. The intuition for this principle is that the same kind of interaction of "noisy" market agents that caused a stock to "random walk" would cause similar kind of a random scatter of price and volume across the market. The assumptions regarding the behaviour of indicators in random market are detailed below in the "Technical indicators used" section.

Let T be a technical indicator and let ND[T,d] be the best normal distribution fit for the empirical distribution of indicator T across the actual market on a given date d. On most days covered in this research there will be a significant number of values of T that are highly improbable given ND[T,d] (for example values outside the six-sigma confidence interval). In general, if α is a chosen confidence level and I_α = [u,v] is the respective confidence interval for ND[T,d] then u and v are regarded as strong signal thresholds. A value of T that is either smaller than u or larger than v is a *strong signal in T* at confidence α .

There were six technical indicators employed in this research. We have seen 160 or more values of these indicators across the S&P 1500 on average per day that were outside the respective 99% confidence intervals. A random sampling of these values was cross-checked against the available news, press releases and earnings data (by human review process which was not automated at this stage). We have found that in most cases the outlying values of indicators appeared to be responses to recent events.

Often strong signals of the day clustered together to highlight movement of money between sectors, as well as sector upgrades/downgrades.

We have also observed the *temporal clustering* of signals, whereby strong signals in an S&P 1500 issue XYZ would be seen for several consecutive days.

An example of a day worth of strong signal analysis for 30th November 2007 is given in the "Case Study" section below.

The main result of this paper is an empirical proof of concept based on statistical analysis of historical price/volume for S&P 1500. This Author is satisfied that measuring the strength of technical indicator values based on the excess kurtosis of the empirical distributions for indicators is a viable method for detecting strong signal issues in the stock market. This is only the first step towards in-depth market signal analysis (as outlined in the "Further Directions" section).

2 Technical indicators used

2.1 Moving average trend strength: relative and logarithmic

To measure the trend strength in the underlying use k-day moving averages of the closing price, denoted [k]dMA. The strength measure that is most amenable to the statistical analysis is

TS[k](date) = [k]dMA(date) / [k]dMA(previous trading date)

TS[k] (d) > 1 iff k-day moving average is trending up on date d and TS[k](d) < 1 iff it is trending down. Under the assumption of the "random walk" market TS[k] is log-normally distributed and thus log(TS[k]) has normal distribution.

The sufficient statistic for the short-term signal research here has been collected for log(TS[5]) and log(TS[20]) and it turned out that either of these measures is leptokurtic across the actual market on most trading days.

2.2 Relative strength: log(RS)

Relative strength (RS) is the basis of the widely used Relative strength index (RSI, [7]). For a chosen moving window, the relative strength of a stock price curve is defined as RS = (Average gain)/(Average loss).

For our purposes we used a 20 day accumulation window (which was found empirically to be more robust than the usual 14 day window).

For a "random walk" market RS is distributed log-normally, so it is **Log(RS)** that was the indicator most suitable here. The Log(RS) appears to be leptokurtic across the real market with typical excess kurtosis between 0.3 and 1.7

2.3 Accumulation rate (normalized)

For a chosen accumulation window of n OHLC bars, the accumulation/ distribution rate is defined as

$$AR = \sum_{i=1}^{n} \frac{(2Close_i - Low_i - High_i)}{(High_i - Low_i)} Volume_i$$

(cf. [8]). The underlying is said to be "under accumulation" if AR is positive and to be "under distribution" if it is negative.

While this measure makes perfect sense along a single price/volume time series, for cross-market comparison the rate must be normalized to trading volume, so that comparison between high volume and low volume securities is possible. Therefore the measure actually used was $ARN = AR/V_a$, where V_a is the mean trading volume.

Strictly speaking ARN is not normally distributed over a "random walk" market. The core model for this indicator there is $\sum_{i=1}^{n} U_i V_i$ where all the variables are independent, each U_i is uniformly distributed on the [-1,1] and all V_i have the same log-normal distribution. However, for a reasonable choice of the random market assumptions, this distribution is going to be mesokurtic, typical excessive kurtosis not to exceed 0.1

2.4 "Day trader index" and ROI

A new indicator introduced specifically for this research is parameterized by a "trading window" of n days and a "trading threshold" t , which is a small positive number, typically between 0.005 and 0.015. For a daily OHLC bar of a given price curve on i-th day define the

$$P_i = (High_i - Open_i)/Open_i \,;\, L_i = (Close_i - Open_i)/Open_i$$

and

$$DR_i = if\,(P_i > t)\,then\,P_i\,else\,L_i$$

Now define $DTI = \sum_{i=1}^{n} DR_i$

DR_i rates a day as "losing" if the price never rises high enough above the opening price and the closing price is lower than the opening one. The day is rated "winning" otherwise. Therefore DR_i scores a win for a day when the underlying had sufficient upward momentum. Conceptually DTI represents returns for a severely idealized model day trader, who always buys at Open and never holds past Close. Technically the indicator relates to both the upward momentum of the underlying and its benign intraday volatility.

Along with the DTI this Author also used a more sophisticated index generically dubbed ROI which does not have a closed form description and had been computed dynamically. ROI related to a trader model that allowed overnight holding and used adaptive day-to-day adjustments of the threshold t. It is somewhat amusing that on average across S&P 1500 DTI and ROI were tied.

3 Signal strength and signal clustering

If $N(\mu,\sigma)$ is the best normal distribution fit for empirical distribution of indicator T across the market then we define the *strength of signal* T=v as

$$S(T=v)=\left|2\Phi(^{(v-\mu)}\!/\!_{\sigma})-1\right| \text{ where } \Phi \text{ is the probit function.}$$

As per this definition the strength of values close to "market mean" $T=\mu$ is close to 0, whereas the strength of a value on either fat tail of the empirical histogram would be close to 1. For example, $S(T=\mu+3\sigma)=S(T=\mu-3\sigma)=0.9973$.

An important concept that requires further research is the *joint signal strength* for a collection of signals. Generalizing the above, the joint signal strength should be derived from the joint cumulative normal proxy of the signals. The complication here is that all indicators are computed from the same body of price/volume data and therefore cannot be automatically considered independent.

For a selected strength threshold t we may see strong signal(s) in one or more indicator for a stock XYZ for L consecutive trading days starting date d. When this is the case, we say that the stock exhibits *strong signal clustering sequence* of length L. For L > 1 it is usually the case that the number and strength of signals increases then decreases as the clustering sequence unfolds.

4 Results: indicator and clustering statistics

The signal strength analysis has been run on 12 months worth of historical S&P 1500 day OHLC/Volume price/volume quotes bars.

We have found that the logarithmic measures based on Relative Strength, Trend Strength for 5-day and 20-day Moving Averages are strongly discriminating in that that they practically always leptokurtic across the actual market. The indicators (and/or their combinations) can be therefore used to measure the strength of signals on most trading days. DTI and ROI were leptokurtic on about 92% of days.

Table 1 describes typical monthly changes in excess kurtosis of indicators used in this research. As one can see the normalized A/D is not strongly leptokurtic, and thus should be used as an auxiliary measure on days when its kurtosis is sufficiently high.

A strong signal in a particular stock would be a part of *temporal signal cluster* in approximately 50% of all instances. The durations of such signal clusters have a highly skewed distribution that tails-off exponentially. An example of a histogram for strong signal lifetimes in a month window is shown in Figure 1.

There were overall 660 incidences of strong signals at confidence level 99% in December 2007. Among these, 343 instances lasted for just one day. On the right end of the spectrum there was one stock (IMB)(IndyMac Bancorp's year-long meltdown has been sealed on Dec 11 when its credit rating has been cut to Junk) that exhibited strong signals for 15 consecutive days.

Table 1: Monthly changes in excess kurtosis of indicators used.

Indicator	Log(RS)	Log(TS[5])	Log(TS[20])	Norm. A/D	DTI	ROI
Mean Ex.Kurtosis	1.014	9.43	6.0	-0.075	9.1	0.9
Ex. Kurtosis StDev	0.345	3.46	1.93	0.28	6.4	0.64

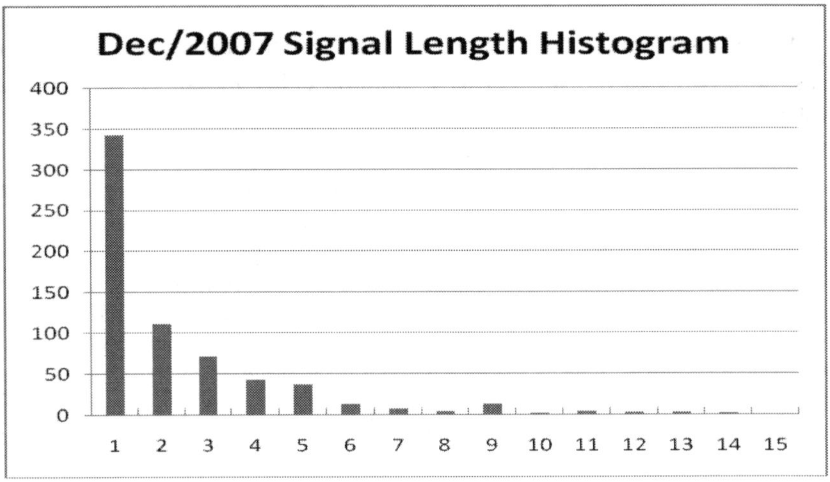

Figure 1: Strong signal lifetimes in December 2007 (length in days).

5 Case study

For case study we were looking for outlier values of indicators that were outside the 99% confidence intervals of the respective empirical normal distributions, i.e. signals with strength 0.99 or higher. There were around 160 outlying values registered per day for the S&P1500 data (on average), so the study was limited to symbols with more than one strong indicator value.

Example . November 30 2007

The 11/30/2007 has been randomly selected for detailed discussion. The market on that day was unremarkable in terms of direction, yet offered a broad variety of signals of many interesting types. Table 2 below highlights 35 issues with multiple strong signals. (There were more than 90 issues, showing strong signal in just a single indicator, which could not be covered here for obvious lack of space). For 31 of the issues in table 2 the reasons for the strong signals are

Table 2: Strong market signals on 11/30/2007.

Symbol	Outliers	Strength	Sign	Apparent reasons *)	Start	End date
AAPL	TS[20],TS[5]	0.99, 0.99	++	iPhone to China, France	11/12	11/30/07
ACAT	TS[5],ROI	0.992, 1	--	"global warming"	11/26	12/06/07
ADS	ROI, A/D	0.991, 0.998	-+	Buyout rumour	11/28	12/04/07
AMD	DTI,ROI	0.998, 0.993	--	Outlook, downgrade	10/18	Unknown
ARM	TS[20],RS	0.994, 0.992	--	Loss, weak USA sales	11/14	12/06/07
ASHW	TS[5],DTI	1,1	++	Trend Reversal **)	11/19	11/30/07
CBG	TS[5],DTI	1,0.998	++	Shares buyback	11/23	12/03/07
CBM	TS[20],RS	1,0.999	--	Downgrade	11/05	12/06/07
CENT A	TS[5],TS[20], DTI	1,1,1	--+	Trend reversal **)	11/28	12/10/07
DITC	TS[20],A/D	1,0.997	--	Neg. earnings outlook	11/1	Unknown
DSL	TS[5],DTI	0.999,0.999	++	Investor stake revealed	11/19	12/03/07
ETFC	TS[20],ROI	1, 0.993	--	Subprime exposure	11/12	Unknown
FBTX	TS[20],TS[5]	1,1	--	Neg. analyst coverage, loss outlook	11/19	12/06/07
FINL	TS[5],DTI	0.994, 1	++	Speculation around lawsuit	11/26	12/10/07
FLE	TS[20], TS[5]	1, 0.995	--	Guidance, loss anticip.	11/1	12/07/07
FNM	TS[20], TS[5], DTI	1, 0.998, 0.998	-++	Gov. probe, losses, benign insider buying	10/06	12/06/07
FRE	TS[20], TS[5],DTI	0.999, 1,1	-++	Gov. probe, $2B losses, good capital plan	10/06	12/06/07
GCO	TS[20],DTI	0.996,1	-+	Lawsuit, insider buying	11/19	12/28/07
GVA	TS[5],DTI	0.99, 0.996	++	Business expansion	11/24	11/30/07
GVHR	TS[20],TS[5], RS,ROI	1, 0.999, 1, 0.999	----	Weak earnings, outlook	11/05	12/03/07
HANS	TS[20],RS	1,0.992	--	Negative earnings	11/08	12/03/07

Table 2: Continued.

ISRG	TS[20],TS[5]	0.995, 0.995	++	Pos. analyst coverage	11/27	12/07/07
LYV	TS[20],ROI	0.996, 0.998	--	Negative earnings	11/08	12/06/07
MDRX	TS[20],RS	1,1	--	Neg. earnings surprise	11/09	Unknown
MHO	TS[20], TS[5]	1,1	--	Housing slump	10/19	12/06/07
MTG	TS[20],TS[5], DTI volume	1,1,1	+++	Change of mortgage standards	11/28	12/10/07
NLS	TS[5],DTI	0.998, 0.994	++	Trend reversal **)	11/21	12/07/07
PENX	A/D,RS,DTI, ROI, volume	0.993, 0.998, 1, 0.995	----	Plans stock offering	11/28	12/03/07
PMTI	TS[20],RS	0.992, 1	--	Weak earnings	10/25	12/07/07
RAI	RS, A/D	0.99, 0.995	++	PR, Dividend	11/27	12/05/07
SAM	TS[20],RS	1,0.991	--	Negative earnings	11/06	12/05/07
SMRT	TS[5],ROI	0.994, 0.995	--	Downgrade, loss	11/22	Unknown
THC	TS[5],TS[20], DTI	1,1,1	+++	Business deal	11/27	12/10/07
URI	TS[20],RS	0.998, 0.994	--	Lawsuit	11/14	1/10/08?
VTIV	TS[20],RS	0.996, 0.997	--	Falls against positive earnings	11/07	12/06/07 ?

*) Apparent reasons: recent event(s) bound to cause the price/volume change.
**) Rebound from apparent support level in absence of major published news.

clear from the historical data. Trend reversals in ASHW, CENTA, NLS happen in absence of recent publicly available news, so the reversals, while technically valid, lack fundamental explanation as of this writing. VTIV is the most interesting of the four ambiguous rows. Despite positive earnings surprise on 11/7/2007 VTIV shares slid 25% over the next few days and stayed depressed until at least 12/17/2007. There were no public disclosures or sector events to explain the decline. The issue does not appear to be fully valued. This may point to a body of tightly kept investor knowledge defining the price. Overall in 11/30 example the ambiguity is limited to 11.5% of the "strong signal" issues surveyed, and it can be perhaps resolved by using better news sources or looking at subcritical values of other indicators.

Note that many of the patterns identified on 11/30/2007, especially the down trends, break down around the same date of 12/06/2007. This is due to market-wide "sucker rally" of 12/05 – 12/10, 2007 in course of which many issues were broadly bought, especially the oversold stocks of healthy companies. It is interesting to note also that the November/December strong signals reflect the key developements of the period such as iPhone craze, subprime mortgage crisis, restructuring in finance, rush of smart money into pharma and bio and, amusingly, the global warming.

6 Conclusion

In the context of daily price/volume data, the statistics that we have collected and analysed offers strong evidence that certain (log-transformed) technical indicators have strongly leptokurtic distributions across stock market of S & P 1500 size. When these same indicators are expected to be normally distributed under the time/breadth equivalence principle, the excess kurtosis of the actual empirical distributions can be used to measure the strength of outlying indicator values. Spot checks performed around randomly selected strong signal instances suggest significant correlation between the signals and recent business events. The scope of strong signals registered for an individual stock spanned across a sequence of consecutive days ("signal clustering") in approximately half of the cases thus suggesting some degree of signal autocorrelation.

7 Further directions

1) Technical indicators used in this research were derived from Relative Strength,s Accumulation/Distribution and Moving Average measures. It is important to investigate how other popular technical indicators can be applied for signal filtering and whether using additional indicators provides significant quality lift to the filtering. The key technical step for this is describing joint distributions of technical indicators under the random market hypothesis.

2) It is practically important to investigate whether the above results scale down to the level of hourly price/volume distributions and thus address the problem of measuring the strength of intraday signals.

3) For efficient validation of results in future it is necessary to develop automated news analysis agents in order to automate the search for correlation between strong signals and market news.

Acknowledgements

The Author wishes to thank Michael Trott for discussing theoretical statistical distributions of some indicators, Chris Meek for comments on the concept of this paper and John Bocharov for extensive editorial help.

References

[1] T. Bollerslev, R. J. Hodrick, Financial Market Efficiency Tests, NBER Working Papers 4108, National Bureau of Economic Research, Inc., 1992

[2] J. Knight, S. Satchell, Return Distributions in Finance, Reed, 2001
[3] C. Brooks, Introductory Econometrics for Finance, Biddels, UK, 2002
[4] M. Fischer, Skew Generalized Secant Hyperbolic Distribution: Unconditional and Conditional Fit to Asset Returns, Austrian Journal of Statistics, Volume 33, 2004, PP.293 – 304
[5] B. Mandelbrot, R. Hudson, Richard L., The (mis)Behaviour of Markets : a Fractal View of Risk, Ruin and Reward, London : Profile, 2004,
[6] R. Kitt, J. Kalda, "Leptokurtic Portfolio Theory", The European Physical Journal B, Volume 50, 2006, PP. 141 - 145
[7] J. Welles Wilder, New Concepts in Technical Trading Systems , TR, 1978
[8] M. Chaikin, unpublished, (see http://en.wikipedia.org/wiki/Accumulation_distribution)
[9] The constituent list of S&P Composite 1500 can be downloaded from the Strandard & Poor's web portal http://www.standardandpoors.com . (ANDW, CHZ, EDO, LYO were excluded from this analysis due to S&P 1500 rotations.)

Section 5
Risk management

Modeling spark spread option and power plant evaluation

Z. Li
Global Commodities, Bank of America, New York, USA

Abstract

Spark spread is an important feature in the electricity industry. The spark spread option pricing framework is presented in this paper. We start from a one-factor model and then provide a two-factor model. Closed form solution is derived. Numerical examples of spark spread option and power plant evaluation are studied. Because of the complexity of real-life constraints, we also use Monte-Carlo simulation in a more complicated example.
Keywords: spark spread, power plant evaluation, stochastic processes, hedging, real option.

1 Introduction

With the deregulation and liberalization of power markets in the last decade, electric markets have seen rapid changes. The power forward market is getting more and more liquid. The old cost-recovery pricing structure for electricity must adapt to market based pricing. A generator's choice can be summarized by the choice of transforming fuel into power or not. In another word, without real-life constraints, a plant can thus be thought of as a series of call options to exercise this gross profit margin, often referred to as spark spread: the difference between the prices at which power can be sold, minus the fuel costs for generating the power. The magnitude of the spark spread depends on the market prices for power and fuel as well as the heat rate, or the conversion efficiency factor of the plant:

- When the plant heat rate is lower than the market heat rate, then the unit should operate. The unit owner should buy fuel, produce power and sell to customers to take profit. The bigger the differences, the bigger the profit margin;

WIT Transactions on Information and Communication Technologies, Vol 41, © 2008 WIT Press
www.witpress.com, ISSN 1743-3517 (on-line)
doi:10.2495/CF080161

- When the plant heat rate is higher than the market heat rate, then the unit should be shut down. This makes economical sense.

The unique characteristics of electricity and electricity markets present new challenges to the risk-management discipline. The most important of these are the challenges of the non-storable nature of electricity and less liquidity in power market. Our focus in developing the pricing and hedging models is on capturing the relationship of each underlying commodity, volatility of each forward as well as correlations between them.

This paper is organized as followings: Section 2 introduces the model framework. Section 3 gives some numerical example, including a power plant evaluation. Section 4 has some comments on the model.

2 The model

The spark spread, in its simplest form, is defined as the difference between the electricity price and the cost of generation. The payoff of the spark spread option on date T_e is then defined as

$$V(T_e) = \max(\varepsilon(F_p(T_e, T_p) - H \cdot F_f(T_e, T_f) - K), 0) \tag{1}$$

where
$F_p(t, T)$: the price of a power future's contract at time t, for delivery at time T,
$F_f(t, T)$: the price of a fuel future's contract at time t, for delivery at time T,
T_e: Exercise date,
H: Heat rate,
K: Strike price,
ε: 1 for call and -1 for put.

Heat rate is the electricity generator's efficiency. It is defined as the number of British thermal units (BTUs) of the input fuel (measured in millions) required generating one-megawatt hour (MWH) of electricity.

2.1 One factor normal model

We first introduce one factor model. The spread is treated as one underline. In this case, we can use a normal model for the spread. The spark spread option is then

$$V(0) = P(0, T_e)(\varepsilon(F_p(0, T_p) - F_f(0, T_f) - K)\Phi(\phi d) - \sigma\sqrt{T_e}\phi(d)), \tag{2}$$

where

$$d = \frac{F_p(0, T_p) - F_f(0, T_f) - K}{\sigma\sqrt{T_e}},$$

and σ is the annualized volatility of the spark spread. $\Phi(x)$ is the cumulative distribution function for the standard Gaussian distribution. $\phi(x)$ is the probability density function for the standard Gaussian distribution.

This one factor normal model is useful when the power prices are quoted as heat rate, such as the case in ERCOT region. It is natural to assume that the spread is one underline.

2.2 Two-factor Log-normal model

Often we can only observe the power and fuel option market separately. So in this section we present a two-factor Log-normal model.

Consider a power future price $F(t, T)$. Assuming that we are in a probability space where information is generated by a vector-Brownian motion $W(t)$, the usual representation theorems imply that, under risk-neutral probability measure,

$$dF_p(t, T_p)/F_p(t, T_p) = \sigma_p(t, T_p)dW_p(t) \tag{3}$$

$$dF_f(t, T_f)/F_f(t, T_f) = \sigma_f(t, T_f)dW_f(t) \tag{4}$$

where $\sigma_p(t, T_p)$ and $\sigma_f(t, T_f)$ are local volatilities for $F_p(t, T_p)$ and $F_f(t, T_f)$ respectively and $dW_1(t)dW_2(t) = \rho dt$.

Hence the spark spread option value is

$$V(0, T) = P(0, T_e)(\varepsilon F_1 A_1 - \varepsilon F_2 A_2 - \varepsilon K A_3), \tag{5}$$

where

$$A_1 = \int_{-\infty}^{\infty} f(x)N(\varepsilon d_1(x))dx$$

$$A_2 = \int_{-\infty}^{\infty} f(x)N(\varepsilon d_2(x))dx$$

$$A_3 = \int_{-\infty}^{\infty} f(x)N(\varepsilon d_3(x))dx$$

$$f(x) = \frac{1}{\sqrt{2\pi}}e^{-x^2/2}$$

$$d_1(x) = \frac{\ln \frac{F_1}{F_2 \exp(x\sigma_2\sqrt{T_e} - \frac{1}{2}\sigma_2^2 T_e + \rho\sigma_1\sigma_2 T_e) + K} + \frac{1}{2}\sigma_1^2 T_e + \rho\sigma_1 x\sqrt{T_e}}{\sqrt{(1-\rho^2)\sigma_1^2 T_e}}$$

$$d_2(x) = \frac{\ln \frac{F_1}{F_2 \exp(x\sigma_2\sqrt{T_e} + \frac{1}{2}\sigma_2^2 T_e) + K} - \frac{1}{2}\sigma_1^2 T_e + \rho\sigma_1 x\sqrt{T_e} + \rho\sigma_1\sigma_2 T_e}{\sqrt{(1-\rho^2)\sigma_1^2 T_e}}$$

$$d_3(x) = \frac{\ln \frac{F_1}{F_2 \exp(x\sqrt{T_e}\sigma_2 - \frac{1}{2}\sigma_2^2 T_e) + K} - \frac{1}{2}\sigma_1^2 T_e + \rho\sigma_1 x\sqrt{T_e}}{\sqrt{(1-\rho^2)\sigma_1^2 T_e}}$$

$$F_1 = F_p(0, T_p)$$

$$F_2 = H \cdot F_f(0, T_f)$$

$$\sigma_1 = \frac{1}{T_e}\sqrt{\int_0^{T_e} \sigma_p(t, T_p)^2 dt}$$

$$\sigma_2 = \frac{1}{T_e}\sqrt{\int_0^{T_e} \sigma_f(t, T_f)^2 dt} \tag{6}$$

Since the solution is closed-form, the calculation is fast. The integral can be computed using the Gauss-Hermite quadrature method (see Press et al [2] for details).

Note $\sigma_i, i = 1, 2$ are the implied volatilities from time 0 until time T_e. In most situations the spark spread is for day ahead or real time, so the local volatilities are not critical. In the case that local volatilities structure is necessary, some other technique can be used.

As we know, a lot of new power generation use natural gas as fuel. The shape of power markets reflect this and they also display strong seasonality.

L. Anderson [1] provided an interesting two-factor mean reverting model for natural gas. Our model can easily expand with this model. We can also apply jump diffusion model to power market.

3 Numerical example

In this section, we give a few examples on the application of the spark spread option. The power curve is taken from PJM West region and natural gas is from Transco Zone 6 on the close of September 17th, 2007. The forward prices are from January 2008 until December 2010 and they are shown in Figure 1.

The average PJM West power prices is \$78.47 per MWH and the Transco Zone 6 gas prices is \$9.87 per MMBTU. So the market heat rate is 7950 MMBTU per KWH. Assuming a correlation of 85%, Figure 2 shows the premiums with different heat rate. In reality, the variable operation and maintenance costs are often non zero. Figure 2 also shows the premiums with different heat rate, giving a variable operation and maintenance (VOM) costs of \$2.5 per MHW.

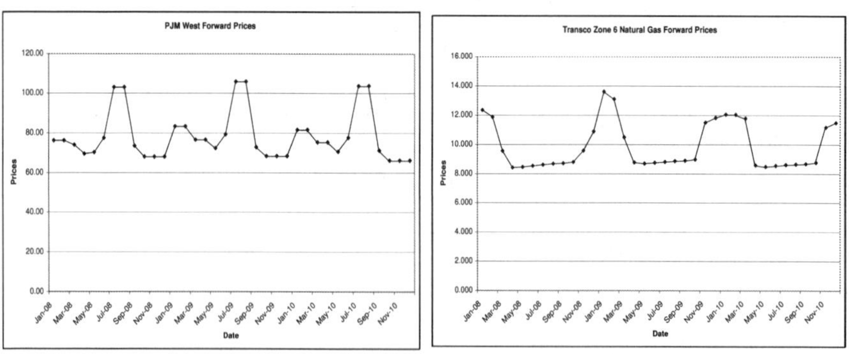

Figure 1: Power and natural gas forward curves.

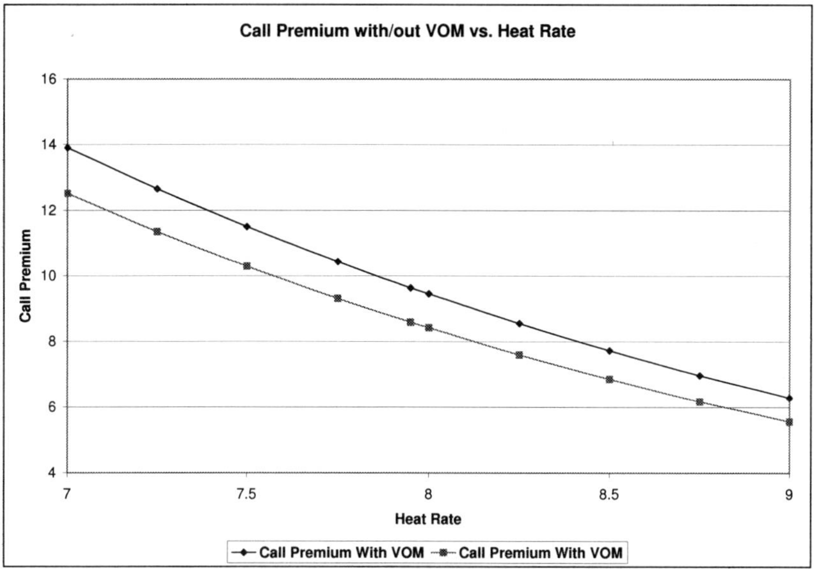

Figure 2: Call premium with/out VOM vs. heat rate.

Power plant evaluation is eventually to price a spark spread option. However, it is much more complicated. In most cases, you will see some or all of the following operation characteristics: minimum/maximum capacity, startup time, number of startups, minimum run time, startup costs, non-maintenance and variable operation maintenance, etc.

In order to properly price this kind of complicated option, we have to use Monte-Carlo simulation. Suppose the power and gas future follow equations (3) and (4), we build up a two-dimensional Monte-Carlo simulation. Here we just give an example on spark spread option with VOM and startup cost.

Assuming a heat rate of 8000 MMBTU per KWH and a VOM of \$2.5 per MHW, the call without start-up cost is flat and obviously has the highest premium. Figure 3 shows the premium with different start-up cost. For comparison, the flat premium without start-up cost is also shown in the figure.

4 Comments

Spark spread is the primary cross-commodity transaction in electricity markets. This spread is to gauge the benefits of generating electric power with natural gas, coal and oil versus buying power directly from the electricity grid. Among all the fuels, the spark spread between electricity and natural gas is the most common spread. Options on spark spread are probably the most important cross-commodity derivatives in the electricity market.

We set up a reasonable framework to price this kind of structure. The closed-form solutions are provided for the one and two-factor models. With the help of

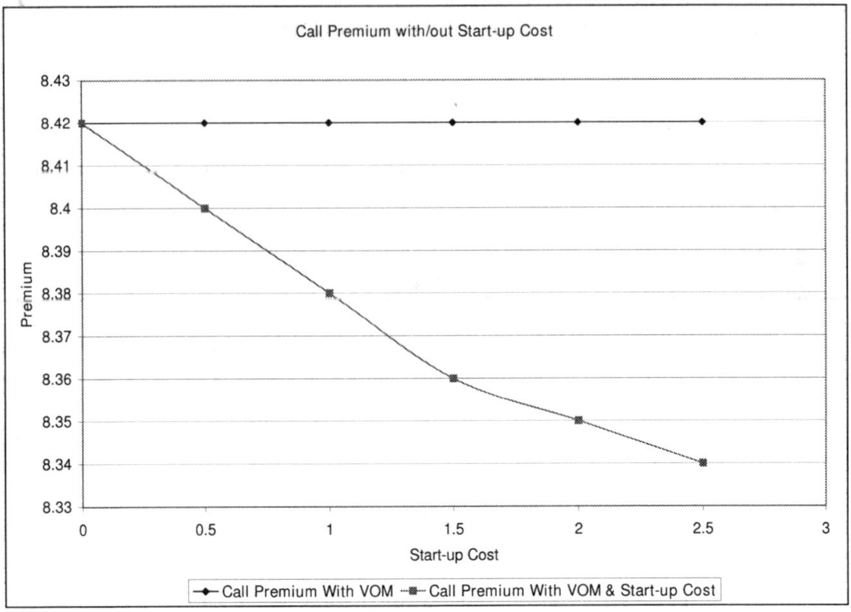

Figure 3: Call premium with/out start-up cost.

Monte-Carlo simulation, we can perform more complicated real life power plant evaluation.

There are some limitations of the models, in particular it does not incorporate "jumps" and seasonality explicitly, though volatility itself already includes this information. L. Anderson [1] provided an interesting direction to resolve these issues and his approach can be applied directly to our framework. Correlation between electricity and fuels are the input of the model, but it is hindered by the lack of market prices to calibrate them to. Our future modeling efforts will be focused in these directions. This is also dependent on the improvement of the market liquidity and more price observance.

Acknowledgement

I thank my colleagues at Global Commodities, Bank of America for their suggestions and many fruitful discussions during the course of this work.

References

[1] Andresen, L. (2007), "Notes on Gas Commodities", Bank of America internal notes.
[2] Press, H. et al. (1988), "Numerical Recipes in C", Cambridge University Press.

Computation and asymptotic properties of estimated coherent risk measures

D. J. Miller & M. Kim
Department of Economics, University of Missouri, USA

Abstract

Recent advances in mathematical finance established linkages among several key concepts related to coherence, distorted risk measures, and information theory. The purpose of this paper is to extend these theoretical results for empirical applications in computational finance. First, we use a concentrated (dual) entropy approach to derive a computational algorithm for estimating the parameters of a distorted probability model associated with a coherent risk measure for a given sample of observed data. Second, we derive the asymptotic sampling properties of the estimated model parameters, which may be used to conduct classical hypothesis tests or to form other statistical inferences based on the estimated coherent risk measure. Third, we note that researchers may also require an estimate of the net loss distribution, and we propose an information theoretic procedure for jointly estimating the net loss probability model and the distorted probability distribution associated with a particular coherent risk measure.
Keywords:coherence, distorted risk measure, entropy, extremum estimator, information theory.

1 Introduction

Risk measures based on the distribution of potential asset losses or returns are widely used in empirical finance, and prominent applications of these tools include determining insurance premia, option prices, margin deposits for hedged and speculative positions in futures markets, and capital reserve requirements for banks and other firms (e.g., see Wirch and Hardy [1]). To be specific, suppose an asset has risk or net loss represented by random variable X with cumulative distribution function (CDF) $F(x) = P(X \leq x)$. A risk measure is a mapping $\rho(X) : \mathbb{R} \rightarrow \mathbb{R}^+$

WIT Transactions on Information and Communication Technologies, Vol 41, © 2008 WIT Press
www.witpress.com, ISSN 1743-3517 (on-line)
doi:10.2495/CF080171

that represents the price or cost associated with holding the risky position. For example, the value–at–risk (VaR) with confidence level $1 - \alpha$ for an asset with a strictly continuous distribution is defined as

$$\rho_{VaR}(X) = F^{-1}(1 - \alpha) \tag{1}$$

In words, the VaR risk measure is the $100(1 - \alpha)\%$ quantile of the net loss distribution.

VaR is one of the most widely used risk measures because it is relatively easy to compute from estimates of the net loss distribution and is very convenient to interpret — the largest possible loss with lower tail probability $1-\alpha$. Although VaR is commonly used in practice, several authors have noted that this risk measure is flawed because it does not properly account for added risks. Artzner, *et al.* [2] define an improved class of risk measures under the following conditions on random variables X and Y in class $\mathcal{X}$:

A1 Monotonicity: if $F_X(z) \geq F_Y(z)$ for all $z \in \mathbb{R}$, then $\rho(X) \leq \rho(Y)$
A2 Positive homogeneity (of degree one): $\rho(\lambda X) = \lambda\rho(X)$ for all $\lambda \in \mathbb{R}^+$
A3 Linear invariance: $\rho(aX + b) = a\rho(X) + b$ for all $a, b \in \mathbb{R}$
A4 Subadditivity: $\rho(X + Y) \leq \rho(X) + \rho(Y)$

If these conditions are satisfied for all random variables X and Y in class $\mathcal{X}$, then the risk measure is said to be *coherent* over the class (Definition 7, Artzner, *et al.* [2]).

The limitations associated with value–at–risk arise because VaR does not satisfy the subadditivity property (A4) and is not coherent. Consequently, researchers in the mathematical finance literature have developed coherent risk measures that are designed to satisfy all four conditions (A1–A4) and should improve on VaR. For example, Artzner, *et al.* [2] propose the conditional tail expectation (CTE) or Tail–VaR risk measure with confidence level $1 - \alpha$ defined as

$$\rho_{CTE}(X) = \mathrm{E}[X \mid F(X) > 1 - \alpha] \tag{2}$$

For practical purposes, the CTE risk measure is based on roughly the same information required to compute VaR and should be relatively easy to use. However, VaR remains to be widely used in practice, and researchers in this field have worked to develop other coherent risk measures that are suitable for particular applications.

2 Coherence, distortion, and entropy

The conceptual challenges associated with deriving coherent risk measures have been eased by recent research outcomes that link coherence to other established concepts and methods in the fields of mathematical finance and statistical information theory. The key contributions in the recent literature are provided by McLeish and Reesor [7], who show that

- Distorted risk measures based on distortions or transformations of the net loss distribution are closely related to coherent risk measures

- Distorted risk measures may be derived from the net loss distribution under an information theoretic (entropy) optimization approach

Thus, we can use the information theoretic approach outlined by McLeish and Reesor [7] to derive coherent risk measures.

Following Definition 4 presented by McLeish and Reesor [7], a *distortion function* g is a right–continuous and non–decreasing function on the unit interval $[0, 1]$ with the end–point properties $g(0) = 0$ and $g(1) = 1$. Given g, the associated distorted cumulative distribution function F^* based on the original CDF for a net loss variable (F) may be formed as

$$F^*(x) = 1 - g(S(x)) \tag{3}$$

where $S(X) \equiv 1 - F(X)$. The distorted probability density function is

$$f^*(x) = f(x)g'(S(x)) \tag{4}$$

where $g'(z) = dg(z)/dz$. Finally, following Definition 6 in McLeish and Reesor [7], we can form a *distorted risk measure* as

$$\rho_g(X) = \int_0^\infty g(S(x))dx + \int_{-\infty}^0 (g(S(x)) - 1)dx = E_{F^*}(X) \tag{5}$$

where the expected value of X is computed as a Choquet integral with respect to the distorted probability distribution. Choquet integrals may be used to represent non–additive probability measures but reduce to the common Lebesgue integral under additive measures (see Denneberg [4] and Groes, et al. [13] for more details).

Distorted probability models and risk measures have been used by a large number of researchers in empirical finance, especially in insurance pricing problems (for example, see Wang [8] and Wirch and Hardy [14]). For purposes of this paper, the key property of distorted risk measures is provided by Theorem 5 in McLeish and Reesor [7], which claims that the following statements are equivalent:

- The distortion function g is concave.
- The distorted risk measure ρ_g is coherent over the class of all random variables.

Thus, we can use the distortion approach to derive coherent risk measures as long as the distortion function is concave.

McLeish and Reesor [7] also propose an information theoretic approach to derive distorted probability models, and their approach is based on the classical maximum entropy and minimum cross–entropy procedures that Jaynes [9, 10] originally developed for discrete probability distributions. The minimum cross–entropy method may also be extended for use with continuous probability distributions, and the details are outlined in Appendix 3. A of the book by Golan, et al. [5]). In either case, the basic purpose of the method is to recover a probability distribution that satisfies some moment conditions (e.g., mean, variance). In general, a probability distribution cannot be uniquely characterized by a finite number of moments, so there are multiple candidate distributions for any particular problem. Accordingly, Jaynes recommends choosing the distribution that satisfies these conditions and is closest to some target or reference distribution, and the "closeness" of the distributions is measured with the Kullback–Leibler cross–entropy functional (see Kullback [6]). One of the key contributions provided by McLeish and Reesor [7] is the set of moment conditions, $\mathrm{E}[G_k(S(x))] = \mu_k$, required to derive five of the most commonly used distorted probability models by the minimum cross–entropy method (see their Table 1).

Specifically, the information theoretic approach for deriving the distorted probability model is to minimize the cross–entropy objective function

$$I(f^*, f) = \int \ln\left(\frac{f^*(x)}{f(x)}\right) f^*(x)dx \tag{6}$$

subject to the known constraints

$$\int G_k(S(x)) f^*(x)dx = \mu_k \quad \text{and} \quad \int f^*(x)dx = 1 \tag{7}$$

McLeish and Reesor [7] note that the entropy problem may be solved for f^* by the method of Lagrange multipliers (i.e., calculus of variations), and the Lagrange equation is

$$\mathcal{L}(f^*, \boldsymbol{\lambda}) = I(f^*, f) + \sum_{k=1}^{K} \lambda_k \left[\mu_k - \int G_k(S(x)) f^*(x)dx\right] + \gamma\left[1 - \int f^*(x)dx\right] \tag{8}$$

where $\boldsymbol{\lambda} = (\lambda_1, \ldots, \lambda_K)'$, λ_k is the Lagrange multiplier for the kth moment constraint, and γ is the Lagrange multiplier on the additivity constraint in (7). Although McLeish and Reesor [7] do not provide the minimum cross–entropy solution for the distorted probability model

$$f^*(x) = \frac{f(x)\exp(\sum_{k=1}^{K} \lambda_k G_k(S(x)))}{\int f(x)\exp(\sum_{k=1}^{K} \lambda_k G_k(S(x)))dx} \tag{9}$$

we can use this expression to derive

$$g'(S(x)) = \frac{f^*(x)}{f(x)} = \frac{\exp(\sum_{k=1}^{K} \lambda_k G_k(S(x)))}{\int f(x)\exp(\sum_{k=1}^{K} \lambda_k G_k(S(x)))dx} \tag{10}$$

By integrating (10), we can derive the implicit solution for the distortion function provided by McLeish and Reesor [7] in their Equation (10)

$$g(S(x)) = \int_0^{S(x)} \exp\left(\sum_{k=1}^{K} \lambda_k G_k(S(z)) - \psi(\boldsymbol{\lambda})\right)dz \tag{11}$$

where $\psi(\boldsymbol{\lambda}) \equiv \ln(\int f(x)\exp(\sum_{k=1}^{K} \lambda_k G_k(S(x)))dx)$ is the natural log of the normalizing constant from (9). Finally, McLeish and Reesor [7] present their

Theorem 4, which claims that the distortion function is concave if and only if

$$\sum_{k=1}^{K} \lambda_k G_k(S(z)) \tag{12}$$

is non–increasing in z. Under this condition, a distorted risk measure derived by the information theoretic approach will also be a coherent risk measure. The relationship between the concavity of the distortion function g and coherence (especially subadditivity) is also examined by Wang and Dhaene [11] and by Wirch and Hardy [14].

3 Concentrated entropy approach to computation

The theoretical developments outlined in the preceding sections have greatly expanded the conceptual range of risk measures available to researchers in mathematical finance. However, much of this effort has been focused on the analytical properties of these tools, and researchers in empirical finance need information about the computational and statistical properties of these tools in order to apply them in practice. In this section, we outline a computational algorithm based on a natural extension of the information theoretic approach developed by McLeish and Reesor [7], and we use this approach to derive the asymptotic sampling properties of the estimated risk measures in the following section.

To begin, suppose we have the sample moments for a given minimum cross–entropy estimation problem, and we denote these sample estimates as $\widehat{\mu}_1, \ldots, \widehat{\mu}_K$. The key computational challenge to forming an empirical version of the distortion function in Equation (8) is to derive the optimal value of the Lagrange multipliers, $\widehat{\lambda}_1, \ldots, \widehat{\lambda}_K$. Although it may be feasible to solve the problem in primal form as stated in Equations (6) and (7), the number of software packages that can solve such constrained numerical optimization problems is quite limited. Fortunately, we can convert this estimation problem to an unconstrained maximization problem that can be solved by a much wider range of numerical optimization software.

The key step is to form a concentrated or dual optimization problem by substituting the implicit solution for the distorted density function (9) back into the Lagrange expression for the primal version of the problem, (8). After simplifying terms, the concentrated Lagrange equation is

$$\mathcal{M}(\boldsymbol{\lambda}) = \sum_{k=1}^{K} \lambda_k \widehat{\mu}_k - \ln\left[\int f(x) \exp\left(\sum_{k=1}^{K} \lambda_k G_k(S(x))\right) dx\right] \tag{13}$$

which is a function of the K-vector of Lagrange multipliers. If the minimum cross–entropy problem has a unique interior solution, we can use the saddle–point properties of the Lagrange equation to show that the concentrated objective function $\mathcal{M}$ is a strictly concave function of $\boldsymbol{\lambda}$ such that

$$\mathcal{M}(\hat{\boldsymbol{\lambda}}) > \mathcal{M}(\boldsymbol{\lambda}) \tag{14}$$

for all $\boldsymbol{\lambda} \neq \hat{\boldsymbol{\lambda}}$. Thus, we can compute the optimal values of the Lagrange multipliers by maximizing $\mathcal{M}$ with respect to $\boldsymbol{\lambda}$ without constraints. Further, we note that the gradient of $\mathcal{M}$

$$\frac{\partial \mathcal{M}}{\partial \lambda_k} = \widehat{\mu}_k - \int G_k(S(x)) f^*(x) dx \quad \text{for } k = 1, \ldots, K \tag{15}$$

is simply the set of moment conditions for the primal minimum cross–entropy problem from (7), and this gradient information may be used to compute the Lagrange multipliers under the Newton–Raphson or related numerical optimization algorithms. For example, the maximum entropy algorithm proposed by Ormoneit and White [12] may be extended to the minimum cross–entropy version of the estimation problem.

4 Asymptotic properties of the model parameter estimator

Although the authors in the preceding literature do not focus on the interpretation of the Lagrange multipliers, these values represent the marginal change in distortion (uncertainty) between the distorted distribution (F^*) and the reference distribution (F) given a small increase in the associated moment values. In empirical research, the estimated values of the Lagrange multipliers may be very useful for model diagnostic and specification purposes. For example, we may wish to test the statistical significance of one or more of the moment conditions in a candidate probability model, and a model specification test for the jth moment may be conducted under the null hypothesis $H_0 : \lambda_j = 0$.

To begin, we assume the K-vector of sample moments $\hat{\boldsymbol{\mu}} = (\widehat{\mu}_1, \ldots, \widehat{\mu}_K)'$ imposed in the minimum cross–entropy problem (i.e., in the first constraint in (7)) are based on samples of size n and are

- Consistent such that $\hat{\boldsymbol{\mu}} \xrightarrow{p} \hat{\mu}_0$ as $n \to \infty$ where $\hat{\mu}_0$ is the set of true population moments under the distorted probability measure
- Asymptotically normal such that $\sqrt{n}(\hat{\boldsymbol{\mu}} - \hat{\mu}_0) \xrightarrow{d} N(\mathbf{0}, \boldsymbol{\Omega})$ as $n \to \infty$

Following the results on extremum estimation presented in Theorems 2.7 and 3.1 by Newey and McFadden [3], we can show that the K–vector of Lagrange multipliers $\hat{\boldsymbol{\lambda}}$ is consistent such that $\hat{\boldsymbol{\lambda}} \xrightarrow{p} \boldsymbol{\lambda}_0$ as $n \to \infty$ where $\boldsymbol{\lambda}_0$ is the set of true Lagrange multipliers under the distorted probability model. We can also derive the limiting normal distribution of the Lagrange multiplier estimators as

$$\sqrt{n}(\hat{\boldsymbol{\lambda}} - \boldsymbol{\lambda}_0) \xrightarrow{d} N(\mathbf{0}, \boldsymbol{\psi}^{-1}\boldsymbol{\Omega}\boldsymbol{\psi}^{-1}) \tag{16}$$

where

$$\boldsymbol{\psi} = \mathrm{E}\left[\frac{\partial^2 \mathcal{M}}{\partial \boldsymbol{\lambda} \partial \boldsymbol{\lambda}'}\bigg|_{\boldsymbol{\lambda}=\boldsymbol{\lambda}_0}\right] = -\mathrm{E}_{F^*}[(\mathbf{G}(S(X)) - \hat{\mu})(\mathbf{G}(S(X)) - \hat{\mu})'] \tag{17}$$

is the negative variance matrix of $\mathbf{G}(S(X)) = (G_1(S(X)), \ldots, G_K(S(X)))'$ under the distorted probability model F^*.

To estimate the asymptotic variance matrix of $\hat{\boldsymbol{\lambda}}$, we could directly evaluate the elements of $\boldsymbol{\psi}$

$$\widehat{\Psi}_{kk} = -\int (G_k(S(x)) - \widehat{\mu}_k)^2 f^*(x)dx \tag{18}$$

$$\widehat{\Psi}_{jk} = -\int (G_j(S(x)) - \widehat{\mu}_j)(G_k(S(x)) - \widehat{\mu}_k) f^*(x)dx \tag{19}$$

by numerical integration under the distorted distribution f^*. Alternatively, we can rely on the special structure of the distorted density function f^* to estimate $\boldsymbol{\psi}$ by importance sampling from the reference distribution f. Given m random draws from f (denoted $x_1, \ldots, x_m$), we can form the variance estimates as

$$\widehat{\widehat{\Psi}}_{kk} = -m^{-1} \sum_{i=1}^{m} (G_k(S(x_i)) - \widehat{\mu}_k)^2 w_i \tag{20}$$

$$\widehat{\widehat{\Psi}}_{jk} = -m^{-1} \sum_{i=1}^{m} (G_j(S(x)) - \widehat{\mu}_j)(G_k(S(x)) - \widehat{\mu}_k) w_i \tag{21}$$

where

$$w_i \equiv \frac{\exp(\sum_{k=1}^{K} \widehat{\lambda}_k G_k(S(x_i)))}{m^{-1} \sum_{i=1}^{m} \exp(\sum_{k=1}^{K} \widehat{\lambda}_k G_k(S(x_i)))} \tag{22}$$

Under random sampling from f, the simulated variance components in (20) and (21) converge in probability to the estimates in (18) and (19) as $m \to \infty$.

We can also use importance sampling to estimate the coherent risk measure ρ_g for a particular data set. Although we could substitute (11) into (5) and use direct numerical integration to compute $\widehat{\rho}_g(X)$, the importance sampling estimator

$$\widehat{\rho}_g(X) = m^{-1} \sum_{i=1}^{m} x_i w_i \tag{23}$$

is consistent under random sampling from f as $m \to \infty$. For example, suppose we have a net loss variable X that is distributed as a standard lognormal random variable with mean 1.649 and variance 4.671. The VaR with $\alpha = 0.05$ from (1) is $\rho_{VaR} = 5.18$, and the CTE at the same level of significance from (2) is $\rho_{CTE} = 8.55$. Using these actual values as benchmarks, we can evaluate the performance of the importance sampling estimators of VaR and CTE based on $m = 5,000$ replications and various sample sizes (n). The simulation results are presented in Table 1, and the sample bias and estimated standard errors decline as n increases, as expected.

5 Joint estimation of the reference and distorted models

In practice, we may also have limited information about an appropriate specification of the reference distribution f for the net loss outcomes. In this section,

Table 1: Importance sampling results, VaR and CTE.

Sample size n	$\widehat{\rho}_{VaR}$	Std. error	$\widehat{\rho}_{CTE}$	Std. error
250	5.0020	0.6529	8.3020	1.5030
500	5.1518	0.4792	8.5591	1.1368
1000	5.1673	0.3411	8.5339	0.7936
2500	5.1740	0.2209	8.5520	0.5087

we show how the minimum cross–entropy approach may be extended to jointly estimate f and f^* from available data. In this case, we assume that we have a reference distribution $q(x)$ that represents our initial (pre–sample) estimate of f, and we use some sample moments related to the original data distribution (F) to update this estimate and form f. In particular, we can minimize the cross–entropy between f^* and q under the following Kullback–Leibler objective function

$$I(f^*, q) = \int \ln\left(\frac{f^*(x)}{q(x)}\right) f^*(x)dx \tag{24}$$

subject to an expanded set of moment conditions

$$\int G_k(S(x)) f^*(x)dx = \mu_k \quad \text{and} \quad \int H_j(x) f^*(x)dx = \theta_j \tag{25}$$

for $k = 1, \ldots, K$ and $j = 1, \ldots, L$ plus the additivity constraint in (7). Here, we use L additional moment conditions of the form $\mathrm{E}_{F^*}[H_j(x)] = \theta_j$ to describe the properties of f and f^*.

Following the discussion in Section 2, we can show that the minimum cross–entropy solution for the distorted probability model is

$$f^*(x) = \frac{q(x)\exp(\sum_{j=1}^{L} \delta_j H_j(x) + \sum_{k=1}^{K} \lambda_k G_k(S(x)))}{\int q(x)\exp(\sum_{j=1}^{L} \delta_j H_j(x) + \sum_{k=1}^{K} \lambda_k G_k(S(x)))dx} \tag{26}$$

where δ_j is the Lagrange multiplier for the jth moment constraint imposed on f^* in (25). The implicit form for the reference distribution is

$$f(x) = \frac{q(x)\exp(\sum_{j=1}^{L} \delta_j H_j(x))}{\int q(x)\exp(\sum_{j=1}^{L} \delta_j H_j(x))dx} \tag{27}$$

and the derivative of the distortion function is

$$g'(S(x)) = \frac{\exp(\sum_{k=1}^{K} \lambda_k G_k(S(x))) \int q(x)\exp(\sum_{j=1}^{L} \delta_j H_j(x))dx}{\int q(x)\exp(\sum_{j=1}^{L} \delta_j H_j(x) + \sum_{k=1}^{K} \lambda_k G_k(S(x)))dx} \tag{28}$$

such that $f^*(x)/f(x) = g'(S(x))$. Finally, the distortion function g may be recovered from (28) by integration as in (11).

To derive the large–sample properties of the model parameter estimators, we let $\boldsymbol{\beta} = (\delta_1, \ldots, \delta_L, \lambda_1, \ldots, \lambda_K)'$ and $\boldsymbol{k} = (\theta_1, \ldots, \theta_L, \mu_1, \ldots, \mu_K)'$, and we then assume that $\hat{\boldsymbol{k}} \xrightarrow{p} \boldsymbol{k}_0$ and

$$\sqrt{n}(\hat{\boldsymbol{k}} - \boldsymbol{k}_0) \xrightarrow{d} N(\mathbf{0}, \boldsymbol{\Phi}) \tag{29}$$

as $n \to \infty$. The results for extremum estimators provided by Newey and McFadden [3] may be used to show that the vector of Lagrange multiplier estimators is consistent such that $\hat{\boldsymbol{\beta}} \xrightarrow{p} \boldsymbol{\beta}_0$ as $n \to \infty$, and the limiting distribution of the estimators is

$$\sqrt{n}(\hat{\boldsymbol{\beta}} - \boldsymbol{\beta}_0) \xrightarrow{d} N(\mathbf{0}, \boldsymbol{\Gamma}^{-1}\boldsymbol{\Phi}\boldsymbol{\Gamma}^{-1}) \tag{30}$$

where

$$\boldsymbol{\Gamma} = -\mathrm{E}_{F^*}[(\mathbf{A}(X) - \boldsymbol{k})(\mathbf{A}(X) - \boldsymbol{k})'] \tag{31}$$

and $\mathbf{A} = (H_1(X), \ldots, H_L(X), G_1(S(X)), \ldots, G_K(S(X)))'$. As we show in the preceding section, we can use importance sampling or other convenient numerical integration tools to estimate the components of the asymptotic variance matrix for $\hat{\boldsymbol{\beta}}$. Then, we can use the estimated asymptotic variance matrix to conduct classical hypothesis tests or form other inferences related to the fitted probability model and estimates of the coherent risk measure.

6 Conclusions

In summary, the proposed methods allow us to apply the recent theory related to coherence, distorted risk measures, and information theory to problems in empirical finance. The key innovations in this paper include an unconstrained computation algorithm and the statistical properties of the coherent risk estimators, and we use a few brief but familiar examples to demonstrate these claims.

References

[1] Wirch, J. and Hardy, M., A synthesis of risk measures for capital adequacy. *Insurance: Mathematics and Economics*, **25**, pp. 337–47, 1999.

[2] Artzner, P., Delbaen, F., Eber, J.M. and Heath, D., Coherent measures of risk. *Mathematical Finance*, **3**, pp. 203–28, 1999.

[3] Newey, W. and McFadden, D., Large sample estimation and hypothesis testing (Chapter 36). *Handbook of Econometrics, Volume IV*, eds. R. Engle and D. McFadden, Elsevier Science: New York, pp. 2111–2245, 1994.

[4] Denneberg, D., *Non–Additive Measure and Integral*. Kluwer Academic Publishers: Dordrecht, the Netherlands, 1994.

[5] Golan, A., Judge, G. and Miller, D., *Maximum Entropy Econometrics: Robust Estimation with Limited Data*. John Wiley and Sons: Chichester, UK, 1996.

[6] Kullback, S., *Information Theory and Statistics*. John Wiley and Sons: New York, 1959.

[7] McLeish, D. and Reesor, R.M., Risk, entropy, and the transformation of distributions. *North American Actuarial Journal*, **7**, pp. 128–44, 2003.
[8] Wang, S., A class of distortion operators for pricing financial and insurance risks. *The Journal of Risk and Insurance*, **67**, pp. 15–36, 2000.
[9] Jaynes, E.T., Information theory and statistical mechanics, I. *Physical Review*, **106**, pp. 620–30, 1957.
[10] Jaynes, E.T., Information theory and statistical mechanics, II. *Physical Review*, **108**, pp. 171–90, 1957.
[11] Wang, S. and Dhaene, J., Comonotonicity, correlation order, and premium principles. *Insurance: Mathematics and Economics*, **22**, pp. 235–42, 1998.
[12] Ormoneit, D. and White, H., An efficient algorithm to compute maximum entropy densities. *Econometric Reviews*, **18**, pp. 127–40, 1999.
[13] Groes, E., Jacobsen, H., Sloth, B. and Traneas, T., Axiomatic characterizations of the Choquet integral. *Economic Theory*, **12**, pp. 441–48, 1998.
[14] Wirch, J. and Hardy, M., Distortion risk measures: Coherence and stochastic dominance, 2000. working paper, Heriot–Watt University.

An empirical investigation of the short-term relationship between interest rate risk and credit risk

C. Cech
University of Applied Science of BFI, Vienna, Austria

Abstract

Empirical results from several studies indicate that changes in interest rates and changes in credit spreads are negatively related in the short run. These findings are further investigated by examining the dependence structure between interest rate and credit risk factor changes that are computed from sovereign and corporate bond indices. Several copulas (Gaussian, Student t, BB1, and Frank copula) are calibrated and their goodness-of-fit is compared. No clear pattern of the dependence structure can be observed as it varies substantially with the duration and – concerning the credit risk factor changes – the rating of the obligors. The Student t copula's fit in terms of the AIC goodness-of-fit measure is superior to that of all other copulas. The null hypothesis of a specific copula being the true copula can be rejected for the Student t copula in the least cases. Additionally employing a likelihood-ratio test, the null hypothesis of a Gaussian copula can be rejected in favour of a Student t copula. The Gaussian copula seems to underestimate the probability of joint strong risk factor changes, while the Student t copula seems to overestimate it.

Keywords: copula, dependence, short-term, interest rate risk, credit risk, risk measurement.

1 Introduction

Credit spreads, the difference in yield between corporate and government bonds of similar maturity, reflect the credit risk associated with corporate bonds. The dependence of interest rate risk, i.e. the risk associated with changes of the interest rate term structure, and credit risk, i.e. the risk associated with rating-migrations or defaults of obligors, is an interesting topic to explore in the context

WIT Transactions on Information and Communication Technologies, Vol 41, © 2008 WIT Press
www.witpress.com, ISSN 1743-3517 (on-line)
doi:10.2495/CF080181

of risk measurement, as it enables an improvement of the risk aggregation process.

Several empirical studies report that short-term *changes* in the level of interest rates are negatively related with *changes* of credit spreads: when interest rates rise, credit spreads tend to narrow and vice versa (Longstaff and Schwartz [10], Duffee [5], Neal et al. [12], Collin-Dufresne et al. [3], and Papageorgiou and Skinner [13] find a negative relationship for monthly changes, Leake [9] and Pape and Schlecker [14] for weekly changes and Leake [9] and Wagner et al. [18] for daily changes. However, Neal et al. [12] report a positive relationship for a long-term horizon (36 months) which is not supported by the theoretical literature) This is sometimes interpreted as a high level of interest rates being related to a low level of credit spreads. Such a relationship is in accordance with the widely used structural credit risk models based on the contingent claim approach by Merton [11] if one assumes that an increase in interest rates does not trigger a drop in the obligors' asset values. It is also consistent with business cycle developments, where in times of contraction the interest rates and the credit quality tend to decrease jointly, while in times of expansions they tend to increase jointly. This is associated with central banks' cyclical adaptation of the interest rates.

This paper focuses on the explicit dependence structure, or copula, for one-day interest rate and credit risk factor changes that are computed from sovereign and corporate bond indices. Copulas are rather a new instrument in risk management that have attracted a lot of attention recently. One advantage of copula-based approaches is that they allow for a separate modelling or calibration of the marginal distributions and the dependence structure (the copula). Copulas allow to combine arbitrary marginal distributions to a joint distribution.

The paper is structured as follows. Section 1 explains the computation of the risk factors. Section 2 gives a short introduction to copula-based approaches and section 3 contains the empirical investigation.

2 Data and computation of the risk factors

The data base includes daily sovereign and corporate bond indices from the iboxx € index family for Euro-denominated fixed-coupon bonds for the period from January 31st, 2000 to September 15th, 2006. For both sovereign and corporate bond indices, subindices with specific maturity bands are considered. These maturity bands are: (i) all maturities, (ii) 1Y to 3Y maturities, (iii) 3Y to 5Y maturities, (iv) 5Y to 7Y maturities, and (v) 7Y to 10Y maturities.

The corporate bond indices' constituents are further grouped according to their ratings. These ratings are: (i) all ratings, (ii) AAA-rated, (iii) AA-rated, (iv) A-rated, and (v) BBB-rated.

We are interested in the dependence structure of joint risk factor changes, specifically of joint interest rate and credit risk factor changes. We define the interest rate risk factor changes at day t as the log-returns of the sovereign bond indices, $i_{j,t}$, with maturity bands j

$$i_{j,t} = \ln P_{sov,j,t} - \ln P_{sov,j,t-1} \qquad \forall j \in \{1,\ldots,5\}\,. \tag{1}$$

If there is an upward shift in the yield curve, we will observe negative interest rate risk factor changes, while the contrary holds for a downward shift of the yield curve. The credit risk factor changes at day t, $c_{j,k,t}$, are defined as the excess returns of corporate bonds over sovereign bonds for a given maturity band and a given rating

$$c_{j,k,t} = \ln P_{j,k,t} - \ln P_{j,k,t-1} - i_{j,t} \qquad \forall j \in \{1,\ldots,5\},\ k \in \{1,\ldots,5\}\,. \tag{2}$$

The corporate bond indices' log-returns are adjusted by subtracting the sovereign bond indices' log-returns such that the resulting risk factor changes $c_{j,k,t}$ only display the change in the value of the corporate bond indices that is due to a change in the credit quality of the constituents, assuming a similar composition of the sovereign and corporate bond indices with identical maturity band concerning duration, and assuming a constant risk-appetite of the market participants and constant premia for the corporate bonds' liquidity risk.

From these riskless returns and excess returns, we construct data pairs that consist of $(i_{j,t}, c_{j,k,t})$ for maturity bands j and rating classes k, resulting in 25 bivariate empirical sample pairs.

A closer look at the risk factor changes shows that they all are non-Gaussian. Using a Jarque-Bera test (Jarque and Bera [8]), the null hypothesis of normally distributed marginal distributions can be rejected at the 1% significance level in all cases (in fact they can be rejected even at the 0.012% significance level). Hence, a copula-based approach clearly seems preferable to the assumption of a multivariate Gaussian distribution for the data sample at hand.

For many of the risk factor changes, autocorrelation is detected. To adjust the data for autocorrelation, an AR(2)-model is fitted where the observed risk factor changes are modelled as

$$r_t = \beta_1 + \beta_2 r_{t-1} + \beta_3 r_{t-2} + \varepsilon_t \tag{3}$$

where r_t is either $i_{j,t}$ or $c_{j,k,t}$. The coefficients and their statistical significance are estimated using the standard OLS-estimates of a classical normal linear regression.(generally, in the context of estimating AR models, alternative estimation methods are preferred to the OLS-method, as the estimated standard errors of the coefficients are downward biased. However, the estimates of the coefficients are consistent and the bias reduces as the sample size increases) If the estimates of either β_2 or β_3 turn out not to be statistically significantly different from 0 at the 5% significance level, models of the type $r_t = \beta_1 + \beta_2 r_{t-1} + \varepsilon_t$ and $r_t = \beta_1 + \beta_3 r_{t-2} + \varepsilon_t$, respectively are estimated. If both β_2 and β_3 turn out not to be statistically significantly different from 0, $r_t = \beta_1 + \varepsilon_t$ is modelled, where $\hat{\beta}_1 \equiv \bar{r}$. For 21 out of the 25 credit risk factor changes, AR(2) models are fitted. For only one of the interest rate risk factor changes, autocorrelation is detected. Here, an AR(1)-model is fitted.

Being interested only in the innovations that cannot be explained by lagged values of the observed returns, the autoregressions' residuals are used as the empirical return observations in what follows. (A part of the empirical analysis was also conducted for the unadjusted data. The results do not differ strongly from the results obtained from the autocorrelation-adjusted observations.) The 25 autocorrelation-adjusted data pairs include 1,727 observations each.

3 Copulas

This paper focuses on the investigation of the goodness-of-fit of selected copulas. The term copula was introduced by Sklar [17] in 1959 (a similar concept for modelling dependence structures of joint distributions was independently proposed by Höffding [7] some twenty years earlier).

Copulas are functions that combine or couple (univariate) marginal distributions to a multivariate joint distribution. Sklar's theorem (using a slightly different notation in the original article) states that a n-dimensional joint distribution function $F(x)$ evaluated at $\mathbf{x} = (x_1, x_2, \ldots, x_n)$ may be expressed in terms of the joint distribution's copula C and its marginal distributions $F_1, F_2, \ldots, F_n$ as

$$F(\mathbf{x}) = C(F_1(x_1), F_2(x_2), \ldots, F_n(x_n)), \qquad \mathbf{x} \in \mathbf{R}^n. \tag{4}$$

The copula function C is itself a multivariate distribution with uniform marginal distributions on the interval $\mathbf{U}_1 = [0,1], C : \mathbf{U}_1^n \to \mathbf{U}_1$.

As far as the calibration of joint distribution functions from empirical data is concerned, copula-based approaches allow for a separate modelling of (i) the marginal distributions (in the present case the univariate distributions of the interest and credit risk factor changes) and (ii) the dependence structure (the copula).

We shall restrict our empirical investigation to some selected copulas from the family of elliptical and Archimedean copulas. These are: the Gaussian and Student t copula (elliptical copulas), the BB1 copula and its two special cases, the Clayton and the Gumbel copula, and the Frank copula (Archimedean copulas). Arbitrary marginal distributions that are combined by a copula to joint distributions are referred to as meta-distributions (meta-Gauss, meta-Student t, meta-BB1, etc.).

The above-mentioned copulas assign different probabilities to joint extreme observations. For example, a Student t copula assigns a higher probability to joint extreme observations than does a Gaussian copula. This is referred to as *positive tail dependence*.(formally, lower and upper tail dependence are defined as $\lambda_L = \lim_{\alpha \to 0} P(u_1 \leq \alpha \mid u_2 \leq \alpha)$ and $\lambda_U = \lim_{\alpha \to 1} P(u_1 > \alpha \mid u_2 > \alpha)$. Positive tail dependence is prevalent if λ_L and/or λ_U is positive) Some copulas assign different probabilities to joint extreme positive deviations from the median than to joint extreme negative deviations (*asymmetric tail dependence*).

Figure 1 displays contour plots of bivariate meta-Student t, meta-Clayton, meta-Gumbel, and meta-Frank distributions with standard normal marginal distributions with a Spearman's rho of 0.4 (top row) and 0.8 (bottom row). Additionally, for reasons of comparison, contours of a Gaussian distribution with identical marginal distributions and identical correlation are displayed. It can be seen that the Student t copula assigns a higher probability to joint extreme co-movements than does the Gaussian copula. Also the symmetric nature of the tail dependence can be identified visually. The Clayton copula's lower tail dependence and the Gumbel copula's upper tail dependence can also be identified well. The Clayton copula's lower tail dependence exceeds the Gumbel copula's upper tail dependence. The Frank copula assigns a lower probability to joint extreme co-movements than a Gaussian copula.

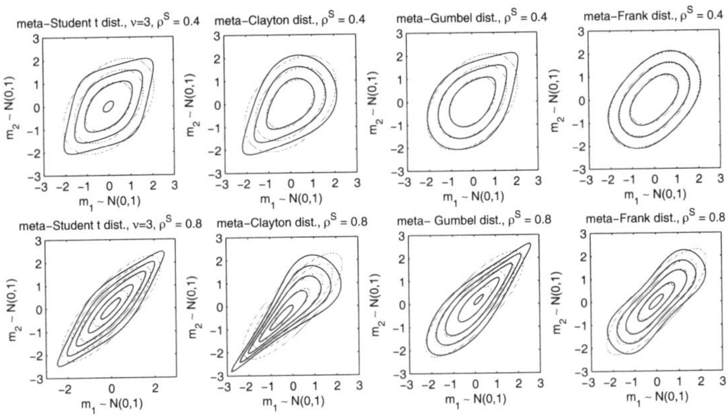

Figure 1: Contour plots of bivariate meta-Student t (parameter $\nu = 3$), meta-Clayton, meta-Gumbel, and meta-Frank distributions with standard normal margins an a Sperman's rho of 0.4 (top row) and 0.8 (bottom row).

Some copulas allow to model both positive and negative dependence in their 'standard' versions by assigning appropriate copula-parameters. Amongst these copulas are e.g. the Gaussian, Student t and Frank copula. Other bivariate copulas like e.g. the BB1 copula and its two special cases, the Clayton and Gumbel copula in their 'standard' version allow to model positive dependence only.(in fact, the Clayton copula may also be used in its standard version to model negative dependence if the copula parameter $\theta \in [-1, 0)$. Such a parameterisation is not further considered in this paper) *Copula rotation* allows to transform copulas such that they may be used to model negative dependence also. Further, copula rotation allows to transform (bivariate) copulas depending on whether and/or where the empirical data at hand requires the copula to display positive tail dependence.(we use rotated copulas C^{--}, C^{+-} and C^{-+} with densities $c^{--}(u_1, u_2) = c(1\text{-}u_1, 1\text{-}u_2)$, $c^{+-}(u_1, u_2) = c(u_1, 1\text{-}u_2)$, and$c^{-+}(u_1, u_2) = c(1\text{-}u_1, u_2)$. C^{--} is also referred to as 'survival copula'.)

To calibrate the copula parameters the *pseudo-log-likelihood method* (also referred to as CML – canonical maximum likelihood – or semiparametric method) is employed in this paper. Here, no assumptions have to be made on specific parametric marginal distribution. Scaillet and Fermanian [16] who conduct a Monte Carlo study to assess the impact of misspecified marginal distributions suggest that 'if one has any doubt about the correct modeling of the margins, there is probably little to loose but lots to gain from shifting towards a semiparametric approach'.

To measure the goodness-of-fit of the calibrated copulas, we use the Akaike information criterion *AIC* (Akaike [1]). This measure takes into account that the likelihood increases with the number of copula parameters by adjusting the measure accordingly.

Concerning statistical tests that explicitly test whether a parameterised copula at hand is indeed the true copula, one standard test does not yet exist. A widely used test is based on Rosenblatt's [15] *probability integral transform*.(this test is presented e.g. in Dias [4], pp. 27f) Statistical tests based on the probability integral transform suffer from the fact that they test for the whole joint distribution (i.e. the copula and the marginal distributions) while the focus should indeed be on the copula. An alternative test that, roughly speaking, examines the null hypothesis of the Gaussian copula being the true copula against the Student t copula can be conducted with a likelihood ratio test, where the Gaussian copula is regarded as a limiting case of the Student t copula with $\nu \rightarrow \infty$. Research on statistical tests examining the goodness-of-fit of copulas is still ongoing. Other tests than the ones presented above have been proposed by e.g. Fermanian [6] and Berg and Bakken [2].

The *computing time* for the copula-parameter estimation procedure and for the simulation of copulas varies considerably, depending on the copula.(the computations were done on a 'standard' personal computer (3.5 GHz processor, 1 GB RAM), using the software 'Matlab', version 7.2, in a MS-Windows environment) The parameter estimation for a Student t copula takes about 150 times as long as for the Gaussian copula. Simulations of a Gumbel and BB1 copula take much (roughly 1,000 times) longer than those for the other copulas. This is due to the necessity of using numerical optimisation for the simulation of these two copulas.

4 Empirical investigation

This section contains the empirical investigation of the dependence structure of daily joint interest rate and credit risk factor changes described in section 1. Table 1 shows sample estimates of Spearman's rho for the 25 bivariate empirical samples and reports whether they are statistically significantly different from 0. In all but 3 samples, the Spearman's rho correlation measure is negative, which is in line with the reported empirical evidence on the short-term relationship between interest and credit risk factor changes.

Bivariate Gaussian, Student t, BB1, Clayton, Gumbel, and Frank copulas are calibrated to the 25 data-pairs, using the pseudo-log-likelihood method. For the BB1, Clayton and Gumbel copulas also the rotated versions are fitted. Results are reported only for the rotated version with the best goodness-of-fit in terms of the AIC. The average AIC that is obtained by the copulas is displayed in table 2. One can see that the Student t copula on average yields the best goodness-of-fit, followed by the BB1 copula. Both copulas yield a better goodness-of-fit than their restricted versions, the Gaussian and the Clayton and Gumbel copulas, respectively. The Frank copula yields a substantially worse goodness-of-fit than the Student t and BB1 copulas.

Table 1: Spearman's rho for the 25 bivariate observation pairs.

	maturity bands					
rating	all	1Y-3Y	3Y-5Y	5Y-7Y	1Y-10Y	*mean*
all	-0.53***	-0.04*	-0.25***	-0.28***	-0.35***	*-0.29*
AAA	-0.78***	-0.08***	-0.28***	0.00	-0.08***	*-0.24*
AA	-0.26***	0.10***	-0.05**	-0.13***	-0.29***	*-0.12*
A	-0.43***	0.09***	-0.20***	-0.22***	-0.29***	*-0.21*
BBB	-0.56***	-0.21***	-0.23***	-0.28***	-0.30***	*-0.32*
mean	*-0.51*	*-0.03*	*-0.20*	*-0.18*	*-0.26*	

Statistically significantly different from 0 at the * 10%, ** 5%, *** 1% significance level.

Table 2: Mean AIC and number of times that H_0: 'copula at hand is the true copula' can be rejected for the 25 data samples.

		No. of times that H_0 can be rejected at significance level		
	mean AIC	10%	5%	1%
Gaussian	-204	22	19	14
Student t	-266	3	1	0
BB1	-237	12	11	6
Clayton	-186	19	17	6
Gumbel	-225	15	13	7
Frank	-207	17	11	10

The Student t copula is also the copula for which the null hypothesis of the copula at hand being the true copula can be rejected in least of the cases (see table 2). The null hypothesis of the BB1 copula being the true copula is rejected more often than the analogous null hypothesis for the Student t copula. The null hypothesis of the Gaussian copula being the true copula is rejected in most of the cases.

Additionally conducting a likelihood ratio test, the null hypothesis of the true copula being the Gaussian copula can be rejected in all of the cases in favour of the Student t copula at the 1% (and even at the 0.2%) significance level. This result is not surprising when the parameter distribution of the estimate of Student t copula parameter ν is regarded (as the Gaussian copula corresponds to a Student t copula with $\nu \rightarrow \infty$): The highest value is 12.09, the lowest 2.83. The mean (median) value is 5.68 (5.17).

The results suggest that 'positive tail dependence'(as the risk factor changes for the data sample at hand are generally negatively correlated, we define lower and upper 'positive tail dependence' for negatively correlated sample pairs in this paper as $\lambda_L = \lim_{\alpha\to 0} P(u_1>1-\alpha \mid u_2\leq \alpha)$ and $\lambda_U = \lim_{\alpha\to 0} P(u_1\leq\alpha \mid u_2>1-\alpha)$. This definition differes from the 'official' definition of lower and upper tail dependence $\lambda_L = \lim_{\alpha\to 0} P(u_1\leq \alpha \mid u_2\leq \alpha)$ and $\lambda_U = \lim_{\alpha\to 1} P(u_1>\alpha \mid u_2>\alpha)$) could be prevalent as the Student t and BB1 copulas that display positive tail dependence in all cases have a better goodness-of-fit than the Gaussian and Frank copula, which do not. The data sample at hand is large enough so that we may examine the potential existence of tail dependence in more detail. To do so, we introduce the concept of corner dependence, which is an empirical counterpart to the measure of positive tail dependence.

For positively correlated pairs in terms of Spearman's rho, we define the empirical lower and upper corner dependence as

$$\hat{\lambda}_{L,\alpha}^{empirical} = P(\hat{u}_1 \leq \alpha \mid \hat{u}_2 \leq \alpha),\ \hat{\lambda}_{U,\alpha}^{empirical} = P(\hat{u}_1 > 1-\alpha \mid \hat{u}_2 > 1-\alpha) \qquad (5)$$

where û1 and û2 are empirical estimates of the quantiles of the interest rate and credit risk factor changes.

For negatively correlated pairs in terms of Spearman's rho, we define the empirical lower and upper corner dependence as

$$\hat{\lambda}_{L,\alpha}^{empirical} = P(\hat{u}_1 > 1-\alpha \mid \hat{u}_2 \leq \alpha), \hat{\lambda}_{U,\alpha}^{empirical} = P(\hat{u}_1 \leq \alpha \mid \hat{u}_2 > 1-\alpha) \qquad (6)$$

To compute e.g. the empirical lower corner dependence for positively correlated pairs, we first identify the observation pairs for which $\hat{u}_2 \leq \alpha$. The empirical lower corner dependence is the fraction of these pairs for which $\hat{u}_1 \leq \alpha$.

Furthermore, for the Gaussian, Student t and Frank copula (symmetric copulas), we define the corner dependence that is implied by a specific copula with parameters θ for positive or negative Spearman's rho respectively as

$$\hat{\lambda}_{L,\alpha}^{implied} = \hat{\lambda}_{U,\alpha}^{implied} = \frac{C(\alpha,\alpha;\hat{\boldsymbol{\theta}})}{\alpha},\ \hat{\lambda}_{L,\alpha}^{implied} = \hat{\lambda}_{U,\alpha}^{implied} = \frac{\alpha - C(1-\alpha,\alpha;\hat{\boldsymbol{\theta}})}{\alpha} \qquad (7)$$

For the BB1 copula (asymmetric copula) and its rotated versions we define

$$\hat{\lambda}_{L,\alpha}^{implied} = \frac{C(\alpha,\alpha;\hat{\boldsymbol{\theta}})}{\alpha} \text{ and } \hat{\lambda}_{U,\alpha}^{implied} = \frac{2\alpha - 1 + C(1-\alpha,1-\alpha;\hat{\boldsymbol{\theta}})}{\alpha} \qquad (8)$$

for C and C^{-+} copulas, and

$$\hat{\lambda}_{L,\alpha}^{implied} = \frac{2\alpha - 1 + C(1-\alpha,1-\alpha;\hat{\boldsymbol{\theta}})}{\alpha} \text{ and } \hat{\lambda}_{U,\alpha}^{implied} = \frac{C(\alpha,\alpha;\hat{\boldsymbol{\theta}})}{\alpha} \qquad (9)$$

for C^{-}- and C^{+}- copulas.

For symmetric copulas (Gaussian, Student t and Frank) table 3 summarises in how many of the 25 cases the implied corner dependence exceeds both the lower and upper empirical corner dependence and in how many cases it is below for $\alpha \in \{0.05, 0.1\}$. The most evident observation is that the Frank and the Gaussian copula tend to underestimate the empirical corner dependence in all/most of the cases. The Student t copula overestimates the corner dependence in a lot more cases for $\alpha = 0.05$ than it does for $\alpha = 0.1$.

The corner dependence that is implied by the Student t and BB1 copulas is more closely examined in table 4, where the number of cases in which the lower and upper empirical corner dependence is over- or underestimated is reported. The Student t copula overestimates both lower and upper cornerdependence more frequently than it underestimates these measures for α = 0.05. No such behaviour can be observed for the BB1 copula.

Table 3: Number of cases where the implied corner dependence are below/exceed the empirical corner dependence for symmetric copulas.

$a = 0.1$	$\hat{\lambda}^{implied} < \min\{\hat{\lambda}_L^{emp.}, \hat{\lambda}_U^{emp.}\}$	$\hat{\lambda}^{implied} > \max\{\hat{\lambda}_L^{emp.}, \hat{\lambda}_U^{emp.}\}$
Gaussian	22	0
Student t	4	5
Frank	25	0

$a = 0.05$	$\hat{\lambda}^{implied} < \min\{\hat{\lambda}_L^{emp.}, \hat{\lambda}_U^{emp.}\}$	$\hat{\lambda}^{implied} > \max\{\hat{\lambda}_L^{emp.}, \hat{\lambda}_U^{emp.}\}$
Gaussian	20	0
Student t	1	12
Frank	24	0

Table 4: Number of cases where the implied upper and lower corner dependence of the Student t and BB1 copula are below/exceed the empirical corner dependence.

$a = 0.1$	$\hat{\lambda}^{implied} < \hat{\lambda}_L^{emp.}$	$\hat{\lambda}^{implied} > \hat{\lambda}_L^{emp.}$	$\hat{\lambda}^{implied} < \hat{\lambda}_U^{emp.}$	$\hat{\lambda}^{implied} > \hat{\lambda}_U^{emp.}$
Student t	10	15	14	11
BB1	14	11	15	10

$a = 0.05$	$\hat{\lambda}^{implied} < \hat{\lambda}_L^{emp.}$	$\hat{\lambda}^{implied} > \hat{\lambda}_L^{emp.}$	$\hat{\lambda}^{implied} < \hat{\lambda}_U^{emp.}$	$\hat{\lambda}^{implied} > \hat{\lambda}_U^{emp.}$
Student t	6	19	8	17
BB1	14	11	10	15

Focussing on the deviation of the implied corner dependence from the empirical corner dependence, the values in table 5 reported for 'diff. Ga λL', 'diff. Ga λU', 'diff. t λL', 'diff. t λU', 'diff. B λL', and 'diff. B λU' are the mean, median, and standard deviation of the log-differences of the implied and the empirical lower and upper corner dependence measures, $\ln \hat{\lambda}_{L,\alpha}^{implied} - \ln \hat{\lambda}_{L,\alpha}^{empirical}$ and $\ln \hat{\lambda}_{U,\alpha}^{implied} - \ln \hat{\lambda}_{U,\alpha}^{empirical}$, for the Gaussian, Student t and BB1 copula, respectively. Negative values indicate that the implied corner dependence is lower than the empirical corner dependence, which means that the parameterised copula underestimates the probability of joint excessive observations. The values presented in table 5 show that the Gaussian copula seems to systematically underestimate the probability of joint excessive events while the Student t copula overestimates them; in addition, these deviations are in absolute terms higher for α = 0.05 than they are for α = 0.1. However, the corner dependence implied by the Student t copula does not deviate as much from the empirical corner dependence as does the corner dependence implied by the Gaussian copula. For the BB1 copula, the deviations for $\alpha = 0.05$ are less pronounced than they are for the other two copulas, so one might infer that the BB1 copula's fit in that region is better than that of the Student t copula. Still, remember that the Student t copula's goodness-of-fit (indeed for the whole unit cube region) is superior in all cases to that of the BB1 copula, which allows for a flexible modelling of asymmetric corner dependence. This suggests that either this asymmetry is of minor importance as far as copula parameterisation for the data sample at hand is considered or that other asymmetric copulas than the BB1 copula should be employed.

Table 5: Log-Differences between implied and empirical corner dependence.

$a = 0.1$	Diff. Ga λ_L	Diff. Ga λ_U	Diff. t λ_L	Diff. t λ_U	Diff. B λ_L	Diff. B λ_U
mean	-0.22	-0.23	0.04	0.03	-0.04	-0.08
median	-0.17	-0.23	0.05	-0.03	-0.04	-0.04
std.dev.	0.18	0.13	0.10	0.13	0.12	0.13

$a = 0.05$	Diff. Ga λ_L	Diff. Ga λ_U	Diff. t λ_L	Diff. t λ_U	Diff. B λ_L	Diff. B λ_U
mean	-0.36	-0.39	0.14	0.12	0.00	-0.07
median	-0.42	-0.40	0.13	0.09	-0.03	0.02
std.dev.	0.42	0.23	0.24	0.24	0.31	0.27

5 Conclusion

Several studies have reported that changes in interest rates and changes in credit spreads are negatively related in the short run. These results are more closely examined in the present paper, which focuses on the dependence structure, i.e. the copula, between daily interest rate and credit risk factor changes that are computed from Euro-denominated sovereign and corporate bond indices for the time period from January 31st, 2000 to September 15th, 2006. The time series were adjusted for autocorrelation.

The empirical investigation shows that the daily risk factor changes are negatively correlated, which is in line with the empirical literature on this subject. However, the dependence structure seems to be very heterogeneous in an unsystematic way, depending on the rating of the obligors (credit risk) and the time until maturity of the financial instruments. As none of the marginal distributions of the risk factor changes are normally distributed, a multivariate Gaussian distribution should not be assumed for risk measurement purposes. Copula-based approaches are a promising and easily implementable alternative.

Gaussian, Student t, BB1, Clayton, Gumbel and Frank copulas were calibrated to the data sample, employing the pseudo-log-likelihood method. The best fit in terms of the AIC goodness-of-fit measure is achieved by the Student t copula. A likelihood ratio test rejects the null hypothesis of a Gaussian copula in favour of a Student t copula in all cases considered. The BB1 copula also yields good results (in terms of the AIC) and the goodness-of-fit is considerably better than for its two special cases, the Clayton and the Gumbel copula. However, the null hypothesis of the BB1 copula being the true copula is rejected quite often compared to the Student t copula. The Frank copula yields inferior results for the data sample at hand. Concerning the computing time needed for the estimation and simulation of copulas it is found that for Student t copulas parameter estimation takes very long while simulation is comparably fast and that the contrary can be said about the BB1 copula. One advantage of the Student t copula over the BB1 copula is that the former easily allows for a modelling of multidimensional copulas with a reasonable computational effort as far as simulation time is concerned – the simulation of a 5-dimensional copula takes only about 3 times as long as that of a bivariate copula.

Finally, the implied probability of joint strong risk factor movements is compared to the empirical probabilities. The Gaussian copula seems to systematically underestimate the probability of joint strong risk factor changes while the Student t copula seems to overestimate it. No such pattern can be found for the BB1 copula.

Acknowledgement

This paper was sponsored by the Austrian Research Promotion Agency under the FH*plus* programme.

References

[1] Akaike H., *A new look at the statistical model identification*, IEEE Transactions on Automatic Control, 1974, Vol. 19, No. 6

[2] Berg D., Bakken H., *A Goodness-of-fit Test for Copulae based on the Probability Integral Transform*, Statistical Research Report No. 10, University of Oslo, Department of Mathematics, ISSN 0806- 3842, 2005

[3] Collin-Dufresne P, Goldstein R., Martin, S., *The Determinants of Credit Spread Changes*, Journal of Finance, 2001, Vol. 56, No.6

[4] Dias, A., *Copula Inference for Finance and Insurance*, PhD thesis, Swiss Federals Institute of Technology (ETH) Zurich, 2004

[5] Duffee, G., *The Relation Between Treasury Yields and Corporate Bond Yield Spreads*, Journal of Finance, 1998, Vol. 53, No.6

[6] Fermanian, J.-D., *Goodness-of-fit tests for copulas*, Journal of Multivariate Analysis, 2005, Vol. 95

[7] Höffding W., *Maßstabinvariante Korrelationstheorie*, PhD thesis, 1940

[8] Jarque C., Bera A., *A test for normality of observations and regression residuals*, Internat. Statist. Rev., 1987, Vol. 55

[9] Leake J., *Credit spreads on sterling corporate bonds and the term structure of UK interest rates*, Bank of England, working paper no. 202, 2003

[10] Longstaff F., Schwartz E. *A Simple Approach to Valuing Risky Fixed and Floating Rate Debt*, Journal of Finance, 1995, Vol. 50 No.3

[11] Merton, R., *On the pricing of corporate debt: the risk structure of interest rates*, Journal of Finance, 1974, Vol. 29
[12] Neal R., Doug R., Morris C., *Interest Rates and Credit Spread Dynamics*, working paper, 2000
[13] Papageorgiou N., Skinner F., Credit spreads and the zero-coupon treasury spot curve. Journal of Financial Research, 29(3):421–439, 2006
[14] Pape U., Schlecker M., *Are Credit Spreads and Interest Rates co-integrated? Empirical Analysis in the USD Corporate Bond Market*, ESCP-EAP working paper No. 25, 2007
[15] Rosenblatt M., *Remarks on a multivariate transformation*, Annals of Mathematical Statistics, 1952, Vol. 23
[16] Scaillet O. and Fermanian J.-D., *Some statistical pitfalls in copula modeling for financial applications*. In: Capital Formation, Governance and Banking, pages 57–72. Nova Science Publishers, 2005.
[17] Sklar A., *Fonctions de Répartition à n dimension et leurs Marges*, Publications de l'Institut de Statistique de l'Université de Paris, 1959, Vol 8
[18] Wagner N., Hogan W., Batten J., *Interest Rates, Stock Returns, and Credit Spreads: Evidence from German Eurobonds*, working paper, 2005

Value at risk, outliers and chaotic dynamics

C. Kyrtsou[1] & V. Terraza[2]
[1]*University of Macedonia, Department of Economics, Greece*
[2]*CREFI-LSF, University of Luxembourg, Luxembourg*

Abstract

Financial returns series typically exhibit excess kurtosis and volatility clustering. The GARCH is often applied to describe these two stylized facts. Nevertheless, all excess kurtosis in stock returns cannot be captured by this model. In presence of such dynamics, a non-linear model in variance cannot take into account all the non-linearity in returns. The aim of this work is the study of relationships between chaotic dynamics, and outliers as well as their impact on Value at Risk. In this paper, our empirical study is based on the daily Nikkei returns series from 06/01/1987 to 14/03/2001. We apply the traditional GARCH and the Mackey-Glass-GARCH (Kyrtsou and Terraza (2003)) both to the initial and the filtered Nikkei returns series without outliers. The performance test of Lopez (1988) for Value at Risk models is then applied to determine the best model. We show that during the period of estimation, the GARCH and the Mackey-Glass-GARCH VaR models with (without) outliers at 95% overestimate (underestimate) risks. The filtering of outliers lead to underestimation of risk more accentuated during the Asian crisis period confirming the presence of severe distortions in the underlying structure of the series when removing extreme events. During this period, the Mackey-Glass-GARCH is better than the GARCH comparing the hedging rates.

Keywords: GARCH model, Mackey-Glass GARCH model, Value at Risk, outliers.

1 Introduction

The new regulations on banking supervision gave new dimensions in the application of Value-at-Risk (VaR) technique. During the last 10 years, VaR measures as well as its parametric estimation based on the volatility of stock returns have been considered as the standard measure of risk [1,7,21,22,23].

WIT Transactions on Information and Communication Technologies, Vol 41, © 2008 WIT Press
www.witpress.com, ISSN 1743-3517 (on-line)
doi:10.2495/CF080191

Recent studies have shown the temporal dependence of squared returns. To capture this type of dependence, different variants of ARCH models have been used. The Riskmetrics system proposed by the JP Morgan Bank (1996) could eventually explain the popularity of the traditional stochastic approach using an IGARCH process without constant to model the variance. However, Pafka and Kondor [21] provided evidence that this model is inadequate to describe volatility behaviour. Even if alternative models have been proposed to estimate the Value at Risk (PGARCH, APARCH), the strong remaining structure in the standardised residuals is a proof that pure stochastic models cannot isolate and filter complex underlying dynamics. The discovery of high-dimensional chaotic dynamics has changed our point of view on the source of financial fluctuations and excessive returns. Financial markets are governed by more complicated and richer dynamics. In an uncertain and volatile world, assumptions about rational and homogenous investors, linear incorporation of the information into stock prices, and pure stochastic nature of fluctuations cannot hold out against critics. We think that a mixed theory containing both endogenous and exogenous explanations of the observed anomalies would be more rational and realistic. Recent empirical works on noisy chaos of Kyrtsou and Terraza [15,16] Kyrtsou and Labys [10,11], Kyrtsou and Serletis [12], Kyrtsou et al. [13] have revealed the existence of chaotic structures in the mean of macroeconomic and financial returns series. The interactions between endogenous and exogenous forces in the market lead to complex dynamics that are incorporated into prices. Financial returns series typically exhibit excess kurtosis and volatility clustering. That is, large observations occur more often than one might expect for a normally distributed variable. The GARCH model often applied to describe these two stylized facts cannot capture all excess kurtosis and high Jarque-Bera. This is mainly due to the fact that some outliers or extreme values contaminate series so that the conditional distribution looks heavy tailed. Some researches suggested to correct the data for outliers when using GARCH models (Franses and Ghijsels [4], Van Dijk et al [2]. They found that neglecting outliers could erroneously suggest misspecification or inadequate descriptive models for financial modeling. However, outliers can be the result of the system behaviour itself and as a structural attribute its removal can destroy valuable information in the underlying generating mechanism (Kyrtsou [9]). In that case treating outliers only as an exogenous distortion of the series can deteriorate the explicative power of the modelling.

The aim of this work is the study of relationships between chaotic dynamics, and outliers as well as their impact on Value at Risk. Theoretical conclusions of Kyrtsou and Malliaris [14] on the removal of outliers find their application here. In this paper we compare the traditional VaR-GARCH with the VaR-Mackey-Glass-GARCH modeling both to the initial and the filtered NIKKEI returns series i.e. the series where outliers have been removed.

2 Methodology and empirical results

The economic market behaviour is governed by complex dynamical systems, which are typically marked by interactions and feedbacks between their components or subsystems. These feedbacks can efficiently be described by a time-delayed self-interaction of the subsystems. The resulting delayed feedback dynamics have been modelled successfully by delay equations.

2.1 Noisy chaotic dynamics and outliers

Well-known example of non-linear equation is the Mackey-Glass process (discrete version) [19]:

$$X_t = a\frac{X_{t-\tau}}{1+X_{t-\tau}^{c}} - \delta X_{t-1} \tag{1}$$

The choice of lags τ and c in eqn. (1) is crucial since determine the dimensionality of the system. Kyrtsou and Terraza [16] have developed a stochastic version of the deterministic Mackey-Glass model, where the error term is supposed to follow an ARCH(1) process.

$$X_t = a\frac{X_{t-\tau}}{1+X_{t-\tau}^{c}} - \delta X_{t-1} + \varepsilon_t \tag{2}$$

where: $\varepsilon_t \mid I_t \sim N(0,h_t)$ with h_t the conditional variance

$$h_t = \alpha_0 + \alpha_1 \varepsilon^2_{t-1} + \beta_1 h_{t-1} \tag{3}$$

This chaotic model is interesting because of its similarity to economic and financial series; it is non-linear in mean and variance. The economic data look rather random and show weak significance of low-dimensional non-linear dynamics. They are the outcome of a high-dimensional (noisy chaotic) attractor produced by a more or less simple delayed feedback system. The subtraction of the detected outliers (outliers are identified using the Freedman et al. definition. (Freedman, D., Pisani, R., and Purves, R., (1978): *Statistics*, New York: W.W. Norton)) from the initial returns series gives the filtered series. The GARCH and the Mackey-Glass-GARCH will be applied both to the Nikkei and the filtered returns series.

2.2 Empirical analysis

First, we carry out a preliminary analysis showing the existence of linear and non-linear structures in the daily Nikkei returns series (from 06/01/1987 to 14/03/2001). The series is widely asymmetric with skewness=-0.142 and leptokurtic with kurtosis=12.205, i.e. non-normal with Jarque-Bera=13084.83. Several other tests for general and neglected non-linearity are used i.e. White [26], Theiler et al. [24], Hinich [5,6], McLeod-Li [20], Engle [3] and Tsay [25] tests (see Kyrtsou and Terraza [17]). Hereafter, we use dlnikkei for the initial returns and adlnikkei for the filtered returns. For presentation purposes, obtained results are not reported here. They are however available upon request. Running the tests for non-linearity lead to the conclusion that the dlnikkei series is non-linear in mean and variance while the adlnikkei series is non-linear only in variance.

In the aim to identify the hidden dynamics causing abnormal returns and likely extreme observations we will employ a Mackey-Glass-GARCH process. The results from the estimations of the benchmark simple GARCH and the new chaotic GARCH models are given in tables 1 and 2 for the dlnikkei series and in tables 3 and 4 for the adlnikkei series.

Table 1: The Mackey-Glass-GARCH model (dlnikkei).

Coefficient	Value	t-Statistic
a	13.02	1.68*
δ	12.98	1.68*
α_0	5.38 e-06	2.84**
α_1	0.169	3.129**
β_1	0.827	18.99**
Standardized residuals	Kurtsosis=11.92	Jarque-Bera=12461.53

* Significant at 10%, ** significant at 5%.

Table 2: The GARCH model (dlnikkei).

Coefficient	Value	t-Statistic
α_0	4.10 e-06	2.65*
α_1	0.136	3.04*
β_1	0.857	23.21*
Standardized residuals	Kurtsosis=13.31	Jarque-Bera=16671.37

* Significant at 5%.

Table 3: The Mackey-Glass-GARCH model (adlnikkei).

Coefficient	Value	t-Statistic
a	0.022	0.84
δ	0.011	0.59
α_0	1.13 e-06	3.14*
α_1	0.066	7.23*
β_1	0.928	92.89*
Standardized residuals	Kurtsosis=3.92	Jarque-Bera=134.13

* Significant at 5%.

Table 4: The GARCH model (adlnikkei).

Coefficient	Value	t-Statistic
α	1.17 e-06	3.22*
α_1	0.066	7.23*
β_1	0.927	92.13*
Standardized residuals	Kurtsosis=3.92	Jarque-Bera=134.76

* Significant at 5%.

Comparing the results, outliers filtering seems to diminish the sample statistics of the standardized residuals. Justifying the absence of non-linearity in mean based on the inexistence of outliers is not as simple as it looks. Recent empirical works show that similar results can be spurious due to the distortions induced by the removal procedure of outliers. Certainly we cannot deny the possibility that the dynamics, which are modelled by the feedback-trading rule of the mean chaotic equation, are part of the underlying forces producing sudden changes in market prices. However the fact that eliminating extreme events removes important information should make us more cautious about accepting similar statements. One we need in order to cross-validate such an assumption is to estimate risk on the filtered series and then check if improvements are achieved. This issue will be addressed in the next section.

3 Performance tests for value at risk models

To test the performance of VaR models in the binomial approach, the number of failures or exceptions is counted on the observation period, and then expected returns are compared with estimations of VaR. If, the loss exceeds the amount of the VaR, an exception is observed. In fact, the test is based on a binary measure from an indicator variable noted I_t.
We use the Lopez [18] test:

$$I_t = \begin{cases} 1 + (r_{i,t+1} - VaR_{i,t})^2 & if \quad r_{i,t+1} \prec VaR \\ 0 \quad otherwise \end{cases} \tag{4}$$

The number of exceptions divided by the observation period defines the failure rate. This ratio compared with the probability of the VaR model gives the proportion of times where the VaR amount is exceeded. From this measure, a hedging index may be constructed to facilitate the interpretations of results.

3.1 The dlnikkei series

In Tables 5 and 6 we report the number of exceptions, the failure rate and the hedging index of the VaR GARCH and the VaR Mackey-Glass-GARCH models at 95%. More precisely, for each sample, we show overestimations of risks. The obtained results show that on average the models hedge the negative losses, since the hedging index is 95% for the GARCH model and equal to 95.2% for the Mackey-Glass-GARCH model.

Table 5: Number of exceptions at 95% for the GARCH (dlnikkei).

Samples	Observed Exceptions	Expected exceptions	Failure rate	Hedging index
All the period	186	185	0.050	0.95
06/01/1987 - 31/12/1990	42	52	0.040	0.96
01/01/1991 - 30/12/1994	51	52	0.048	0.952
01/01/1995 - 31/12/1998	65	52	0.062	**0.938**
01/01/1999 - 14/03/2001	28	29	0.048	0.952

One exception appears in bold, the period from 01/01/95 to 31/12/1998, which includes the Asian crisis 1997--1998. During this period, the Value at Risk is underestimated, and so our models are not valid. However, the Mackey-Glass-GARCH gives the best estimations of the hedging rate (94.1%) against 93.8% for the GARCH model. So, it seems that the noisy chaotic model is able to take into account extreme risks occurring over volatile periods (crises).

Table 6: Number of exceptions at 95% for the Mackey-Glass-GARCH (dlnikkei).

Samples	Observed Exceptions	Expected Exceptions	Failure rate	Hedging index
All the period	177	185	0.048	0.952
06/01/1987 - 31/12/1990	42	52	0.040	0.96
01/01/1991 - 30/12/1994	49	52	0.047	0.953
01/01/1995 - 31/12/1998	62	52	0.059	**0.941**
01/01/1999 - 14/03/2001	24	29	0.041	0.959

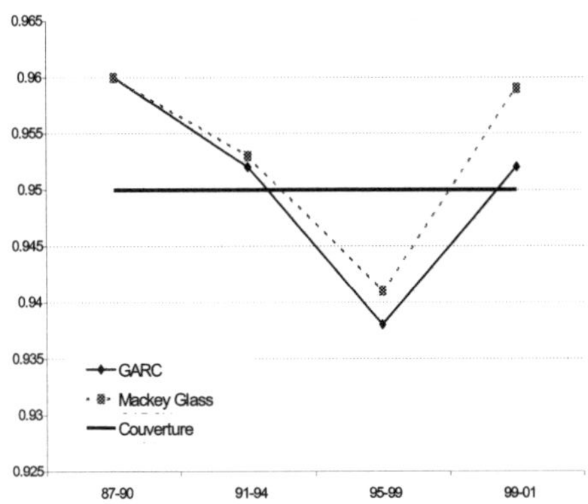

Figure 1: Hedging indexes.

Comparing the number of observed exceptions in Tables 5 and 6, it is obvious that the Mackey-Glass-GARCH model outperforms the simple GARCH model. This means that within periods where exceptional risks are observed, the noisy chaotic approach can be more efficient than the traditional stochastic. This conclusion is concretised in figure 1.

As we can see there are under-hedge periods where the probability is inferior to 95%. From 06/01/1987 to 14/03/2001, on average, risks are overestimated at 95%. Similar results have been obtained in Alexander and Leigh [1]. They provided evidence that the ARCH type models (particularly the Riskmetrics model) are generally accepted at 95%.

3.2 The adlnikkei series

The second stage of our analysis is to repeat the same procedure this time for the adlnikkei series (without outliers). Tables 7 and 8 give the number of exceptions at 95% for both models.

The conclusions are quite different comparing Tables 5, 6 and 7, 8. The VaR is underestimated at 95% by the two models, even more in the case of the Mackey-Glass-GARCH model. More precisely, for each sample, there are no significant differences concerning the number of exceptions between the two models. During the period of crisis (01/01/1995 to 31/12/1998), hedging index is equal to 94% and 93.7% for the GARCH and the Mackey-Glass-GARCH models respectively. An important characteristic is that figures 1 and 2 keep the same shape.

Table 7: Number of exceptions at 95% for the GARCH model (adlnikkei).

Samples	Observed Exceptions	Expected exceptions	Failure rate	Hedging index
All the period	**212**	**185**	**0.064**	**0.936**
06/01/1987 - 31/12/1990	52	52	0.05	0.95
01/01/1991 - 30/12/1994	63	52	0.060	0.940
01/01/1995 - 31/12/1998	66	52	0.064	**0.936**
01/01/1999 - 14/03/2001	31	29	0.030	0.97

Table 8: Number of exceptions at 95% for the Mackey-Glass-GARCH model (adlnikkei).

Samples	Observed Exceptions	Expected exceptions	Failure rate	Hedging index
All the period	214	185	0.057	0.943
06/01/1987 - 31/12/1990	52	52	0.05	0.95
01/01/1991 - 30/12/1994	63	52	0.061	0.938
01/01/1995 - 31/12/1998	67	52	0.065	**0.935**
01/01/1999 - 14/03/2001	31	29	0.030	0.97

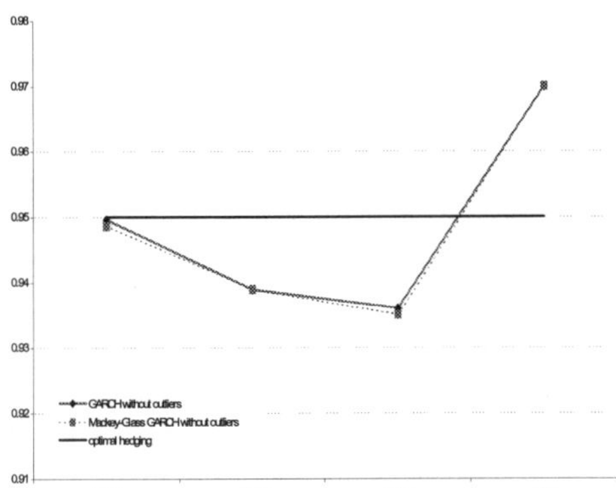

Figure 2: Comparison of hedging indexes.

4 Conclusion

The use of a Mackey-Glass-GARCH model for filtering non-linear structures in stock series can reduce the potential informational bias in the estimation of risk involving underestimation of risk (during crises period). Indeed, extreme risks come from both heterogeneous behaviors of agents and external events. GARCH models are not sufficient for taking into account these two risk sources. Interactions between endogenous and exogenous dynamics in financial returns contain information that is valuable for risk estimation.

Furthermore, it seems that the removal of extreme observations is not the solution to the problem of risk overestimation. During extreme events, the removal of outliers calls into question the VaR methodology. Important characteristics of the nature of shocks can be lost. This result is quite evident since as Kyrtsou [9] underlines: "removal (of outliers) may lead to serious distortions of the structure of the signal". In turn, the filtering of high-dimensional structures employing the Mackey-Glass-GARCH directly on the initial returns series improves the estimation of risk. Other financial applications on market indexes are needed to comfort our results. Technically, an eventual extension of the present paper could concern further investigation of alternative high-dimensional chaotic schemas and their impact on VaR calculation. These works will be presented in the near future.

References

[1] Alexander C.O, Leigh C.T., (1997): On the covariance matrices used in value at risk models, *Journal of Derivatives* pp. 50–62 spring 1997

[2] Dijk DJC Van, Franses PH HBF, Lucas A., (1999): testing for smooth transition non linearity in the presence of outliers, *Journal of Business and Economic Statistics* 17(2), pp. 217–235.

[3] Engle R.F., (1982): Autoregressive conditional heteroskedasticity with estimates of the variance of United Kingdom inflation, *Econometrica*, vol.50, n°4, pp.987–1007.

[4] Franses PH HBF, Ghijsels H., (1999): Additive outliers, GARCH and forecasting volatility, *International Journal of Forecasting*, 15 pp 1–9.

[5] Hinich M.J., (1982): Testing for Gaussianity and linearity of a stationary time series, Journal of Time Series Analysis, vol.3, n°1, pp. 169–176.

[6] Hinich, M. Patterson, D.M., (1995): Detecting epochs of transient dependence in white noise, *Working Paper*, University of Texas at Austin.

[7] Jorion P (1997): *Value at risk: The new benchmark for controlling market* risk, McGraw – Hill.

[8] JP Morgan (1996): Riskmetrics: technical document.

[9] Kyrtsou C., (2008): On the role of complexity in economic time series: New evidence for the crude oil and Gasoline price series relationship, accepted under revisions, *Energy Economics*.

[10] Kyrtsou C., Labys W., (2006): Evidence for chaotic dependence between US inflation and commodity prices, *Journal of Macroeconomics*, 28(1), pp. 256–266.
[11] Kyrtsou C., Labys W., (2007): Detecting positive feedback in multivariate time series: the case of metal prices and US inflation, *Physica A*, 377(1), pp. 227–229.
[12] Kyrtsou C., Serletis A., (2006). Univariate tests for nonlinear structure, *Journal of Macroeconomics*, vol. 28, 1, 154–168
[13] Kyrtsou C., Labys W., Terraza M., (2004): Noisy chaotic dynamics in commodity markets, *Empirical Economics*, 29 (3), pp. 489–502.
[14] Kyrtsou C., Malliaris A., (2008): The impact of information signals on market prices, when agents have non-linear trading rules, *Economic Modelling,* accepted subject to revisions.
[15] Kyrtsou C., Terraza M., (2002): Stochastic chaos or ARCH effects in stock series? A comparative study, *International Review of Financial Analysis*, vol.11, n°4, pp.407–431.
[16] Kyrtsou C., Terraza M., (2003): It is possible to study chaotic and ARCH behaviour jointly? Application of a noisy Mackey-Glass equation in the *Paris Stock Exchange returns series, Computational Economics*, 21, pp. 257–276.
[17] Kyrtsou C, Terraza V., (2003): Evidence for mixed non-linearity in daily stock exchange series, *Political Economy,* 13, pp. 71–97.
[18] Lopez J.A (1998): Methods for evaluating value at risk estimates, *Working Paper, Federal reserve bank of New York #9802.*
[19] Mackey M, Glass L., (1977): Oscillation and chaos in physiological control systems, Science, 50, pp 287–289
[20] Mcleod, A.I., Li, W.K., (1983): Diagnostic checking ARMA time series models using squared-residuals autocorrelations, *Journal of Time Series Analysis, 4, pp. 269–273.*
[21] Pafka S, Kondor I (2001): Evaluating the riskmetrics methodology in measuring volatility and value at risk in financial markets, *Working Paper*, March 2001.
[22] Terraza V., (2002): Modélisations de la Value at Risk du CAC 40. Un essai d'amélioration de l'approche RISKMETRICS par la modélisation hétéroscédastique saisonnière. *Actes de Colloque Journée d'économétrie de Paris X Nanterre, April 2002.*
[23] Terraza V., (2002): Modélisations de la Value at Risk, une évaluation de l'approche Riskmetrics, *Thèse de Doctorat*, université Paris 2.
[24] Theiler J., Eubank S., Longtin A., Galdrikian B., Farmer D., (1992): Testing for nonlinearity in time series: the method of surrogate data, *Physica D*, 58, pp. 77–94
[25] Tsay R.S., (1986): Nonlinearity tests for time series, *Biometrica*, 73, pp. 461–466.
[26] White, H., (1989): Some asymptotic results for learning in single hidden layer feedforward networks models, *Journal of the American Statistical Association*, Vol. 84, pp. 1003–1013.

Numerical modelling of operational risks for the banking industry

R. Barreira, T. Pryer & Q. Tang
Department of Mathematics, Sussex University, UK

Abstract

In Basel II Capital Accord, the Advanced Measurement Approaches (AMA) is stated as one of the pillar stone methods for calculating corporate risk reserves. One of the common yet cumbersome methods is the one known as loss distribution approach. In this article, we present an easy to implement scheme through electronic means and discuss some of the mathematical problems we encountered in the process together with proposed solution methods and further thought on the issues.
Keywords: loss distribution, bottom-up approach, operational risk, Monte-Carlo simulation.

1 Introduction

In Basel II Capital Accord, the use of top-down or bottom-up method to calculate risk provisions are recommended as the ways to model and compute corporate risk value (VaR – values at risk). We mainly discuss the bottom-up approach. For this approach, there are process based models, actuarial models and proprietary models.

The process based model splits banking activities into simple business steps, the management evaluates the situation according to these steps to identify risks. This is mainly a time series type of model. Regressional analysis tools are often used when there are multi-factors in the problem (cf. [1, 2, 5–7]).

The actuarial models or statistics models are generally parametric statistical models. Various statistical fitting techniques are used (see extensive discussions in [3]). In this article, we present an efficient, direct way for this approach and we also discuss some of the technical difficulties that need to be solved.

WIT Transactions on Information and Communication Technologies, Vol 41, © 2008 WIT Press
www.witpress.com, ISSN 1743-3517 (on-line)
doi:10.2495/CF080201

The advantage of our actuarial model is that once it is set, the model itself will give results very close to historic expected total loss. However, extensive Monte-Carlo disturbance to the multi-parameter model can be made on various levels and simulate a complicated business operation. It can also incorporate features such as management control impact on reduction of losses. We only discuss the general philosophy of algorithm design but not the details of how to implement various technical control issues. Our final program operates in the world-wide-web environment.

The proprietary models are mainly developed by major finance service companies. The approach involves a variety of bottom-up, top-down and qualitative analysis schemes. It is mainly spreadsheets based. It was mentioned in [3] that the currently available proprietary software include Algo OpVantage by Algorithmics Inc, Six Sigma by Citigroup and GE Capital, and Horizon by JP Morgan Chase and Ernest & Young. Interested readers should go to the internet search engines to obtain more information.

2 The modelling approach

In order to describe the loss profile of a corporate entity, it is important to collect the past data from the company. If the company has accumulated enough data over the past three to five years, then we can use the method defined in this section to model the company risk. The method falls into the general category of LDA but without the parts of estimating parameters and fitting to an existing distribution function, the model is based on direct modelling of the existing loss data.

The reason for using direct modelling rather than fitted to an existing probability distribution is as follows:

1) Computational techniques make the handling of thousands of data automatic and instant, it can also highlight many critical issues automatically (such as few observations among some risk classes, very high loss values in a risk class etc) to alert the management in a mechanical manner.
2) The estimate of the loss value and frequency can now be done by Monte-Carlo simulation. When hundreds or thousands of data are involved, the Monte-Carlo simulation of the business operation becomes much more closer to real life situations.

Our discussions are based on real industrial consultancy experience, the modelling problems / challenges mentioned are real world situations. In each subsequent section, we concentrate on one particular issue, we give the background information on why these issues are arising, what is the expectation of the company management and what we can do to build a robust mathematical model.

According to past discussions, it is a common agreement that the risks faced by a company should be classified according to

Company
Business Departments
Individual risk events
↓

At the lowest level, it is common now to give a label to each individual risk events (just an example) in the way of

110 corresponding to "Default on payment"
320 corresponding to "Falsified identity"

etc. To simplify the discussion, these events are regarded as probabilistically independent events for the business.

Of course, they can also be treated as dependent events, then the aggregation of different probability distribution functions will be different from what we present now, we postpone the discussion to Section 7.

The business departments within a company will be directly responsible to a number of risk events. It is a common practice not to let different departments to share same risk events. So the structure looks like

Department 1	Department 2	••• •••
Risk 110	Risk 210	••• •••
Risk 120	Risk 220	••• •••
••• •••	••• •••	

It is common that risk are analysed per risk event and aggregated back to departmental and company level. The labelling of the risks provides a convenient way for the assessment and analysis using internet web forms and programmed algorithm.

2.1 The data collection system

A web based reporting system installed across the business's offices, departments should provide a reporting form as:

Table 1: Possible risk report form from a web reporting system.

Risk No	Time reported	Loss value	Impact	Probability
110	02/02/2003	312,227.71	M	L
210	03/07/2003	0	L	M
300	07/10/2003	536.24	H	L

The reported event with loss value "0" in the report form is called a "near-miss" event, where an event has happened against the interest of the company and has been observed, but there is no immediate observable money loss. However, it cannot be excluded that hidden loss has happened or will happen.

In real life reporting, the front line management should type in the information of Risk number, Time reported and Loss value. The remaining columns should be generated automatically according to the risk number. They are perceptions of the management regarding this particular risk number and are pre-defined in the program.

The meanings of the quantities involved in the table are as follows:

- Risk No – an identity number given to the risk event.
- Time reported – the time when the report of the loss is made OR the actual date when this event happened.

- Loss value – the actual recorded value of loss – this may be inconclusive as hidden losses may appear later.
- Impact – the perceived severity of loss for such event should it happens. This could be visible financial losses and/or invisible reputation losses.
- Probability – the perceived probability that such event can occur.
- Range – the perceived range of loss should such event happens. Usually this is linked to the Impact column, may not be directly linked to the reported visible loss.
- L=low, M=medium, H=high. They have associated values depending on the circumstances of the company.

For example, for impact, H could mean loss values are between 2m and 5m, M could mean 0.5m to 2m, and L could mean below 0.001m and 0.5m. Particularly small losses below 0.001m may be ignored.

For probability, it is the same, H could mean 20% to 10%, M could be 10% to 4% and L could be 4% to 0.1%.

It is widely agreed that "low impact, low probability" events can be ignored, "High impact, low probability" events have to be modelled separately. That leaves us with the 7 or so remaining categories (various kinds of L, M and H combinations).

2.2 Construction of probability distribution

Based on this reporting system, we can accumulate and sort all data for Risk No 10, for example, we list all loss data in increasing order (here time factor has been ignored, it could also be ordered according to the time when it happens), if the loss observation x_j has occurred p_j (≥ 1) times, the associated frequency will be p_j. The loss observations will be in the following format

Observations for risk No k

Loss sum	x_{k1}	x_{k2}	...	x_{kS}
Frequency	p_{k1}	p_{k2}	...	p_{ks}

Remark: The index can be arranged in any convenient order.

We can then construct a probability distribution around each loss value, say

$$g_s(\mu_s, \sigma_s)$$

where g_s is a probability density function, μ_s is the "assigned" expected loss and σ_s is the "assigned" spread of the loss (risk of the loss). The strategy for computing these parameters should be decided by using neighbouring loss data.

For example, if loss x_s is one of the actual loss observations, to construct the probability distribution $g_s(\mu_s, \sigma_s)$, we can use

$$x_{s-p} < x_{s-p+1} < \ldots < x_s < \ldots < x_{s+q}$$

to calculate the expected loss and risk. Here loss observations are from the same risk number.

Remark:

1) The distribution function can be normal, gamma or any other appropriate distribution. For example, if normal distribution is used, truncation at 0 (loss values are all regarded as positive) and re-weighting is necessary.
2) The assigned expected loss and assigned spread of the loss will depend on the neighbouring loss values. Different models have different ways of computing.
3) This requires that the parameters are calculated "locally", eliminating the need for estimating the parameters of the probability distribution.
4) The "localization method" can give large rare loss a large associated spread (risk), therefore smoothing the probability distribution associated. It will also concentrate sharply where a large number of losses are observed.

The probability loss function can then be constructed using weighted sum, the weight is the frequency of ith loss value (the number of times it appeared) over the total frequency in that risk number.

Remark: It is easy to check that if the loss distribution thus constructed for risk number i is f_i, we have

$$\text{Expectance of } [f_i] \approx \text{Expectance of frequency} \times \text{Expectance of Loss}$$

Here we do not have equality because of truncation and re-weighting errors. This conforms to the insurance risk modelling principle.

After constructing the probability distribution for losses in each risk number, we can aggregate them by using weighting coefficient

$$\frac{\text{total number of observations in this risk number}}{\text{total number of observations for the whole business}}$$

The resulting probability distribution gives the basis of modelling of company risk.

Finally, random perturbations can be given to each loss value and its frequency. The perturbed model will exhibit rather complicated behaviour and resembles to a real business operation. The perturbation pattern can be decided by the company need. After many simulations, an estimated loss interval can be extracted using certain percentage confidence.

3 Give different weights to different years of data

Background: Assuming that the management system is reasonably efficient, gradual improvements will be in place for controlling high / medium impact losses. Considering the delay in time in the management process, it is anticipated that j-year-old data will have less impact on current operation that (j-1)-year-old data for any j.

Solutions: design the program to detect how many observations are there in the past three years, if the observation number is low, do not subdivide the observations into annual subgroups, treat the 3–5 year data as one group and apply a reduction factor according to how many data in year two, how many data in year two etc.

1) Standard approach (there are enough observations): we apply reduction factors as follows

Table 2: Reduction factor.

Year from current time	The 1st year	The 2nd year	The 3rd year	The 4th year	The 5th Year
Factor of Importance	A_1	A_2	A_3	A_4	A_5

where $A_j \geq 0$ for j=1,2,3,4,5, usually $A_1 > A_2 > A_3 > A_4 > A_5$.

Remark: *It is OK for some of the* A_j*s to be than 1, for example, the choice* $(A_1, A_2, A_3, A_4, A_5) = (1.4, \quad 1.0, \quad 0.7, \quad 0.4, \quad 0.2)$ *is perfectly OK.*

If we use 5-year past data all in one group and with total observations as follows

Table 3: Probability distribution function for different years.

Year from current time	The 1st year	The 2nd year	The 3rd year	The 4th year	The 5th Year
Probability distribution for that year	f_1	f_2	f_3	f_4	f_5

The adjusting factor applied new probability distribution should have been

$$F = \frac{\sum_{j=1}^{5} A_j B_j f_j}{\sum_{j=1}^{5} A_j B_j}$$

in front of the standard probability distribution we produce. This will have the effect that given more stress to recent losses to distant losses.

Here B_j is the total frequency of the risk in j^{th} year

2) Non-standard approach (there are not enough observations):

There is no weighting problem, just proceed with construction of loss distribution function and calculate number of loss expected lose value using the formulas

$$\int_a^b F dx \times \frac{\sum_{j=1}^{5} A_j B_j}{\sum_{j=1}^{5} {}_j} \qquad \text{and} \qquad \int_a^b xF(x)dx$$

as above.

4 Insufficient number of observations

Background: because of subdivision of risk into categories such as business lines and risk types, it is often that in the construction of the probability loss function, we end up having just a few observations or no observations at all. Recall that to construct loss distribution function, we need neighbouring data to define local data spread (risk) and expected loss, few neighbouring data means that the reliability of analysis is reduced.

For example, if 4 neighbouring (different) observed loss values are need to calculate expected losses and data spread (risk), and there are only three different loss values observed in that category, then we have to compromise the way we compute these quantities.

Solutions: Again here, management participation is necessary. It is understood that the in the <<Impact>> column of the report form (see Table 1 and the bulleted explanation below that table), the indicator H, M and L have their corresponding "loss range", this is the management judgement of possible range of loss for events in this particular risk. If your loss falls inside this range, then the end data of this range and the actual loss(es) can be used to form a computational strategy.

It has to be pointed out that this "range" is usually very wide and may not be refined, it may not be a good idea to use them directly as imaginary possible loss values in the computation, some adjustment of their values based on the actual loss values is desirable.

However, in this case, the column in the report form containing the statement concerning the probability for this risk number by the management should be ignored. The fact that there are few observations speaks for itself.

5 Near-misses

Background: Near-misses are observed events that have led to no quantifiable immediate losses. Near-misses are actually quite frequently reported in real life. In the institutions we worked with, as many as about 8% of total reports are about near-misses. They spread also over many different risk numbers.

Solutions:

5.1 Loss value = 0

To design a probability loss distribution, we can use a fixed percentage of the expected loss in that category (risk number).

Correspondingly, a reduction in the total number of observations must also be applied.

5.2 Single loss value with a large number of observations

From risk assessment point of view, we should view this with certain suspicion. The interpretation of this phenomenon is that either the fraudsters find this particular value attractive, or in the reporting procedure, the reporter simply added the various losses and took an average. So the loss values should have the space to spread out.

One way to solve the problem is to reorder the data according to the time it occurs or it is reported. However, this may or may not solve the problem as data may still stay together.

In our approach, if such an event happens, the program will automatically detect it, and give a warning, asking the management if an adjusting factor to the risk (spread) factor should be applied, usually this adjusting factor f(m) is a function of m, the total number of observations for this event in consideration.

That is, if σ is the standard risk (spread) for the probability distribution for this loss, the adjusted risk (spread) is $f(m)\sigma$. We used $f(m) = m^{\phi}$ for some $\phi \in (0,1)$, a constant to be decided and tested by the management. An explanation has been added in the program warning message and gives advice on what value of ϕ should be inputted.

6 Incorporating high impact, low probability events

Background: It is often true that if a risk number is labelled as having high impact (in terms of value of loss) and low probability (in terms of appearance frequency), we may find that in the period of data collection, there is no actual observation of such event (notice here this is not for one year period observations, it has to be for the whole time period of observations, say over the whole 3-5 years).

Solutions: First, a detection mechanism should be in place to warn that such an event has got no observations in the time interval concerned. If no data is added, just set the probability density = 0. If data is added, the modelling should have followed the approach in Section 3, the number of observation (frequency) in this case should be less than one and should be decided by the management with appropriate advice through warning issued from inside the program.

7 Issues arising from Monte-Carlo simulations

In the Monte-Carlo simulations, we perturb the observed loss values and the associated frequencies. We repeat the simulation many times and pick the confidence interval. This approach agrees with the BASEL II requirement that the simulations must be based on models using true company data.

8 Example and conclusion

The following is the probability distribution of "frequency against loss" constructed using part of the data file received from a company (no name disclosed for confidential reasons) and its 1000 Monte-Carlo simulations averaged. It is not the whole picture as the range goes from zero to positive infinity, there are some other concentration areas further beyond the range we plotted. But the effects are smaller.

In summary, based on a consistent web reporting system, our algorithm has the following advantages:

1) It is numerically very efficient to construct a probability distribution.
2) The Monte-Carlo simulation can high light distribution anomalies and smooth out large number of small losses.
3) The form of the probability distribution is fully adapted to the past situation of the company.
4) It is easy to decide what impact people give to distant past data, what to do with near-misses and the Monte-Carlo simulation is highly similar to real life situations.
5) The computation speed can be designed efficiently (to complete one cycle, the time consumed is $< 10^{-2}$ seconds on an ordinary PC).
6) The program can simulate over the whole interval, can simulate over some pre-indicated loss value interval, it can also simulate on any arbitrary group of risk numbers, can incorporate imagined large loss events or reduce the scale of an unexpected large loss observation which is unlikely to happen again.

Finally, we point out that the program also incorporated a feature of adapting management control measures into the numerical simulation.

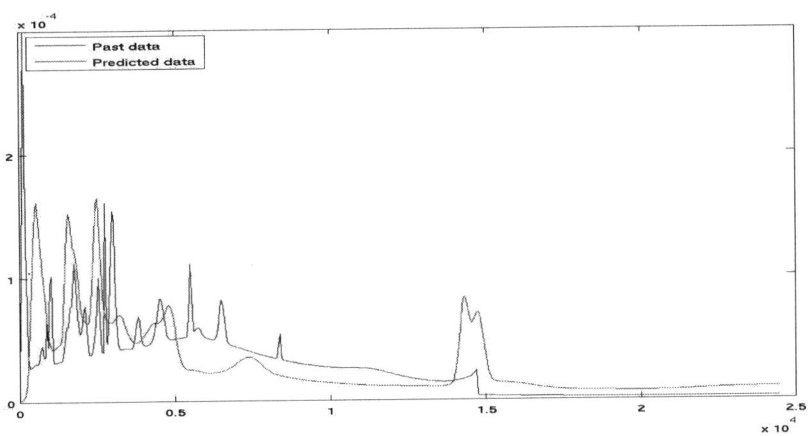

Figure 1.

References

[1] C Alexander and J Pezier, Taking control of operational risk, Futures and Options World 366, 2001.

[2] L Allen, J Boudoukh and A Saunders, Understanding Market, Credit, and Operational Risk: The Value-at-Risk Approach, Blackwell Publishing, Oxford, 2004.

[3] A S Chernobai, S T Rachev and F J Fabozzi, Operational Risk, a Guide to Basel II Capital Requirements, Models and Analysis, Wiley Finance, 2007.

[4] P Cizek, W Hardle and R Weron eds, Statistical Tools for Finance and Insurance, Springer, Heidelberg, 2005.

[5] P Giudici, Integration of qualitative and quantitative operational risk data: A Bayesian approach, in M G Cruz ed., Operational Risk Modelling and Analysis, Theory and Practice, RISK Books, London, 2004, pp 131–138.

[6] C L Marshall, Measuring and Managing Operational Risk in Financial Institutions: Tools, Techniques, and Other Resources, John Wiley & Sons, Chichester, 2001.

[7] M Neil and E Tranham, Using Bayesian Network to Predict Op Risk, Operational Risk, August 2002, pp 8–9.

[8] J V Rosenberg and T Schuermann, A general approach to integrated risk management with skewed, fat-tailed risks, Technical Report, Federal Reserve Bank of New York, 2004.

[9] B W Silverman, Density Estimation for Statistics and Data Analysis, Chapman & Hall, London.

Conditional Value-at-Risk under ellipsoidal uncertainties

M. H. Wong
The Chinese University of Hong Kong, Hong Kong

Abstract

Although Value-at-Risk (VaR) has been widely adapted in financial management, Conditional Value-at-risk (CVaR), which is also known as mean excess loss, mean shortfall, or tail VaR, has also gained importance over the past decade. This is largely owing to the more appealing mathematical properties of the latter. Based on Rockafellar and Uryasev's idea, we are going to look into the CVaR under an ellipsoidal distribution. With the ad-hoc primal-dual interior-point algorithm, we will also focus on the technique that minimizes the CVaR under the framework of portfolio selection.
Keywords: Conditional Value-at-Risk (CVaR), Value-at-Risk (VaR), interior point algorithm, ellipsoidal uncertainties, clustered scenarios, Risk Management, portfolio management.

1 Introduction

Risk Management plays an important role in assets allocation. It entails the exercise of control over some statistical characteristics of the uncertain portfolio return. Conditional Value-at-risk (CVaR), which is also known as mean excess loss or tail VaR, has gained importance in this aspect over the past decade. This is largely owing to the more appealing mathematical properties compared to the VaR. Based on Rockafellar and Uryasev's [1, 2] idea, we are going to look into the CVaR under the ellipsoidal uncertainties. A portfolio selection problem, using CVaR as the objective, will be discussed in the framework of stochastic optimization. To model the ellipsoidal uncertainties, we will propose a "Clustered Tree", which is deviated from the traditional scenario tree [3, 4, 5] in the sense that each discretization in the latter is now represented by an ellipsoidal cluster. We will also work out

WIT Transactions on Information and Communication Technologies, Vol 41, © 2008 WIT Press
www.witpress.com, ISSN 1743-3517 (on-line)
doi:10.2495/CF080211

the solution method using the ad-hoc primal-dual interior-point algorithm [6] followed by numerical results.

2 Derive the conditional Value-at-Risk

Let $f(\phi, r) = -\phi^T r$ be our loss function with the portfolio vector ϕ and uniform random return vector $r \in \mathcal{E} := \{r \in \mathbf{R}^n \mid (r-c)^T Q(r-c) \leq \rho^2\} \subset \mathbf{R}^n$. Without loss of generality, we assume Q to be the identity matrix (otherwise, we can do the transformation $\widetilde{r} = Q^{\frac{1}{2}}(r-c)+c$) so that r lies on a sphere with a density function $p(r)$ equal to the inverse of its volume, i.e. $p(r) := \frac{1}{\Omega_n \rho^n}$ [7], where $\Omega_n := \frac{\pi^{\frac{n}{2}}}{\Gamma(\frac{n}{2}+1)}$. The probability of $f(\phi, r)$ not exceeding a threshold α is then given by

$$\Psi(\phi, r) = \int_{f(\phi,r)\leq\alpha} p(r)dy.$$

As a function of α for fixed ϕ, Ψ is the cumulative distribution function for the loss associated with ϕ. It completely determines the behavior of this random variable and is fundamental in defining VaR and CVaR. With a specified probability level $\beta \in (0, 1)$, the β-VaR and β-CVaR values for the loss random variable associated with ϕ are given by:

$$VaR_\beta(\phi) := \alpha_\beta(\phi) := \min\{\alpha \in \mathbf{R} \mid \Psi(\phi, \alpha) \geq \beta\} \tag{1}$$

$$CVaR_\beta(\phi) := \frac{1}{1-\beta}\int_{f(\phi,r)\geq\alpha_\beta(\phi)} f(\phi, r)p(r)dr \tag{2}$$

In the first formula $\alpha_\beta(\phi)$ comes out as the left endpoint of the nonempty interval consisting of the values α such that $\Psi(\phi, \alpha) = \beta$, since $\Psi(\phi, \alpha)$ is continuous and nondecreasing with respect to α. In the second formula, the probability that $f(\phi, r) \geq \alpha_\beta(\phi)$ is therefore equal to $1 - \beta$. Hence $CVaR\beta(\phi)$ comes out as the conditional expectation of the loss associated with ϕ relative to that loss being $\alpha_\beta(\phi)$ or greater.

Our objective is to minimize the β-$CVaR$, but solving this directly seems to be difficult owing to the nature of its definition in terms of the β-VaR value ($\alpha_\beta(\phi)$) and the often poor mathematical properties of that value. Fortunately, we can handle a far simpler expression introduced by Rockafellar and Uryasev:

$$F_\beta(\phi, \alpha) := \alpha + \frac{1}{1-\beta}\int_{r\in B}[f(\phi, r) - \alpha]^+ p(r)dr.$$

A crucial feature of F_β is its joint convexity with respect to ϕ and α. A very significant result in their paper is that minimizing $CVaR_\beta(\phi)$ over the set of possible ϕ's, say X, is equivalent to minimizing $F_\beta(\phi, \alpha)$ over the set $(\phi, \alpha) \in X \times \mathbf{R}$, i.e.

$$\min_{\phi\in X} CVaR_\beta(\phi) = \min_{(\phi,\alpha)\in X\times\mathbf{R}} F_\beta(\phi, \alpha). \tag{3}$$

Since $F_\beta(\phi, \alpha)$ is convex with respect to (ϕ, α), assuming X to be a convex set, the joint minimization is a convex programming problem. This is a high motivation leading us to explore this function in our settings. We now go into the details of the integration in F_β. As $p(r)$ is also a constant, we omit this term for the time being. Consider the case when $\frac{\alpha+\phi^T c}{\|\phi\|} < \rho$:

$$\begin{aligned}
\int_{r\in\mathcal{E}} [f(\phi, r) - \alpha]^+ dr &= \int_{r\in\mathcal{E}} [-\phi^T r - \alpha]^+ dr \\
&= \int_{\substack{(r-c)^T(r-c)\le\rho \\ \phi^T r \le -\alpha}} (-\phi^T r - \alpha) dr \\
&= \int_{\substack{\tilde{r}^T\tilde{r}\le\rho \\ \phi^T\tilde{r}\le -\phi^T c - \alpha}} (-\phi^T\tilde{r} - \phi^T c - \alpha) d\tilde{r} \\
&= \int_{-\rho}^{\frac{-\alpha-\phi^T c}{\|\phi\|}} (-\|\phi\| t - \phi^T c - \alpha)(\rho^2 - t^2)^{\frac{n-1}{2}} dt \\
&= -(\phi^T c + \alpha) \int_{-\rho}^{\frac{-\alpha-\phi^T c}{\|\phi\|}} (\rho^2 - t^2)^{\frac{n-1}{2}} dt \\
&\quad - \|\phi\| \int_{-\rho}^{\frac{-\alpha-\phi^T c}{\|\phi\|}} t(\rho^2 - t^2)^{\frac{n-1}{2}} dt \\
&= -(\phi^T c + \alpha) g_1(\phi, \alpha) - \|\phi\| g_2(\phi, \alpha),
\end{aligned}$$

where

$$g_1(\phi, \alpha) = \int_{-\rho}^{\frac{-\alpha-\phi^T c}{\|\phi\|}} (\rho^2 - t^2)^{\frac{n-1}{2}} dt$$

$$g_2(\phi, \alpha) = \int_{-\rho}^{\frac{-\alpha-\phi^T c}{\|\phi\|}} t(\rho^2 - t^2)^{\frac{n-1}{2}} dt$$

We writing the constant term as $A_{\beta,n} := \frac{p(r)}{1-\beta} = \frac{1}{(1-\beta)\Omega_n \rho^n}$, the function now becomes

$$F_\beta(\phi, \alpha) = \begin{cases} \alpha - A_{\beta,n}((\phi^T c + \alpha) g_1(\phi, \alpha) + \|\phi\| g_2(\phi, \alpha)), & \dfrac{\alpha + \phi^T c}{\|\phi\|} < \rho; \\ \alpha, & \dfrac{\alpha + \phi^T c}{\|\phi\|} \ge \rho. \end{cases} \tag{4}$$

where, for $\frac{\alpha+\phi^T c}{\|\phi\|} < \rho$,

$$\nabla_\phi g_1 = \left(\rho^2 - \left(\frac{\alpha + \phi^T c}{\|\phi\|}\right)^2\right)^{\frac{n-1}{2}} \left(-\frac{c}{\|\phi\|} + (\alpha + \phi^T c)\frac{\phi}{\|\phi\|^3}\right)$$

$$\frac{\partial g_1}{\partial \alpha} = -\frac{1}{\|\phi\|}\left(\rho^2 - \left(\frac{\alpha + \phi^T c}{\|\phi\|}\right)^2\right)^{\frac{n-1}{2}}$$

$$\nabla_\phi g_2 = \frac{-\alpha - \phi^T c}{\|\phi\|}\left(\rho^2 - \left(\frac{\alpha + \phi^T c}{\|\phi\|}\right)^2\right)^{\frac{n-1}{2}}\left(-\frac{c}{\|\phi\|} + (\alpha + \phi^T c)\frac{\phi}{\|\phi\|^3}\right)$$

$$\frac{\partial g_2}{\partial \alpha} = \frac{\alpha + \phi^T c}{\|\phi\|^2}\left(\rho^2 - \left(\frac{\alpha + \phi^T c}{\|\phi\|}\right)^2\right)^{\frac{n-1}{2}}$$

The above derivatives will be zero otherwise. So, the first and second derivatives are

$$\nabla_\phi F_\beta = \begin{cases} -A_{\beta,n}\left(c g_1 + \frac{\phi}{\|\phi\|} g_2\right), & \frac{\alpha + \phi^T c}{\|\phi\|} < \rho; \\ 0, & \frac{\alpha + \phi^T c}{\|\phi\|} \geq \rho. \end{cases}$$

$$\frac{\partial F_\beta}{\partial \alpha} = \begin{cases} 1 - A_{\beta,n} g_1, & \frac{\alpha + \phi^T c}{\|\phi\|} < \rho; \\ 1, & \frac{\alpha + \phi^T c}{\|\phi\|} \geq \rho. \end{cases}$$

$$\frac{\partial^2 F_\beta}{\partial \phi_i \partial \alpha} = \begin{cases} \frac{A_{\beta,n}}{\|\phi\|}\left(\rho^2 - \left(\frac{\alpha + \phi^T c}{\|\phi\|}\right)^2\right)^{\frac{n-1}{2}}\left(c_i - \frac{(\alpha + \phi^T c)\phi_i}{\|\phi\|^2}\right), & \frac{\alpha + \phi^T c}{\|\phi\|} < \rho; \\ 0, & \frac{\alpha + \phi^T c}{\|\phi\|} \geq \rho. \end{cases}$$

$$\frac{\partial^2 F_\beta}{\partial \phi_i^2} = \begin{cases} \frac{A_{\beta,n}}{\|\phi\|}\left[\left(\rho^2 - \left(\frac{\alpha + \phi^T c}{\|\phi\|}\right)^2\right)^{\frac{n-1}{2}}\left(c_i - \frac{(\alpha + \phi^T c)\phi_i}{\|\phi\|^2}\right)^2 \right. \\ \left. -\left(1 - \frac{\phi_i^2}{\|\phi\|^2}\right) g_2\right], & \frac{\alpha + \phi^T c}{\|\phi\|} < \rho; \\ 0, & \frac{\alpha + \phi^T c}{\|\phi\|} \geq \rho. \end{cases}$$

$$\frac{\partial^2 F_\beta}{\partial \phi_i \partial \phi_j} = \begin{cases} \frac{A_{\beta,n}}{\|\phi\|}\left[\left(\rho^2 - \left(\frac{\alpha + \phi^T c}{\|\phi\|}\right)^2\right)^{\frac{n-1}{2}}\left(c_i - \frac{(\alpha + \phi^T c)\phi_i}{\|\phi\|^2}\right) \right. \\ \left. \left(c_j - \frac{(\alpha + \phi^T c)\phi_j}{\|\phi\|^2}\right) + \frac{\phi_i \phi_j}{\|\phi\|^2} g_2\right], & \frac{\alpha + \phi^T c}{\|\phi\|} < \rho; \\ 0, & \frac{\alpha + \phi^T c}{\|\phi\|} \geq \rho, \end{cases}$$

$$\forall i \neq j$$

3 Single cluster model and numerical algorithm

As the usual portfolio selection model, we would consider the constraint set which includes no shorting selling, meeting (at least) the target return R, and the budget constraint. By (3) and (4), the model of minimizing the β-$CVaR$ becomes

$$\begin{aligned} \min \quad & F_\beta(\phi, \alpha) \\ s.t. \quad & \phi^T e = 1 \\ & \phi^T c \geq R \\ & \phi \geq 0 \end{aligned}$$

We will use the interior point algorithm again to solve the problem. For convenience, we add the slack variables ϕ_{n+1}, $s := (s_1, \cdots, s_n)^T$ to the inequalities and obtain:

$$\begin{aligned} \phi^T c - R - \phi_{n+1} &= 0 \\ -\phi + s &= 0. \end{aligned}$$

The Langrangian function is given as

$$L(x, \alpha, y, z) = F_\beta(\phi, \alpha) + y_1(\phi^T e - 1) + y_2(\phi^T c - R - \phi_{n+1}) - z^T x$$

where $x = \begin{pmatrix} \phi \\ \phi_{n+1} \end{pmatrix} \in \mathbf{R}^{n+1}$, $y = \begin{pmatrix} y_1 \\ y_2 \end{pmatrix} \in \mathbf{R}^2$, and $z = \begin{pmatrix} z' \\ z_{n+1} \end{pmatrix} = \begin{pmatrix} \begin{pmatrix} z_1 \\ \vdots \\ z_n \end{pmatrix} \\ z_{n+1} \end{pmatrix} \in \mathbf{R}^{n+1}$

The first order KKT conditions are

$$\begin{aligned} \nabla_\phi F_\beta(\phi, \alpha) + y_1 e + y_2 c - z &= 0 \\ (\nabla_\alpha F_\beta(\phi, \alpha) =) 1 - A_{\beta,n} g_1(\phi, \alpha) &= 0 \\ (\nabla_{\phi_{n+1}} L(x, \alpha, y, x) =) - y_2 - z_{n+1} &= 0 \\ \phi^T e - 1 &= 0 \\ \phi^T c - R - \phi_{n+1} &= 0 \\ -x + s &= 0 \\ z_i s_i &= 0, \quad i = 1, \cdots, n+1 \\ (z, s) &\geq 0 \end{aligned}$$

Writing the no-shorting selling constraints (with the slack variable ϕ_{n+1}) as a vector function $h(x) = -x$, the Jacobian of it will be $J_h(x) = -I_{(n+1)\times(n+1)}$. Hence, the modified Newton step used for interior-point algorithm for the equality conditions becomes

$$\begin{pmatrix} \nabla_x^2 L & \nabla_\alpha(\nabla_x L) & \nabla_y(\nabla_x L) & J_h(x)^T & 0_{(n+1)\times(n+1)} \\ \nabla_x(\nabla_\alpha L) & \nabla_\alpha^2 L & \nabla_y(\nabla_\alpha L) & 0_{2\times(n+1)} & 0_{2\times(n+1)} \\ \nabla_x(\nabla_y L) & 0_{2\times 1} & \nabla_y^2 L & 0_{2\times(n+1)} & 0_{2\times(n+1)} \\ J_h(x) & 0_{(n+1)\times 1} & 0_{(n+1)\times 2} & 0_{(n+1)\times(n+1)} & I_{(n+1)\times(n+1)} \\ 0_{(n+1)\times(n+1)} & 0_{(n+1)\times 1} & 0_{(n+1)\times 2} & S & Z \end{pmatrix} \begin{pmatrix} \Delta x \\ \Delta\alpha \\ \Delta y \\ \Delta z \\ \Delta s \end{pmatrix}$$

$$= \begin{pmatrix} -\nabla_x L \\ -\nabla_\alpha L \\ -\nabla_y L \\ -(h(x)+s) \\ -SZe+\sigma\mu e \end{pmatrix}$$

where

- $S = \begin{pmatrix} s_1 & & \\ & \ddots & \\ & & s_{n+1} \end{pmatrix}, Z = \begin{pmatrix} z_1 & & \\ & \ddots & \\ & & z_{n+1} \end{pmatrix},$
- $\mu = \frac{s^T z}{n+1}$, $\sigma \in (0, 1)$ is arbitrarily chosen,
- $\nabla_\alpha(\nabla_x L(x, \alpha, y, z)) = \begin{pmatrix} \frac{\partial^2 F_\beta}{\partial\phi_1 \partial\alpha} \\ \vdots \\ \frac{\partial^2 F_\beta}{\partial\phi_n \partial\alpha} \\ 0 \end{pmatrix} = \nabla_x(\nabla_\alpha L(x, \alpha, y, z))^T,$
- $\nabla_\alpha^2 L(x, \alpha, y, z) = \frac{\partial^2 F_\beta}{\partial\alpha^2},$
- $\nabla_y(\nabla_\alpha L(x, \alpha, y, z)) = 0_{1\times 2} = \nabla_\alpha(\nabla_y L(x, \alpha, y, z))^T,$
- $\nabla_y(\nabla_x L(x, \alpha, y, z)) = \begin{pmatrix} 1_{n\times 1} & c \\ 0 & -1 \end{pmatrix} = (\nabla_x(\nabla_y L(x, \alpha, y, z)))^T,$
- $\nabla_x^2 L(x, \alpha, y, z) = \begin{pmatrix} \nabla_\phi^2 F_{SD}(\phi) & 0_{n\times 1} \\ 0_{n\times 1} & 0 \end{pmatrix},$

  and $\nabla_y^2 L(x, \alpha, y, z) = 0_{2\times 2}$

4 Multi-clusters model

We now go to explore the multiple clusters model. Suppose there are m clusters. Our return r could now be $r^{(k)}$ with a probability of $\omega^{(k)}$ and whose expected return are $c^{(k)}$ for $j = 1, \cdots, m$. In other words, each $r^{(k)}$ is in an ellipsoid $\mathcal{E}^{(k)} := \{r \in \mathbf{R}^n \mid (r - c^{(k)})^T Q^{(k)}(r - c^{(k)}) \leq (\rho^{(k)})^2\}$. Again, for simplicity, we assume all $Q^{(k)}$'s are identity matrices and all $\rho^{(k)}$'s are equal to ρ. So, the clusters are now only differed by the centres $c^{(k)}$'s. We would also consider a function like (4) in order to minimize the $CVaR$. In fact, it is a weighted average of (4). Let

$$F_\beta^{(k)}(\phi,\alpha) := \begin{cases} \alpha - A_{\beta,n}((\phi^T c^{(k)}+\alpha)g_1^{(k)}(\phi,\alpha) + \|\phi\| g_2^{(k)}(\phi,\alpha)), & \dfrac{\alpha+\phi^T c}{\|\phi\|} < \rho; \\ \alpha, & \dfrac{\alpha+\phi^T c}{\|\phi\|} \geq \rho, \end{cases}$$

where $g_1^{(k)}$ and $g_2^{(k)}$ are the same as g_1 and g_2 respectively except that c is replaced by $c^{(k)}$. Then our objective function for $\frac{\alpha+\phi^T c}{\|\phi\|} < \rho$ is derived as follows.

$$\begin{aligned} F_{MC} &:= \sum_{k=1}^{m} \omega^{(k)} F_\beta^{(k)} \\ &= \alpha + \frac{1}{1-\beta}\sum_{k=1}^{m}\omega^{(k)} \int_{r\in\mathcal{E}^{(k)}} [f(\phi,r)-\alpha]^+ p(r)dr \\ &= \alpha + A_{\beta,n}\sum_{k=1}^{m}\omega^{(k)} \int_{r\in\mathcal{E}^{(k)}} [-\phi^T r-\alpha]^+ dr \\ &= \alpha + A_{\beta,n}\sum_{k=1}^{m}\omega^{(k)} \int_{-\rho}^{\frac{-\alpha-\phi^T c^{(k)}}{\|\phi\|}} (-\|\phi\|t - \phi^T c^{(k)} - \alpha)(\rho^2-t^2)^{\frac{n-1}{2}} dt \\ &= \alpha - A_{\beta,n}\sum_{k=1}^{m}\omega^{(k)} [(\phi^T c^{(k)}+\alpha) g_1^{(k)}(\phi,\alpha) + \|\phi\| g_2^{(k)}(\phi,\alpha)] \end{aligned}$$

with the derivatives

$$\begin{aligned} \frac{\partial F_{MC}}{\partial \phi} &= -A_{\beta,n}\sum_{k=1}^{m}\omega^{(k)}\left(c g_1^{(k)} + \frac{\phi}{\|\phi\|} g_2^{(k)}\right) \\ \frac{\partial F_{MC}}{\partial \alpha} &= 1 - A_{\beta,n}\sum_{k=1}^{m}\omega_k g_1^{(k)} \\ \frac{\partial^2 F_{MC}}{\partial \phi_i \partial \alpha} &= -A_{\beta,n}\sum_{k=1}^{m}\omega^{(k)} \frac{\partial g_1^{(k)}}{\partial \phi_i} \\ &= \frac{A_{\beta,n}}{\|\phi\|}\sum_{k=1}^{m}\omega^{(k)}\left(\rho^2 - \left(\frac{\alpha+\phi^T c^{(k)}}{\|\phi\|}\right)^2\right)^{\frac{n-1}{2}} \left(c_i^{(k)} - \frac{(\alpha+\phi^T c)\phi_i}{\|\phi\|^2}\right) \end{aligned}$$

$$
\begin{aligned}
\frac{\partial^2 F_{MC}}{\partial \phi_i^2} &= \frac{A_{\beta,n}}{\|\phi\|} \sum_{k=1}^{m} \omega^{(k)} \Bigg[\left(\rho^2 - \left(\frac{\alpha + \phi^T c^{(k)}}{\|\phi\|} \right)^2 \right)^{\frac{n-1}{2}} \left(c_i^{(k)} - \frac{(\alpha + \phi^T c^{(k)})\phi_i}{\|\phi\|^2} \right)^2 \\
&\quad - \left(1 - \frac{\phi_i^2}{\|\phi\|^2} \right) g_2^{(k)} \Bigg] \\
\frac{\partial^2 F_{MC}}{\partial \phi_i \partial \phi_j} &= \frac{A_{\beta,n}}{\|\phi\|} \sum_{k=1}^{m} \omega^{(k)} \Bigg[\left(\rho^2 - \left(\frac{\alpha + \phi^T c^{(k)}}{\|\phi\|} \right)^2 \right)^{\frac{n-1}{2}} \\
&\quad \times \left(c_i^{(k)} - \frac{(\alpha + \phi^T c^{(k)})\phi_i}{\|\phi\|^2} \right) \left(c_j^{(k)} - \frac{(\alpha + \phi^T c^{(k)})\phi_j}{\|\phi\|^2} \right) + \frac{\phi_i \phi_j}{\|\phi\|^2} g_2^{(k)} \Bigg], \\
&\quad \forall i \neq j.
\end{aligned}
$$

We can see that our objective function is a linear combination of convex functions ($F_\beta^{(k)}$), which is still convex. Hence we can apply the same techniques as before to solve the model:

$$
\begin{aligned}
\min \quad & F_{MC}(\phi) \\
s.t. \quad & \phi^T e = 1 \\
& \phi^T \left(\sum_{k=1}^{m} \omega^{(k)} c^{(k)} \right) \geq R \\
& \phi \geq 0
\end{aligned}
$$

In particular, the numerical procedure will be only differed by the derivatives such that those of F_β is now replaced by those of F_{MC}, and the explicit forms are already shown above.

As a reminder, it is worth mentioning that the corresponding β-VaR value (the optimal value of α) comes out as a by-product of the optimization of β-$CVaR$, but this optimal value α is not equivalent to the result of minimizing $\alpha_\beta(\phi)$ directly over the same constraint set. However, since β-$CVaR(\phi) \geq \beta$-$VaR(\phi)$, solutions to our problem should also be good from the perspective of minimizing $\alpha_\beta(\phi)$. We will go through the numerical results in the next session.

5 Numerical results

Suppose there are three scenarios in next stage. We will assume they are all spheres instead of ellipsoids. Here are the expected rates of return for three stocks in each of the cluster. In other words, these are the centres of the spheres. We set a radius of 0.4 for each.

Stocks \ Scenarios	1	2	3
A	2	1.2	0.8
B	1.8	1.3	0.7
C	0.5	1.2	1.9

Table 1: Numerical results for the CVaR model.

β	0.85	0.90	0.95	0.99
portfolio	0.296568668	0.286307431	0.274452573	0.250280625
	0.281468101	0.287049666	0.293294229	0.310341706
	0.421963231	0.426642903	0.432253197	0.439377668
$E[\phi^T r]$	1.250766974	1.250159468	1.249442324	1.248303690
$CVaR$	-1.130975111	-1.092842583	-1.046622223	-0.987803416
VaR	-1.239149005	-1.174644069	-1.100725596	-1.011797682

We may regard cluster 1 and 3 as the two extreme states of the economy, while cluster 2 may be regarded as a stable economy. In this sense, we assign a probability of occurrence arbitrarily to each state as follows.

Cluster	1	2	3
Probability	$\frac{1}{4}$	$\frac{1}{2}$	$\frac{1}{4}$

Applying our notations, we will have the following:

- $c^{(1)} = (2, 1.8, 0.5)^T$
- $c^{(2)} = (1.2, 1.3, 1.2)^T$
- $c^{(3)} = (0.8, 0.7, 1.9)^T$
- $\rho^{(k)} = \rho = 0.5 \quad \forall \quad k = 1, 2, 3$
- $\omega^{(1)} = .25$
- $\omega^{(2)} = .5$
- $\omega^{(3)} = .25$

Using the primal-dual interior-point algorithm with the modified Newton step shown in Section 3, we can solve our model efficiently. By varying the threshold parameter β representing the confidence level, the numerical results are shown in Table 1.

Agreeing with the model, the result shows that R is almost an independent factor unless it reaches its the critical value (1.3) or a higher level of confidence ($\beta > 0.9$) is of our concern. Also, the $CVaR$ as well as the associated VaR is decreasing as we increases our confidence level β, which is in line with our common sense that risk has to be eliminated for a greater certainty (or β).

6 Conclusion

After investigating into the numerical results, we may conclude that the CVaR model is reasonably practical in the sense that the numerical results meet our intuition. As a matter of fact, some other measured can also be derived based on our clustered tree, for instance, the downside risk measure and the probability of a certain level of attainment. The close form solutions are also as nice as the CVaR.

However, there is a hinderance for our clustered tree to develop further into a two-stage tree. The main challenge lies on the recourse problem in the stochastic programming, in which we will suffer from an infinite number of constraints.

Some further directions of this area could be trying to alternate the distribution from the uniform one to others. A step density function that cumulates more "mass" towards the center of the ellipsoid may be considered. Meanwhile, we may also extend our discussion to a broader class of distributions, namely, the radial distribution. If this extension is successful, it may result in a wider application of our tree, since the commonly used Gaussian distribution also falls into this class. An artificial data set is created for the numerical tests instead of data set that generated from proper sampling techniques because we have failed to find a suitable set of sample data so far. Therefore, searching for a set of proper real market data for the implementation is also an important issue.

References

[1] Rockafellar, R. & Uryasev, S., Optimization of conditional value-at-risk. *Journal of Risk*, **2**, 2000.

[2] Rockafellar, R. & Uryasev, S., Coniditional value-at-risk for general loss distributions. *Journal of Banking and Finance*, **26**, 2002.

[3] Kaut, M. & Wallace, W., Evaluation of scenario-generation methods for stochastic programming. *Stochastic Programming E-Print Series (¡spepsorg¿)*, **(14)**, 2003.

[4] Kouwenbery, R., Scenario generation and stochastic programming models for asset liability management. *European Journal of Operational Research*, **134**, 2001.

[5] Hoyland, K. & Wallace, W., Generating scenario trees for multistage decision problems. *Management Science*, **47**, 2001.

[6] Wright, S.J., *Primal-dual interior-point methods*. Philadelphia : Society for Industrial and Applied Mathematics, 1997.

[7] Hotelling, H., Tubes and spheres in n-spaces, and a class of statistical problems. *American Journal of Mathematics*, **61(2)**.

Author Index